Development and Planning Economy

Development and Planning Economy

ENVIRONMENTAL AND RESOURCE ISSUES

P. A. STONE
MSc (Econ), PhD

LONDON   NEW YORK

E. & F. N. SPON

First published in 1988 by E. & F. N. Spon Ltd
11 New Fetter Lane, London EC4P 4EE
Published in the USA by E. & F. N. Spon
29 West 35th Street, New York 10001

Printed in Great Britain by
St. Edmundsbury Press Ltd
Bury St Edmunds, Suffolk

ISBN 0 419 13560 X (Hb)
0 419 13570 7 (Pb)

British Library Cataloguing in Publication Data

Stone, P.A.
    Development and planning economy.
    1. City planning — Great Britain
    I. Title
    711'.4'0941   HT169.G7
    ISBN 0-419-13560-X
    ISBN 0-419-13570-7 Pbk

Library of Congress Cataloging-in-Publication Data

Stone, P.A.
    Development and planning economy.

    Includes bibliographies and index.
    1. Urban economies. 2. City planning–Economic
aspects. I. Title.
    HT321.S76   1987   330.9173'2   87-17534
    ISBN 0-419-13560-X
    ISBN 0-419-13570-7 (pbk.)

To my wife and family

Contents

Contents

Preface

The 'built environment' implies buildings of all types, transport infrastructure, public utilities and other built structures and modifications to the natural environment. Its development has a profound effect on the provision of goods and services, and hence a considerable impact on the standard of living. The scale, quality and distribution of built facilities affects the efficiency with which producers of goods and services operate, and the quality and shape of the environment in which we live. The planning, design and servicing of built facilities has consequences for the use of resources in their construction, maintenance and operation, and for the values of comfort, convenience and appearance which they create, and hence for achieved value for money.

Annual national expenditure on the built environment is substantial. It has important consequences for the operation of the national economy and for government policy for the economy. Governments seek to influence the annual expenditure on the built environment, particularly that involving government and other public funds, to influence the behaviour of the economy. Private expenditure is influenced through monetary and fiscal policy, while public expenditure is controlled directly through controls on public capital and revenue expenditure. Clearly the exercise of such controls has consequences for the scale and quality of the built environment and for the value achieved for the resources used.

Most of the built environment already exists, but annual construction modifies it and can make a profound difference over several decades. Once constructed, built facilities may last for many years, sometimes for centuries. Development is for the long-term future. Individual developers can generally have little conception of the way in which their development contributes to changes in the pattern of the built environment, or of its economic and social consequences, which are only fully revealed when examined in relation to the likely long-term economic and social changes and built development in relation to it. Central and local government (official) planning is concerned with the long-term future of the built environment, and with the scale, quality and distribution most likely to meet future needs for economic and social development.

Economy implies not cheapness but using resources in the most efficient and effective way to generate the greatest benefits. This book attempts to provide a comprehensive analysis of the economic impact of development and land use planning, from the economic and social consequences of individual developments to those of national development on the operation of the national economy. Consideration is given to the operation of the property market and the consequences for private and public development; to likely future changes in the context in which demand for built facilities arise; to the issues for national development in the use of land and the distribution of built environment, and its maintenance and up-dating; to the planning, design, maintenance and management of individual built facilities; and to issues and costs of official planning.

The book is based on the experience and research carried out by the author over some three decades. It is addressed both to professional and general readers who are concerned with the relation between development, official planning and the economy.

I should like to express my gratitude to Professor M. C. Fleming, M.A. (Oxford), Ph.D. of the Department of Economics in the University of Loughborough, who was kind enough to read an early draft and who made some most valuable suggestions. He is, of course, in no way responsible for any shortcomings in the final result. I should also like to thank my daughter, Elizabeth for her patience in typing and retyping the drafts of this book and my wife for her forebearance while it was being written.

P. A. Stone
March 1987

1

Introduction

The built environment is the term used to describe buildings and works, and the other modifications which the human race makes to the natural environment. Development and planning are the functions which create and sustain it. Shelter costs most households, firms and other organizations significant proportions of their income or revenue and creates a substantial proportion of their wealth. Since developing and sustaining the built environment is such a large user of resources and creator of wealth, it is not surprising that these activities have a considerable impact on the functioning of the national economy; it is clearly important that the available resources should be used in the most beneficial way. Economy in the use of resources implies not cheapness but value for money.

PART I

In order to appreciate how the need for development arises and is met, how economy in development and planning can be achieved, and how development interacts with the economy, some elementary understanding of the science of economics and the working of the economy is helpful. This book therefore starts with a brief introduction to economic concepts and principles, and to the working of the national economy. Such a knowledge forms part of the analytical tools useful in understanding the development process and planning issues (Chapter 2).

In the private sector development arises from the demands of people and firms operating through the property market. In the public sector development arises from the need to provide the services required by the public. To understand the forces affecting the supply and demand of the built environment, it is necessary to analyse how the property market integrates the demands for property and its supply, and the construction, financial and other elements in the process. Such knowledge is necessary not only for those who use and take part in the market but also for participants in the planning process. The function of official planning is to guide developers in the context of the wider needs of the community and government purposes. This cannot be achieved satisfactorily without an understanding of how the market functions (Chapter 3).

The built environment is very durable. At any one time most of it already exists; only marginal changes can be achieved in the course of a year. Even single buildings can take several years to develop, while settlements and communication facilities can take several decades to develop. Once developed, built facilities may exist for many decades, even centuries. The context for planning and development is future needs and resources – decisions made today will affect the use of resources and the benefits derived for long periods ahead. It is not possible to predict the future, only to project the past to obtain a measure of the possible limits within which future conditions are likely to lie. There is a need to know the types of information available and the problems which arise in assessing the existing situation, analysing past trends and projecting future ones (Chapter 4).

PART II

The second part of the book concerns itself with the context within which planning and development decisions are made. On the one hand, it is necessary to examine the investment achievements in built environment, the potential of the development industry, the existing stock and its condition and the resources needed to sustain and improve it, and on the other hand, the economic, social and technological factors likely to affect future demand for the built environment and its supply.

Past trends in different types of development in the built environment indicate how the stock has been built up and the current capacity of the industry. The movement of prices provides some guide to changes in levels of efficiency with respect to other industries and to the movement of real costs. An analysis of the existing stock of the built environment and its conditions in relation to measures of demand provides an indication of current shortfalls and a starting point for assessing future demand (Chapter 5).

Before an assessment can be made of likely future demand, it is necessary to obtain some measure of the context in which the forces of demand are likely to be operating. Projecting past trends to provide an indication of the possible limits to future demand depends on the availability and quality of the data. This varies from aspect to aspect. There are extensive statistical data covering the scale, structure and geographical distribution of population and a good deal more on employment, output and floor area for industry and commerce.

Statistical data for social trends such as changes in life style and consumer preferences are far less comprehensive. In some areas there are few or no statistics to provide a basis for projecting the future. Some types of change can emerge over short periods with little early indication of their development. Thus, it is difficult to project changes in fashion and behaviour, and in technological development (Chapter 6).

PART III

The third part of the book deals with the developing built environment: the trends in its growth and decline; the nature of its development and its geographical spread; and the options and strategies available for its control. The first two chapters in this section cover spatial issues, national and regional distribution of populations and economic activities and other major issues concerned with urban and rural development. The second pair of chapters discuss the structure of settlements (the options available), the economics of developing and operating settlements, their growth and decline, and the economic and social consequences.

Because the human population and its activities are generally in a state of change, their environment is subject to growth, decline and adaptation. Settlements and their districts, regions and countries follow the fortunes of their inhabitants. As comparable levels of economic activity and affluence change, standards and scales of built environment change with changing forms and modes of development; economic and social problems arise as settlements prosper, expand or decline. Planning options range from attempting to sustain existing patterns of development to following the full indications of market demand. There is little agreement on whether governments can plan national development more effectively than market forces. In fact governments often attempt to sustain existing national and regional patterns of development, or at least to modify the full economic and social consequences of market-orientated geographical relocation of population and industry. To this end a range of strategies have been developed to assist in sustaining industry and commerce in areas of economic decline and for discouraging movement to areas of rapid economic growth. Such regional and congestion strategies are generally based on financial and tax incentives, and forms of planning control (Chapter 7).

There are a large number of planning issues in addition to those concerned with the broad geographical distribution of population, industry and commerce. There is only space to deal with the more important in this book; most centre around the use of land. A central issue is the spread of settlements, with options relating to urban concentration, size of settlements and their geographical location, giving rise to policies on density, Green Belts, congestion, urban growth and decline, and regional location. Changes in the nature of industry and commerce and the growth of road transport has increased the demand for large open sites with easy access to the trunk road system and the move out of the inner areas of cities to their periphery and to out-of-town sites. Such moves may, for example, leave unwanted land in the inner city which tends to become derelict, reduce the buoyancy of the centres of towns and add to urban spread. Revival of the inner cities is proving difficult and expensive. Roads are imbedded in the built environment of the city; expanding them to meet current traffic loads is expensive both in resources and environmental quality. Despite the slow population growth, the number of households is increasing and with it the demand for additional dwellings. This again leads to demands for urban spread, given the reluctance to develop in the inner city. The pressure for growth is much greater in the south, particularly the south-east, than in the north, where there is relatively more vacant urban land and where urban pressure on the countryside is less. The migration of population, and industrial and commercial activities to the south-east, and the growth of importance of the Channel and East Anglian ports, together with the switch of traffic to the roads, has created the need for large scale road building. While the pressure on the countryside for urban purposes is increasing, so are demands for its protection, giving rise to a range of protective policies. The financial encouragement to farm intensively is transforming the rural scene in ways which meet with considerable disapproval as is the development of coniferous forests. These and other planning issues are considered (Chapter 8).

Town development ranges from single buildings, through various types of estate, to expanded and new settlements. Size, density, form, shape, and other structural features affect initial and running costs, the way the settlement functions economically and socially, and its appearance. Options for settlement development range from villages to cities, from separate buildings in spacious grounds to high density multi-storey developments. Settlements can range concentric to dispersed, circular to linear, continuous to clustered. Transport arrangements can vary from mainly private transport to mainly public, the latter either road or rail orientated. There are generally fewer options for town expansion than for new settlements, the costs and benefits depending to an important extent on the size and form of the existing settlement, and the potential of the existing built facilities. The phasing and adaptability of settlements also have important economic and social consequences (Chapter 9).

Settlements are generally in a state of evolution. Buildings, clusters and even whole districts are gradually adapted or redeveloped to meet economic and social demands. Settlements expand or contract as population changes and the economy prospers or declines. Changing and relocating the urban fabric can reduce or increase benefits, and may use large amounts of resources. While town expansion generally eats into the rural hinterland, it is generally easy to finance since it tends to occur when the economy is buoyant and both private and public finance is available. Town decline tends to create economic, social and administrative difficulties. The effects of decline tend to be widespread rather than concentrated; many buildings become under-used, others become vacant and eventually derelict; taxable capacity tends to decline faster than the demand for services. Economic decline tends to be followed by a fall in the standards of the built environment and in urban services. There tends to be neither the demand nor the finance to redevelop, economic revival tends to be equally difficult, and the economic, social and administrative difficulties tend to increase with the scale of decline (Chapter 10).

PART IV

In the fourth part of the book the discussion turns to the economics of the design and management of buildings and other urban facilities, and to the techniques for the economic evaluation of designs, maintenance and management procedures and planning options. Concern is with the values of comfort, convenience and appearance obtained from the resources used.

The many issues to be considered in specifying and designing a built facility each offer several options. The issues include the necessity of a new facility against adapting the process or an existing facility to new purposes, location, size, shape and form, flexibility, structure and claddings, lighting, heating and ventilation services, and finishes and fittings. Each option has its own initial and running costs, and offers different levels of comfort, convenience and appearance. The costs and benefits need to be evaluated and the balance of advantage for each option compared, to find which offers the best value for money. A considerable amount of research has been carried out into the relative economies of various options: some of the results are given where they offer guidance on design economies (Chapter 11).

The lifespan of a built facility depends on its physical qualities, the maintenance of them and its flexibility and adaptability in meeting new demands. During its life its fabric needs to be maintained, and its fittings and fixtures repaired and replaced. Buildings need to be cleaned, lighted, heated and ventilated, and their equipment serviced and operated. They may need to be adapted or converted to meet changing requirements. Carrying out these functions affects both the costs and returns from the occupation and use of built facilities. Again there are many options both in terms of building technique and in management: alternatives can be compared to determine which offers the best value for money (Chapter 12).

Building facilities affect not only their occupiers and users but create costs and benefits for many groups within the community, that is the external costs. Amongst those affected in addition to occupiers and users are the local authorities, the public utility services, and the central government and its agencies. The two main techniques for evaluating costs and benefits to compare comparative value for money are costs-in-use and cost–benefit analysis. Broadly, the former is concerned with means to achieve a given end and the latter with ends as well as means, attempting to determine which option gives the best return for the capital expended. In both methods the first step is to analyse the incidence of costs and benefits to each interest group affected by the development (Chapter 13).

The final part of the book is concerned with financial and planning machinery, with an understanding of the context in which financial and planning decisions are made, and with the economic and social consequences.

Much of the national building fabric is inadequate for its purpose and provides poor value for money, and there appears to be a large backlog of maintenance work. The inadequacies of the stock tend not only to lead to a waste of building resources but to a reduction in the efficiency of economic activities and to social losses. While some of the poor value for money reflects errors of specification and design, much of it arises from limited vision in framing financial criteria and measures of taxation. Building decisions in the private sector are affected by taxation, financial criteria which give insufficient consideration to the consequences for the built environment and in some cases to a shortage of finance. In the public sector more importance tends to be placed on controlling public investment and resource expenditure than on value for money (Chapter 14).

Official planning is the public watchdog over private and public development. Its value lies in taking a comprehensive, long-term view of the demands on the built environment and guiding developers towards planning decisions which collectively provide the greatest benefits for the resources used. In carrying out its function, it is necessary to project the likely future planning context, to prepare strategies for future development and to make judgements on planning proposals in the light of the proposed long-term strategies. Clearly these functions and the additional work which falls on developers in submitting and negotiating planning proposals have a cost which can be set against the net gains from a rationalized system of national development. If the official planning process is inefficient or needlessly officious, it will add to costs and if it fails to judge demand and the best way to meet it accurately, it will reduce the benefits (Chapter 15).

The final chapter summarizes the more important factors affecting development and planning economy, and their relationships, and the issues and options most in need of consideration.

PART ONE
Analytical tools

2

Economic principles, and planning and development

2.1 ECONOMIC SCIENCE

Economic principles are, broadly speaking, logical reactions to the challenge of expending scarce resources to obtain a maximum return. Most resources are scarce because they are limited, whereas demand for them is unlimited. Producers and consumers will not generally give up more resources than necessary, or give resources of a greater value than the commodity exchanged. For the producer, the businessman, the return from an economic activity is the money surplus or profit left after all the expenses have been deducted from the price realized; this is generally expressed as the return on capital. His object is to find the combination of ends (products) and means (factors of production) which provides the best return. The consumer measures his return in terms of the satisfaction obtained for the time, energy or money spent. These are all limited in amount and the consumer aims to obtain for them the goods and services which gives him the maximum satisfaction.

As illustrated below, in practice an economic decision generally involves balancing a number of factors which interact in a complex way. For example, a choice between sites for a house involves comparing not just prices and site areas, but its shape and soil structure and their effect on development costs, the nature of surrounding property and location relative to local services, and their effect on convenience, and the quality of life.

Economic analysis commences with the simplest situation, other factors being brought into consideration as the simpler ones are understood. Studies of simple situations have resulted in general laws or principles as a guide to decision. Frequently these can be expressed mathematically. Actual situations can be analysed statistically to evaluate the constants in the mathematical relationships which can then be applied to new situations to provide a basis of decision. Because, however, economics is dealing with human reactions, mathematical relations are not immutable as in the physical sciences. Economic laws are more akin to decision theory, operational method and other decision techniques.

Micro-economic problems are concerned with comparatively simple situations involving scarce resources and alternative ends, with operations, firms and so on, such as the effect of increasing the labour force on a development project, or increasing densities and raising prices. The effects of changing one or two factors on a third are usually measurable and hold good, at least in the short run. Macro-economic problems are concerned with changes in the economy as a whole. Development and planning decisions arise in situations in which the economy as a whole is changing. For example, while housing demand is related to prices in the short run, in the longer run the number of households, their incomes and patterns of consumption, tax levels, availability of credit and so on are all changing. While there may be satisfactory evidence of how pairs of factors are related, other things being equal, there is generally less certainty of behaviour patterns where many factors are changing. If house prices rise, for example, fewer may be purchased; this is modified, however, if incomes and the prices of most goods and services are rising or if there is an expectation that general price levels will rise.

Clearly it is not possible in a short chapter to do more than introduce a subject as large as economic theory. It is only possible to give the reader a feel for economic analysis through discussion of some of the basic economic principles used in evaluating the economics of development and planning, and some elementary understanding of the way the economy operates in relation to the development and servicing of the built environment.

2.2 ECONOMIC RENT

Rent in economic theory, as opposed to rent as a payment for the use of a building, can be defined as a surplus obtained for a factor of production with a fixed supply. If the supply of free agricultural land was just adequate and only just worth cultivating, it would earn no economic rent. If the prices of output were to rise or the costs of cultivation fall, marginal land, previously just not worth cultivating, would now be worth cultivating. This marginal land would have no or only a nominal value, while the land formerly cultivated would have a value in excess of that of the marginal land relative to its greater potential output. Clearly a new farmer would be as well off paying the value of the excess output as a rent for the better land, as he would be with rent-free marginal land. Each time cultivation is extended to a lower quality of land, the values of the grades of land previously cultivated will rise, yielding increased economic rents (Fig. 2.1).

The values of urban land arise in a similar way to those for cultivated land. Historically, settlements usually started at a junction of communications, at the crossroads, the most convenient place to do business. As settlements

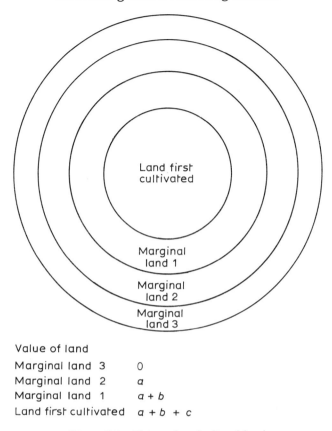

Value of land
Marginal land 3   0
Marginal land 2 a
Marginal land 1 $a + b$
Land first cultivated $a + b + c$

Figure 2.1   Value of agricultural land.

expanded down each of the crossroads, successive sites would be less well sited. A newcomer might have to decide between a free site at the margin of the settlement and a site nearer the junction for which he would need to pay the owner a rent representing the value of the difference in potential of the two sites. Thus there would be a hierarchy of sites commanding a hierarchy of rents equivalent to the comparative advantages of each (Fig. 2.2). The occupier would be equally well off on any site because the comparative advantages would be creamed off by rent. The demand for the best sites exceeds the supply and enables the owner to obtain a rent equal to the value of its advantages over freely available marginal sites.

2.3   INCREASING AND DECREASING RETURNS

The returns on an operation can often be increased relative to cost by optimizing the amount of factors used in production. A classic example is the

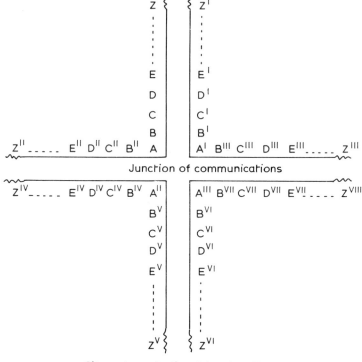

Junction of communications

Site values decline from A to Z

Figure 2.2 The relation between values of sites of development land and their location on the junction of two roads.

application of fertilizer to an area of land. A little might have no effect but each additional unit of fertilizer might, up to a point, result in increasing units of output. Eventually additional units would be likely to add less and less to output (i.e. marginal output) and eventually average output would fall (Fig. 2.3). As a result marginal and average costs would eventually rise (Fig. 2.4).

Consider as an example the development of a site. Generally the value of a site rises as the permitted density of development increases. Up to a point the greater the floorspace developed on the site, the higher the value of the development relative to the costs of development. However, generally beyond a certain point, the more floorspace, the higher the cost of constructing each additional unit of floorspace, while the value of each unit tends not to increase and might even fall. This situation might arise where, in order to develop more units of space, the number of storeys has to be increased, unit floorspace costs tending to rise as more storeys are added, while the higher

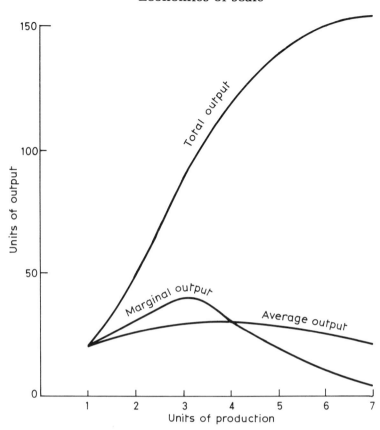

Figure 2.3   Increasing and decreasing returns.

floors might tend to command lower rents than the lower ones. Thus returns tend to increase at first but eventually tend to fall.

2.4   ECONOMIES OF SCALE

Economies of scale imply that unit costs fall as the scale of production is increased; scale implies more than just an increase in output. For example, doubling the labour force and other factors of production to build twenty dwellings at a time rather than ten using the same methods would not produce economies because there would have been no change in technique. If, however, building twenty dwellings rather than ten justified the use of a tower crane for materials' handling, economies in labour and other factors of production would be obtained. Economies of scale are thus obtained when a larger scale of production enables a different and more efficient technique or

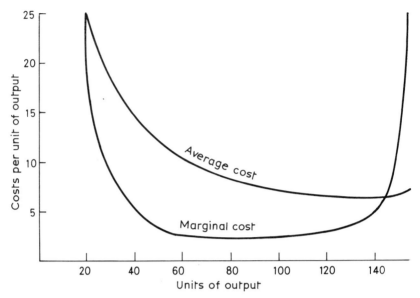

Figure 2.4 Average and marginal costs per unit of output.

machine to be used. Clearly, to obtain the best results, the scale of production must be large enough to utilize the machine at its optimum level of output. As well as the introduction of machinery increasing the scale of production might allow, for example, the bringing in of better management, perhaps a full-time supervisor; it might be possible, in addition, to subdivide the work so that full-time specialists are employed on each type of operation.

2.5 PRICES AND DEMAND

The price a consumer is prepared to pay for a commodity depends on how far his appetite has already been satisfied, an assessment of future satisfaction from further units of a similar kind and of those from other uses of resources. For example, each household needs a dwelling, a second dwelling can be convenient and enjoyable but each additional further dwelling is likely to bring less satisfaction. The lower the price of dwellings, other things being equal, the more each household might purchase. The demand price for units of a commodity available at the same time is the price at which it is just worth purchasing. The total quantity sold depends on the price asked (Fig. 2.5).

While all purchasers normally have to pay the same price for an identical commodity sold at the same time, in the same market – the 'market price' – the satisfaction obtained by each purchaser will vary. Some will place a high value on a dwelling of good quality and location, others will be prepared to sacrifice the standards of their dwelling for cars, boats, holidays and so on.

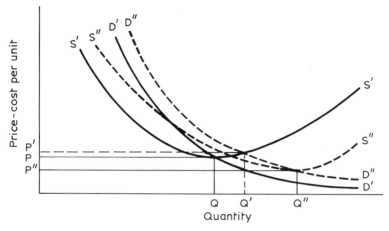

Figure 2.5   Demand and supply curves.

Individuals each have their own scale of values and will aim to use their resources to obtain equal satisfaction from the final unit of resource spent in each direction. This is described as obtaining equal marginal utility. If this is achieved purchasers obtain maximum satisfaction from resource usage, not only resources used to purchase goods and services but those used to invest and to retain as residual cash.

In the business sector the way in which demand varies in relation to prices charged for a commodity is related to the contribution the commodity makes to the surplus of receipts over expenditure in relation to capital employed. For example, additional working space will be purchased or hired if the total costs of the operation are sufficiently lower than the expected revenue. Expected rates of return on capital can be estimated for possible new ventures. Ventures for which the expected rate of return is less than the borrowing rate would not be undertaken. Market prices will be determined by the sum of the demand schedules of each producer.

2.6   EQUILIBRIUM OF NORMAL DEMAND AND SUPPLY

When factors of production used in conjunction with a fixed amount of plant and management reach the amount at which marginal output falls (Fig. 2.3), average and marginal costs rise, marginal costs starting to rise when marginal output falls (Fig. 2.4). In the long run, producers will not generally increase output at a loss. Losses occur if the market price is less than the cost of production, so each producer tends to limit his output at the point at which his marginal costs are at a minimum (supply curve S'S') and equal to market prices (demand curve D'D') (Fig. 2.5). If a producer increased his output by a further unit, costs per unit would rise above market price and there would be a loss; if he produced less, profits would be reduced because market price would have been above his marginal costs of production for the marginal units. Thus producing output (Q) up to the point at which marginal costs are at a minimum (P) and equal to market prices (P) gives the best return (Fig. 2.5). If a producer has a monopoly of supply or can combine with other producers to control supply (possible only if the number of producers is limited) supply can be held at a point at which market price was higher than marginal costs, so securing higher profits.

Of course, if purchasers raise their valuation of a commodity and collectively increase their demand (D"D"), they tend to bid up the price to secure their needs; the higher the level of demand at a fixed level of supply, the higher the price tends to be (P' for Q'). Prices tend to be raised at each level of demand (D"D"). If there is no change in costs, producers' profits rise. This tends to stimulate a higher rate of output from existing and new producers until a new equilibrium is reached between marginal costs and prices. Similarly if demand falls, prices tend to fall, profits are reduced and output is cut back until a new equilibrium is reached. Marginal producers cease production.

2.7   COSTS OF PRODUCTION

In the long run producers take into account all costs together with an allowance for normal profits. These are estimated to cover the cost of their own capital and sufficient to make it worthwhile to incur the risks of production and marketing.

Costs can be divided into prime costs and overheads. Prime costs are the variable costs, those which vary directly with output – generally for labour and materials. Overheads arise from the costs of plant, management and credit, and are fixed in the short term. In order to reduce costs for a level of output beyond the optimum level for existing plant and management, the scale of production has to be changed with a larger and different combination of plant and management. Overheads tend to rise but so does productivity, so that marginal costs do not rise so rapidly as before. The best returns, therefore, are obtained at a higher level of output (O" at P') than formerly (Fig. 2.5). Thus the supply curve is shifted to the right in the same way as the demand curve would be shifted if demand increased.

2.8   MEDIUM-TERM PRICES

In the medium term it might pay a producer to continue with his level of production even when the price does not cover costs plus normal profit and overheads cannot be reduced in the same period. For example, a building contractor cannot instantly dispose of surplus plant and buildings, nor dismiss surplus staff; the shortage of orders might be expected to be temporary, making it worthwhile to maintain capacity. In these circumstances prices might be tendered below costs, since any excess over prime costs would make some contribution towards the overheads. On the other hand, when work is plentiful and enquiries exceed capacity, prices for some contracts might be quoted higher than necessary to cover costs and normal profits. If this situation becomes general throughout the industry, contractors expand and new ones are formed until capacity and demand are once again in balance and competition forces prices back to a level which yields normal profits.

2.9 SHORT-TERM PRICES

Short-, medium- and long-term market conditions vary with the nature of the commodity produced. At one extreme, short term might imply a day or even less. For example, perishable commodities such as fish, might have to be sold within a few hours or destroyed. Initially the seller aims for a price which covers all costs and provides a normal profit. If demand proves to be greater than supply the tendency is to raise prices and obtain above normal profits; if demand is less, prices are lowered in an effort to clear stocks which otherwise might be valueless. In the light of experience the seller adjusts the volume to take to the market on the next occasion but this one individual cannot alone affect the market price. Eventually, however, there is a knock-on effect to the producers who themselves have to sell at prices which do not cover all the costs, including normal profits and who adjust to changes in market demand as indicated above.

At the other extreme supply might be more or less fixed; for example, the supply of Tudor houses and sites suitable for development in the central business district. In the short term the supply of most buildings can only be increased or reduced marginally since annual output is only about 2% of the stock. As well as new stock there will generally be a part of the existing stock on the market. If demand for a type of building declines, it takes some time to adjust supply to demand. Prices tend to fall, yielding lower profits or losses, output tends to decline as marginal producers go out of production and if stocks are high enough, production might cease. While buildings are not perishable if weather-tight, there is a holding cost which broadly amounts to the cost of credit tied up in the building and costs of servicing the building. It pays to accept a reduction in the price for a quick sale if this is less than the holding cost.

2.10 PRICE AND INCOME ELASTICITY

The relationship between price and supply can be expressed more precisely through the concept of price elasticity: the percentage change in the quantity demanded in relation to the percentage change in price. Demand is said to be elastic if the percentage quantity demanded increases more than the percentage fall in price, and inelastic if percentage demand increases less than percentage fall in price. Measures of elasticity can be estimated from past levels of price and demand. Demand is generally elastic for commodities with close substitutes and inelastic for those for which there are no alternatives. For example, demand for use of a toll-bridge where there was no alternative route would tend to be inelastic, while that for a toll-road connecting the same towns as other roads would tend to be elastic.

The concept of income elasticity expresses changes in demand relative to changes in income. Again income elasticity can be estimated from past experience. Generally income elasticity is low for necessities and high for luxuries. As a result as incomes rise, proportionally less tends to be spent on food and other necessities, and increasing amounts on higher quality housing, transport, leisure and other luxuries.

2.11   AGGREGATE NATIONAL DEMAND

Aggregate national demand depends on consumer spending, private investment, public consumption and investment, and net overseas demand.

Consumer spending tends to depend on earnings, pensions and other investment income, social payments, the rates and forms of taxation, and the incidence of savings. The proportions spent and saved tend to depend on expectations about future prices, income and demand. Consumers may try to beat price rises by purchasing ahead but they may save more in periods of rising prices in order to maintain real savings.

Private investment tends to depend on business confidence in the volume of future demand and on expectations of future prices, costs, rates of taxation and interest. The higher taxes and interest rates are expected to be, the smaller the volume of investments likely to be accepted as viable. Investment other than labour-saving investment, tends to be damped by expectations of rising labour costs and lower prices.

Public consumption and investment tend to depend more on political than economic factors. Public investment is only a part of total public expenditure and tends to be easier to control than public consumption. This is because investment generally involves contracts to firms which are of limited duration and can be curtailed or cancelled or not offered. Reducing public consumption generally involves changing laws and reducing staff, both of which are difficult. Public expenditure is financed through taxation, borrowing, sales of government assets and creating credit. The first three of these factors all tend to reduce the money available for private consumption and investment, while creating credit tends to be inflationary. Inflation distorts the economy, reduces the value of incomes and savings, and tends to be self-perpetuating.

Overseas demand depends on such factors as prices, quality and reliability of delivery. If home labour costs rise or quality of work and productivity decline relative to other countries, raising relative prices, exports tend to fall and imports to rise. In such a situation rising home demand may have a greater effect in increasing imports than in increasing home employment.

2.12   NATIONAL INCOME AND THE MULTIPLIER EFFECT

Increases in employment and rises in productivity generate a larger national income, a larger supply of goods and services and an increase in demand. Additional economic activities create a demand for additional labour, materials and plant, creating additional employment and incomes. This in turn creates more demand, employment and incomes and hence yet further demand until the initial effect is exhausted. This is known as the multiplier effect. It provides the basis on which governments are advised to spend their way out of a recession, that is a period when demand is less than the capacity of the economy and resources are idle.

To increase total demand orders can be placed for commodities which cannot easily substitute for those already being produced, such as additional public housing, public health and education buildings, roads and other infrastructures. If the money to pay for these goods is taken through taxation from existing incomes, the demand for other commodities already in the economy tends to decrease, but demand increases as incomes from the additional employment are spent. Of course, if the unemployed are being supported by social security, the net cost of providing them with jobs is reduced by savings in social security payments, but equally their additional incomes and hence spending are reduced by social payments no longer received, reducing the multiplier effect.

This is a very complex subject and only a greatly simplified account is possible here. However, since aggregate national income and government economic measures have a large influence on demand for built environment and on its quantity and quality, it is a subject central to development and planning economy.

2.13   PUBLIC AND PRIVATE INVESTMENT

Public investment is as necessary as private investment. Without it public goods, broadly those for which a direct market price cannot be levied, would not be provided. While public investment generally does not yield a cash return on the capital expended, it can provide an economic return to the community. This can take the form of savings on operating costs to the public service, to firms and the rest of the community and the enhancement of the standard of life. For example, the costs-in-use, that is the equivalent costs of construction and servicing (Chapter 11), of a reconstructed road or school might be less than those of maintaining an old one; the provision of a new road might reduce transport costs to firms and private persons; a new hospital or swimming bath might add to personal satisfaction.

If the services which result from an investment produce either a revenue from leasing or sale, or a saving in the public service comparable with the cost of servicing the capital and operating the investment, no additional public revenue need be raised. (Public investments tend to have long lead times and it may be some years before returns are obtained.) There is in this case little difference in the effect on the economy between public and private investment. Where an investment yields social benefits, for which a charge cannot be made, additional public revenue is needed to service the capital borrowed and to operate the service. In some cases the benefits may take the form of savings to the business economy providing in aggregate a fund for meeting additional taxation. Many investments in the built environment are of a form with potential for creating revenue or generating savings.

Financing public investment through borrowing tends to reduce the capital available for private investment or, by stimulating increased savings, to reduce consumption. If it increases the demand for savings, it tends to result in higher interest rates and to reduce the volume of worthwhile private investments.

Private investment depends on the business ventures available which offer a return on capital compatible with the rate of interest and the risks of the venture. The return has to be large enough to cover the risk of failure based on past experience, adjusted in relation to current expectations about the state of trade, labour relations, prices, government regulations and policies, and so on. Hence the lower the rates of interest and the greater the confidence in future conditions, the more private investment is likely to be undertaken.

2.14 GOVERNMENT AND AGGREGATE NATIONAL DEMAND

Additional investment as indicated above tends to increase aggregate national demand through the creation of more employment, incomes and demand; the total effect being much larger than the additional investment (the multiplier effect). A distinction must be made, however, between increasing the capital stock through investment and increasing the level of economic activities. The latter will have a continuing effect on employment and incomes, while the direct investment effect may be limited to the duration of its development. In such cases in order to maintain the effect on aggregate demand and employment it would be necessary to maintain the level of investment throughout the period to be affected. It is generally agreed, however, that much of the new activity stimulated by the consequences of public development will continue after the original stimulus is withdrawn.

It is usually advocated that public investment should be increased when aggregate demand is below the level necessary to sustain full employment. Problems arise, however, because the effects do not take place immediately and continue beyond the investment period. If, in the meantime, economic activity increases for other reasons, the economy might be over-stimulated with inflationary consequences. Measuring what is happening in the economy and projecting the future is difficult. Investments in hospitals and public baths, for example, give rise to operating costs, so that public costs are increased over the investments and hence well beyond the period during which additional demand may be required. It is neither easy nor necessarily satisfactory to use investment in the infrastructure as an economic stimulus. Some developments may even result in social and economic loss to the community, but investments which result in increasing economic efficiency and reducing product costs relative to those of other countries, tend to have a permanent effect in increasing economic activity and aggregate economic demand.

The general proposition that demand declines as price increases is appropriate to most commodities, including labour costs and rates of interest. Labour costs rise not only because wage rates are increased beyond increases in productivity but also as a result of government employment regulations and taxes on employment such as social insurance. It is now thought that wage levels fail to fall with large numbers of long-term unemployed because they are not in the effective labour market. Some believe that boosting the economy will do little to bring the long-term unemployed back into work unless they are first retrained.

Rates of interest tend to rise as a result of inflation, declining international exchange rates and increases in borrowing. Rising labour costs tend to result in home-produced goods becoming more expensive than overseas goods with the result that exports tend to decline and imports to rise. Such movements tend to reduce the world value of the home currency (i.e. the international exchange rate) but international borrowing is now on such a large scale that the financial consequences of it, may have more effect on international exchange rates than the exchange of goods and services. As a result the home currency may not fall enough in world value to offset sufficiently the rise in home prices and so assist exports and damp down imports.

Many of the factors affecting aggregate demand are difficult or impossible for governments to control, for example, wage rates and overseas exchange rates. Other factors have undesirable as well as desirable effects. For example, while borrowing overseas does not immediately affect investment and consumption at home, and if investment at home raises aggregate income, it also tends to raise the value of home currency resulting in exports becoming more expensive and imports cheaper. In the longer term, meeting the interest on the loan and eventually repaying it, has the reverse tendencies. Determining the best balance between rates of tax, interest and overseas exchange is difficult: achieving them even more so.

2.15   EXTERNAL COSTS

By external costs is meant, not overseas costs, but costs (positive or negative) external to the principal in a transaction. It is necessary to distinguish between costs and benefits to persons, firms, public bodies and the community. In making decisions, developers, purchasers and tenants take account of the costs to themselves but ignore (in fact rarely know) the costs borne by others, the external costs. This applies equally to private and public developers, and users of buildings and works. Most developments create some costs to the community at large which arise from the incidence of such things as noise, fumes, dirt, loss of light, privacy and traffic generation. External costs arise to central and local government for servicing a development and to firms, public enterprises and individuals from the inconveniences created and the costs of trying to avoid them. It is not always easy to estimate external costs and usually there is no machinery to enable the costs to be transferred back to the developers and users of the development.

External costs are an important factor to be considered in planning and planning control. Cost–benefit studies analyse how the costs and benefits arise, who is affected by them and how large they are (Chapter 13). Developments creating excessive external costs can be rejected or modified. While private and public enterprises try to maximize returns to themselves, governments, both central and local, as agents of the community, have a duty to take a wider view. Very detailed cost–benefit analyses have been made for some government developments, particularly in the case of roads and some other transport developments (Chapter 13).

2.16   ECONOMIC TOOLS FOR PLANNING AND DEVELOPMENT

In the final analysis, development and planning decisions are economic and social decisions which affect not only local firms and individuals but national well-being. On the one hand, development and planning decisions affect national output and resources, and on the other hand, national output and resources affect both the demand for built environment and the resources available to develop and maintain it. It is therefore necessary to have some grasp of the economic principles which underly economic decisions. Economic concepts and principles are largely commonsense and applied intuitively in reaching decisions by both organizations and individuals. Complexities arise when several principles need to be considered at the same time, when they are in conflict and when there is some uncertainty as to the relative importance to be attached to each. The value of a formal approach lies in the deeper understanding which this provides in analysing the problems and providing a logical basis for decision. Readers requiring a more complete account than is possible here should refer to an economic textbook [1, 2].

REFERENCES

1. Harvey, J. (1983) *Modern Economics*, 4th edn, Macmillan, London.
2. Lipsey, R. G. (1983) *An Introduction to Positive Economics*, 6th edn, Weidenfeld and Nicholson, London.

3

The market for land and built environment

3.1 DEMAND FOR THE BUILT ENVIRONMENT

The demand for the built environment arises from human activities requiring shelter and developed operational space. People form households and require dwellings and a large range of goods and services. Organizations, both public and private, supplying goods and services (directly or indirectly) require shops, warehouses, industrial buildings, offices, health, education and other social buildings, transport and other public utility facilities (Fig. 3.1). Thus initially demand depends on population and its economic and social activities. By far the greater demand for the built environment is met from stock. Additional development arises where the stock of suitable built facilities at required locations and in relation to price is not available. The shortfall may be met by new buildings or by rehabilitation and conversion of existing stock. Some obsolete facilities may be demolished.

The annual demand for development is small in relation to the demand for built facilities; generally only about 2% of stock (Fig. 3.2). The scale of annual demand for development depends on a large number of economic and social factors related to the scale of economic activity, financial conditions and client preferences. These will be discussed later. The current level of aggregate demand for each class of property depends on activities in the appropriate field. For example, in recent times the demand for offices has increased, reflecting growth and changes in service industry, while demand for shops and cinemas has declined. The higher the costs of new facilities, the more likely is the client to make do with existing ones, particularly when confidence is low. While new development can be postponed for several years, eventually changes in activities, techniques and locations, and growing obsolescence creates an urgent need for new development. Because of the scale of existing stock, demand for development fluctuates more than the demand for built facilities.

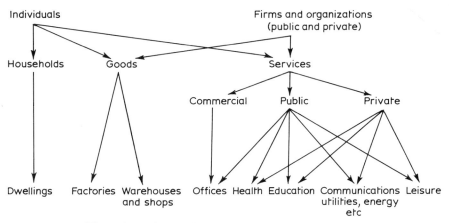

Figure 3.1 Generation of demand for built facilities.

3.2 CLIENTS

The starting point for examining the market for land and the built environment is the client. It is necessary to consider who the clients are, the nature of their demands, the basis of their evaluation and how they influence demand.

The users of the built environment are heterogeneous. They include the occupiers of land, buildings and other built facilities, visitors to them and all those members of the public who pass by, live adjacent to or pass over them. In the private sector buildings' occupiers, whether owners or tenants, are direct clients for land and buildings and can affect demand through their offers to purchase or rent. Occupiers in the public sector concerned with commercial operations are to some extent in a similar position but those in the non-commercial public sector do not usually enter the market directly; the provision of buildings being the responsibility of the administrations of the organizations of which they are a part. Visitors to buildings in the commercial sector are generally customers purchasing goods and services, a category which includes shoppers, audiences, members of clubs, students and patients. They can influence the form of building demand through their patronage of the occupiers. The third group, the general public or the community are affected by the built environment through its appearance, convenience and through the way its use generates noise, fumes, traffic and other nuisances. The community can influence development demand indirectly through political action influencing the official planning process, and through influencing government fiscal, monetary and regional policies.

3.3 OCCUPIERS

Occupiers, whether tenants or owners, are concerned with annual costs.

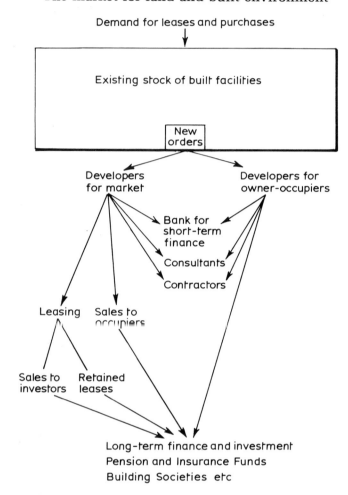

Figure 3.2   Market for built facilities and development.

These include the rent or its equivalent to the owner, rates, other costs of servicing the property and certain costs of operating within it. Some occupiers obtain public assistance towards these costs in the form of subsidies or tax relief. Annual costs can be related to some measure of the capacity of the property such as floor area, rooms, work spaces or beds, to provide a basis for comparing the costs per unit capacity of one property with another and some measure of the value of the property to the occupier. The total annual costs, the costs-in-use [1] that is the amortized equivalent of the capital costs, together with the running costs, depend to a large extent on the volume and design of the property and are within the control of the developer and hence indirectly of the first occupier. Rates, taxes and subsidies depend on central and local government policies. They can affect demand for property nationally and, where they vary from one area to another, locally. Their incidence may also influence design and servicing.

Private non-commercial occupiers, mainly households and charities, are concerned with occupation for shelter, personal satisfaction and investment potential. Benefits are valued in terms of personal satisfaction from appearance, comfort and convenience. These are subjective and difficult to evaluate in money terms (Chapter 11). The more they are valued the more will be spent on acquiring and running the property relative to the occupiers' wealth and income. Generally the higher the income the more will be spent on housing and the higher the standard demanded. On average in western societies households spend about one-fifth of their incomes on housing, including rent and rent equivalent, and running costs. The proportion does not necessarily increase with income although the absolute amount usually does. In the case of charities the actual occupier does not generally bear the cost; costs are borne by the charitable organization which might not experience the benefits directly. This division increases the difficulties of comparing costs and benefits.

Private commercial occupiers are concerned less with the property for its own sake and more with the buildings as a factor of production. The buildings or works are required to provide shelter and an acceptable environment for a production process, whether for goods or services. Their value lies in the way they function in relation to the productive process and how they affect its costs. It is worthwhile increasing the costs-in-use of the building if the extra costs are less than the saving in direct production costs (Chapter 11). Clearly the lower the value of the goods and services produced and the lower the value added by the process, the lower the building costs which can be afforded or are worth incurring. For example, at one extreme, the handling of waste products, wrecked cars and raw materials such as coal, sand and gravel generally takes place in the open air or in old, cheap premises, obsolete for most other purposes. At the other extreme, head offices for banks and oil companies are usually high quality and expensive. Nevertheless, even though turnover and value added per unit output are high there is still some limit on the property costs worth incurring. The buildings are not usually gold plated and even firms producing high added values are amongst those moving out of the high cost central areas, at least for some of their activities. Of course, a large proportion of the cost of a property in the central business district of a capital city arises from the site and property tax rather than the building itself.

Public commercial occupiers are public corporations and other units which operate as commercial organizations. They tend to regard their buildings as a factor of production in the same way as private commercial occupiers. Where, however, they enjoy a monopoly in their field of production, for example the

Central Electricity Generating Board, they are under less pressure to obtain the most economic building because they can meet additional costs of production, up to a point, by raising their prices. Often public commercial undertakings receive subsidies which may be used partly to obtain higher standard buildings than would otherwise be possible.

Public housing occupiers are in a somewhat different situation to private owner-occupiers. The product is the housing service itself and competes with private housing whether for rent or purchase. As indicated above the occupier judges value for money in terms of satisfaction from appearance, comfort and convenience as against costs, an important element of which is rent. The landlord needs to know the potential tenants' likely evaluation and the rent they would be prepared to pay, in order to determine demand for different types of dwellings. Of course, public housing is frequently subsidized both in general and in relation to tenants' means and its supply may be restricted to tenants satisfying certain social criteria. Subsidies increase value for money to the tenants, reduce tenants' preference strengths and hence distort market demand and market guide to potential tenants' preferences. Public housing shares with public non-commercial building a separation of those commissioning the building, meeting the costs and obtaining the benefits; often the agents responsible for servicing the dwellings are separate from those developing them. The separation of responsibility weakens the incentive to provide good value for money. The occupiers of private rented housing are also affected by market distortions but these arise from government rent control rather than subsidies.

Public non-commercial occupiers such as the staffs of schools, hospitals and public offices do not have a market for their products. There is no revenue from the operations against which to judge the benefits derived from the properties. The costs incurred in producing the service are not constrained by sales revenue but only by grants and subsidies. There is no market indication of clients' preferences. Costs are often difficult to identify because they are charged to administrative accounts which bear little relation to function. While benefits of occupation could be analysed in terms of appearance, comfort and function, it is often difficult to identify the occupier to be considered. The property exists to provide a service to pupils, patients, audiences and so on – transient groups difficult to consult. The lead-time for public buildings is often so long that the staff available for consultation and the technology in use at the planning stage have changed by the time the property is ready for occupation. Planning and design decisions are generally taken by administrators and designers who will neither use the property, nor meet its costs. Market constraints are replaced by administrative constraints, often cost targets based on past results. Because capital and revenue funds are obtained from separate sources, cost targets usually only relate to initial costs and there is no guarantee that revenue funds will be available to operate the service in the way it was designed to function or even at all (Chapter 14). Such administrative procedures tend to result in higher costs, in a waste of resources and in reducing the quantity of properties which can be financed.

3.4 OCCUPIERS' COSTS

As indicated above occupiers' costs include rent or its equivalent, running costs and costs arising from the effect of the planning and design of the building on operating within it.

Rent is determined by the supply and demand for the type, style and location of the property. In the short term a rent which covers the landlord's current expenses, that is his prime costs, is worth considering; in the longer term the rent would also need to cover the annual equivalent of the price the development would fetch on the market. In the very long term, properties will not be developed if the expected rents will not cover the annual equivalent costs, that is the amortized costs of land and development, annual expenditure and a profit commensurate with the risks. Some occupiers prefer to own their properties rather than rent them. The capital cost incurred is either the cost of acquiring a site and developing a building (to be considered later in Section 3.10) or the capitalized value of expected future rents. The relationship between rent and capital value depends on the rate of interest (or discount), the expected future economic life of the property and expectations about future changes in rents.

The seller's rate for capitalizing rent may be different from the cost of servicing the capital to the purchaser. Expectations about future events, investment opportunities and the incidence of taxation may reduce the expected cost of servicing the capital cost to the occupier relative to the rent he would expect to pay. On the other hand, the occupier may not be able to raise the capital or prefer to have the ability to invest more in other directions, for example in his business. The effective real rate of interest may be considerably below the nominal rate. For example, an inflation rate of 5% would reduce a nominal rate of interest of 12% to a real rate of about 7%. In the business sector rents and interest are charged against profits, reducing the effective costs by the rate of taxation the business pays. The lower the rate of interest (or discount) the greater the capital equivalent of the rent and the more important the expected future economic life of the property (Fig. 3.3). For example, the capital equivalent at 15% is about 6.6 times the annual payment and this factor increases little after about 45 years, while at 4% the factor is about 24 times and increases little after 80 years.

The annual running costs include rates, maintenance, heating and ventilation, lighting, cleaning, insurance and administration. The costs vary according to the type of property and the type and situation of the building. Rates are likely to be particularly variable, depending on the current rental value,

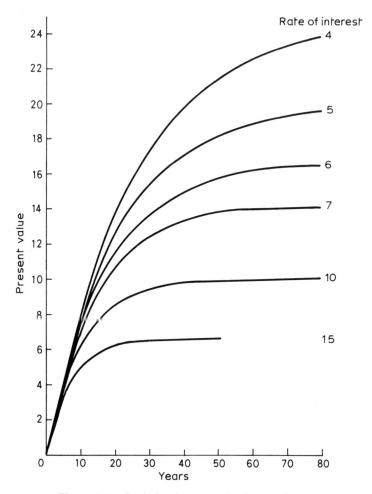

Figure 3.3 Capital value per unit of annual value.

itself being considerably affected by location. Other costs will vary mainly according to the design, layout and use of the property (Chapter 11).

Operation costs depend on the nature of the operation carried on in the building but are also affected by the layout and design of the building (Chapter 11).

3.5 MARKET DEMAND

Market demand for properties depends in the first place on the demand for goods and services to be produced or generated by the use of their facilities. Other factors include the availability of finance to rent or purchase them. For new facilities demand depends in addition on the potential of the existing stock and on the availability of land, developers and appropriate finance. The incidence of demand varies with the type of property.

3.6 HOUSING

Housing need depends on the formation of households by structure and number. Demand depends on need and the ability to meet housing cost. Often the scale and distribution of households does not match the distribution of dwellings. Even if the number is adequate, the dwellings may not be in the locations in which they are required, or of the right size and quality. The greater their incomes, the more households generally will be prepared to pay for their housing and the less they will be prepared to compromise on size, quality and location. Their demands will be reflected in the rents and purchase prices they are prepared to offer. In the public sector greater national affluence usually results in political pressure for better housing. When the economy is buoyant, incomes tend to be increased and migration at its highest, tending to push up the demand for dwellings.

House purchase is generally financed on borrowed money. The amount which can be borrowed depends on the size and stability of the borrower's income and hence the ability to service the loan. In Great Britain mortgage finance is provided mainly by building societies and to a smaller extent by banks and insurance institutions. In some countries the main agencies are housing associations. Whether sufficient funds flow to institutions providing mortgages depends on how their rates of interest and conditions for lenders compare with those of other saving institutions. Although substantial funds flow back to lending institutions as mortgages are repaid, such funds are not usually sufficient to finance new mortgage demand especially when property prices are rising, when additional funds are required even to finance the same number of mortgages. The number of mortgages demanded fluctuates, but it tends to rise as more households aspire to house ownership. When the funds available are below demand, mortgages are rationed both in number and in size in relation to the cost of the dwelling. This has a number of consequences. It tends to dampen prices and to increase the difficulty of obtaining mortgages for poorer property and by borrowers with smaller and less secure incomes. Generally this results in fewer and smaller mortgages for first time borrowers. While lending institutions often try to favour such borrowers, a balance between new and existing borrowers is necessary since the availability of a flow of existing dwellings for sale depends on the provision of mortgages to householders moving up-market or to new locations.

While the demand for dwellings, including new dwellings, depends on the availability of mortgage finance and the ability of purchasers to service the mortgages, the supply of new dwellings is affected by the finance available to developers. This is generally provided by banking institutions rather than mortgage institutions and depends on the availability of finance to the banks, mainly current and deposit accounts, and on other demands on bank finance. Hence the development and sale of dwellings depends on the availability of two types of finance, supplies of which may not move together. The supply of dwellings for sale is increased by the sale of dwellings in the rented sector. In Britain, tenants of public authority housing can generally purchase the dwellings they rent at a considerable discount and large numbers have indeed been purchased in this way.

Demand for rented housing depends on such factors as household incomes, the comparative financial returns from purchasing and renting, availability of personal capital and credit, expected duration of residence and the supply of property. Mortgage payments are usually greater than rents because they are generally repaid over comparatively short periods. The financial returns depend on the incidence of taxation, subsidies and rent controls. Payments for housing do not usually count as an expense for tax purposes but a tax allowance is given currently in Great Britain on mortgage interest which reduces the cost for those without corresponding investment interests. Capital gains on the principal dwelling are currently not taxed in Great Britain. Publicly provided housing is usually subsidized, substantially reducing the cost to the occupier. Private rented dwellings, at least those at the cheaper end of the market, often have controlled rents, reducing costs below market level. Tenants with rents below market prices tend to be reluctant to move, reducing the mobility of this sector of households.

Rent controls tend to reduce the returns to the owners of the property below market levels and hence reduce the market value of such dwellings. Investors who purchase at such prices can generally obtain a fair return on their capital, but those who are owners at the time controls are imposed or increased are likely to incur real losses on selling. Legislation on rented property tends to reduce the amount of property available for letting. Often the capital value of a rent-controlled house is less than the cost of a replacement. It is not surprising, therefore, that where dwellings are subject to rent control and to secure tenancy, there is little building for the private rented market or that existing ones are sold off when the opportunity occurs. In such circumstances the amount of private rented housing tends to be inadequate to meet market demand unless the shortfall is made good by public authorities or housing associations supported by subsidies or tax allowances. Controlled rents are often too low to support adequate mainten-ance, resulting in a deterioration in the stock.

Public housing is allocated according to criteria related to social need. Supply is often well below demand. Generally there is little opportunity to move to another dwelling in the public sector. As a result tenants in this sector tend to be immobile. Despite short supply and subsidized rents, some property is difficult to let, particularly high density flatted estates. The range of standards and forms of housing tend to be limited for those at the lower end of the market. Rents tend not to reflect perceived differences in standards, forms and locations, and little opportunity is provided for tenants who place a high value on housing services to bid for higher-quality dwellings. In the absence of market operations within the public sector, and effective substitutes, there is little indication of the preferences of potential tenants. Decisions on design and location are mainly taken by the sponsors and their officials. There are many reports of technical and social failures, resulting in the need for extensive maintenance in an atmosphere fostering vandalism and crime, and in some cases demolition (Chapter 5).

3.7 COMMERCIAL PROPERTIES

The term 'commercial properties' is intended to include commercial and industrial properties of all types used for the production of goods and services in the private sector or for the market in the public sector. Market demand depends on confidence in future demand for the goods and services themselves and market conditions. There is a demand for new premises in declining as well as growth sectors of the economy. Demand arises from changes in methods and scales of production and distribution, and in location. New and expanding firms and organizations require additional premises. The production of new products and new activities can generally be pursued more efficiently in new or remodelled premises. Migration of customers and changes in location of factors of production often entail new locations for the suppliers.

In this sector firms increasingly rent rather than own the property they occupy. Some firms do not have the capital or credit to purchase or develop their premises, or prefer to use it to develop their business. Often firms already owning their premises sell to investors in order to release capital, leasing the property back. Firms requiring premises frequently enter into leasing arrangements with a developer. After development or remodelling the developer may sell to a property investor, but investors usually require property for which there is likely to be long-term market demand so that there is a reasonable opportunity to relet or sell if required. Generally, demand for premises in this sector is better informed and more selective than for housing. Space and other needs are analysed with care. Developers often only develop building shells, leaving tenants to specify their needs or to complete developments themselves.

3.8 PUBLIC NON-COMMERCIAL PROPERTIES

Demand for public non-commercial development such as buildings for social purposes, roads and other public engineering facilities arises from public need, as determined by public authorities rather than by a market. While an allowance may be made for costs and benefits to the community, this is difficult and value for money judgements tend to be overridden by political judgements and public budgeting (Chapter 14). Demands for public development generally exceed the resources public bodies are prepared or able to make available. It is difficult to devise administrative mechanisms sensitive enough to distribute funds to maximize welfare. There is a tendency for standards for new facilities to be set high in relation to total resources, reducing their number and the resources available to sustain existing facilities at an adequate standard. In this way the best can be the enemy of the good. In order to obtain the maximum benefits in relation to the resources used, it would be necessary to examine the global demand for the built environment and the standards of existing and proposed units, and to consider the consequences of devoting more or less resources to developing and rehabilitating each unit, or to reducing or increasing the number of units developed or brought up to standard (Chapter 14).

3.9   SITE VALUES

The value of a site depends on its natural and built physical attributes, its location and the nature of possible planning consent. Undeveloped land itself has little economic value even today. The bare top of a mountain with no minerals or other attributes of value and no access has virtually no use and hence no economic value, but if a road or cable lift is built, the mountain may have attractions for sport or tourism. If the revenue exceeds the annual equivalent costs of development and operation, the mountain top will have a value. Economic value arises because someone is prepared to pay for the rights to use the site whether for building development, agriculture, sports or other purposes. If the desire to enjoy rights, such as scenic and ecological values is not backed by purchasing power, the site has no economic value for that purpose. Such rights can then only be secured by political pressure to impose planning restrictions to protect such attributes.

Most of the difficulties of development arising from the physical quality of the site can be overcome but the additional development costs will be reflected in the site value. Other things being equal, the sites with the best attributes will be developed first. Sites without adequate communications, on steep slopes, with waterlogged land and poor load-bearing qualities will initially be beyond the margin of development but will gradually be taken into development as the better land is used up. If demand is strong enough, physical difficulties will be overcome as, for example, in Venice and Edinburgh.

The value of the location of a site for a particular person depends on its geographical position, particularly in relation to the development of its locality. Value rises with improvements in communications and services, and with the status of the development around it. Hence the incidence of public and private development is an important factor in determining value. Relative to location value, the value of natural physical attributes may not be high. 'Bygones are forever bygones'. The price of a property depends on its future potential, not on its past. A high-quality building, even one just built, may have little value if the demand it was built to meet disappears and it cannot easily be used for another purpose, or adapted to other needs.

Site prices vary in particular in relation to location, density and use. Prices vary considerably from site to site because sites offer different attributes. There can be tenfold differences within a few streets [2], reflecting differences in economic potential and the consequential differences in economic rent (Chapter 2). Nevertheless, there are broad patterns of site prices. Prices per unit area tend to be highest in the city centre, to decline with city size and with distance from the centre and to be lowest in remote rural areas. Studies of residential land prices in England indicated that at constant densities prices declined exponentially with distance from the centre [3]. They averaged eight times as high in Central London as 60 miles from the centre. Local peaks were found in the areas of large towns with the lowest values in rural areas. Prices were found to increase broadly linearly with the number of dwellings for which planning consent was available. At ten times the density average prices were five to eight times higher. Industrial land was found to be on average two to three times as expensive as residential land, while land for commercial purposes averaged about twenty five times as much. Within these broad patterns prices varied widely with the attributes of sites and of town sectors. The price relationships may vary over time and place. Sites in run-down inner cities, for which there is often little demand, may have little site value (Chapter 10).

Sites and properties are synonymous. Even most virgin sites have some use without further development. Further development will not take place unless the potential value of the new use exceeds that of the existing use by more than the costs of the further development. Values may change without development being necessary. For example, rising affluence may enable turnover to be increased, bringing higher profit margins and making it worthwhile to incur a higher rent. Often the full potential cannot be obtained without further development. Competition for the most valuable sites will push up prices.

In the short run site prices depend on the site's value-in-use and on scarcity. For example, a shop in the centre of a main shopping area of a large town is likely to have a much greater turnover than a similar shop in a village. Generally the larger the turnover the lower the price at which goods can be bought in, the greater the sales per unit floor area and per assistant and the more rapid the turnover: factors favourable to profit margins. Up to a point it is worthwhile to incur a higher rent in order to secure such economies.

Development costs are not generally affected by turnover per unit area, so that site value tends to rise relative to rent. The value of the advantage resides in the site. If sites are in short supply relative to demand, potential occupiers and investors will bid up the price. It can be observed, for example, that the price of sites for residential development tends to rise with the price of dwellings, other things being equal, but tends to fall as development costs increase.

In the long run costs of supply are important. Developers will only purchase land if the expected prices for the completed properties are large enough to meet all the costs of development and leave a reasonable profit. If property prices fall, the prices offered for sites tend to follow suit. Again developers take into account all the development costs in determining what a site is worth to them. Other things being equal, they are not prepared to pay as much for a site which requires high demolition, drainage and underbuilding costs as for a flat, undeveloped, well drained site with good load-bearing characteristics. Again, other things being equal, an industrial site along a wide, metalled road is likely to command a higher value than one to which a road must be built.

The price of a site in a developed area in part reflects the saving in not having to provide the necessary services. A developer of housing, infilling sites along an existing developed road, generally does not incur development costs outside the curtilage of the individual site. If he were developing an estate he would generally have to provide estate roads and paths, areas of landscaping, land for electric substations and other utilities, estate drainage and water mains, and contribute to the costs of providing estate services such as electricity and gas. The developer of a new town needs to purchase a great deal more land than he will eventually have available to sell as properties. An analysis of the use of land in a typical new town indicated that about 17% of the land would be required for roads and public parking [4]. A considerable proportion of the remaining land would be needed for other public purposes and would have returns far less than those of residential, commercial and industrial land. Estimates for a typical new town suggest that the costs of land and engineering services spread over the land available for sale for residential, commercial and industrial purposes raises its cost by a factor of ten [4]. In this way the gap between the price of agricultural land and land with services ready for development tends to be closed. The prices realized for such land will depend on the confidence of developers that the sites will have the promised potential. Initially prices will depend on a rapid build-up of a large enough area of activity with an adequate balance of jobs and labour, housing services and customers. Once a thriving nucleus has been established property prices will tend to rise (Chapter 9).

Site values fluctuate with changes in neighbourhood activity. Sites tend to rise in value when they are part of a city which is expanding or becoming more affluent or of a neighbourhood which is moving up-market. A developer may raise the value of neighbouring sites by carrying out redevelopment and rehabilitation. Sites tend to lose value when the city and neighbourhood are in decline. As a town becomes more prosperous, incomes tend to rise and business activity increases, revenues increase and site values rise. Pressure on space increases, encouraging new development and redevelopment. Demand for sites tends not to rise evenly; some areas are favoured and shifts occur in the centres of activity. Demand for sites and development is also affected by changes in business methods and in the relative importance of different activities. Changes in the locality tend to affect all sites and to shift the distribution of site value over wide areas. Changes in site use usually involve either remodelling or redevelopment. Which is undertaken depends on the future potential of the building and the costs of development work.

Redevelopment is generally more costly than remodelling but usually produces a property with greater current value and a longer potential life (Chapters 11 and 12). The greater the possible increase in space and value from change in use, the more it is worth spending on development. Without redevelopment or remodelling values may decline even though town activity and prosperity is increasing; this would occur where properties in their existing form lack the potential and standards currently required. Even when a neighbourhood has potential, it may not be possible to release it by developing individual sites: they may be too small, wrongly shaped and have poor access, and the layout of the area may be inappropriate to potential new uses. Roads may need to be resited, and car parking and amenity space provided. Such development would involve local authority agreement to road development, possible exchange between public and private land, and public utility cooperation in realigning their service connections. Area redevelopment usually involves considerable problems of land acquisition. It can take many years to acquire sites in separate ownership and tenancies may take many years to run out. The problems of land acquisition and development by a number of developers are considerable. It is easier if the sites are brought into single ownership. The local authority may acquire sites using its powers for compulsory purchase. They may redevelop the area themselves, creating sites for sale or lease to developers, or sell or lease the area to a developer who will undertake to provide land for roads, utilities and amenity areas, and perhaps develop them as a part of the price of the land (Chapter 10).

Fortuitous gains and losses arise because land values change in response to changing demand arising from forces outside the control of the owners of the sites, for example, changes in local affluence, the economy and the local infrastructure. High-class dwellings may cease to be practical for the occupiers; they may be let for multiple occupation and allowed to deteriorate. Such changes to even a few houses may result in demand in that area declining, bringing down the values of all the properties. In other situations affluent people may move into a run-down area, do up the dilapidated property and attract others to follow them, raising property values in the area (Chapter 10). Increasing values may also arise because the demand for higher value property, such as offices, is expanding in a locality. While such changes in use and higher densities are usually dependent on planning permission, higher site values arise from changes in demand, although the absence of planning consent would prevent much of the value being realized. Such windfall gains may be taxed but losses are seldom compensated except where they arise from the withholding of planning consent in an unreasonable way.

3.10 DEVELOPERS

Developers include owners who develop property for their own use, property investors who develop for leasing, speculators who develop for sale to owner-occupiers and investors, and public organizations who develop for their own or public use or speculatively for leasing to households and commercial and industrial firms (Fig. 3.2).

Owners developing for their own occupation are their own clients. The development of property by owners is generally undertaken when their specification of space, quality and location is not met by properties available on the market or from current development. In conjunction with professional advisers they prepare a brief, instruct independent or in-house designers to prepare plans, specifications and bills of quantities, and engage contractors to develop the site and construct the buildings; occasionally they carry out the construction themselves.

Property investors are intermediate clients. They are concerned with what the final clients, the tenants, require and are prepared to rent. The investor must try to understand how potential occupiers are likely to use the building and the value of the various features to them. There will generally be a range of options, each with its own development cost and potential rent. Subject to the potential of the site, they will attempt to find which option provides the best return on their investment. The property investor will then have plans prepared to meet the favoured set of specifications, contracting the development with a construction firm. Alternatively property investors may purchase a completed property from a speculative developer, or enter into a purchasing arrangement with them prior to construction.

There is no clear differentiation between developers building for sale to the market and those building for investment, although the latter are often the larger firms. Property developers may always build for sale, or sometimes for sale and sometimes for renting. Often, particularly when the market is uncertain, they will endeavour to secure a tenant before development is commenced; an agreed lease will assist sale to an investor.

Public developers have a wide range of functions. Local authorities build or renovate dwellings for renting and sometimes for sale, while they and town development organizations also develop commercial and industrial property for renting and prepare sites for leasing to users who wish to construct their own buildings and to developers building for the market. Local authorities, central government and other public organizations develop properties for their own use such as offices, schools and hospitals. As indicated earlier, the customer of the services provided by the properties is also in a sense the final client. Such authorities also develop public service facilities like roads and public utilities for the use of the community.

Developers in the private sector aim to obtain an acceptable return on their investment, that is a return on the capital adequate in relation to the rate of interest paid for borrowed money or forfeited on their capital employed in the enterprise, together with a premium to cover the risks they incur. The rate of interest is determined by market conditions. The risk premium varies with the nature of the development and the extent to which they can reduce the risks by forward sales and other arrangements.

3.11   RISKS

Risks fall as the size of the market increases. The wider the market the greater the number of clients and the lower the risks of delay in disposing of the property or of price fluctuations. The market is wider the larger the class of building, the more standard it is and the more popular the area for that class of building. The market for low-cost housing and standard office, industrial and shop units is far wider than that for specialist units, such as large expensive dwellings and cinemas. Risks are reduced by developing for the average occupier. Building only shells, leaving the occupier to complete them to meet his own needs is a form of risk limitation. Development risks are generally less in growth than in static areas; developers tend to be reluctant to develop in declining areas or those which have not yet become popular.

Economic conditions favourable to development occur when general demand is rising, business confidence is high and rates of interest and inflation are low. At such times firms are likely to be expanding and migrating, and new firms are being born, events likely to increase the demand for additional and better premises. In such situations more households will tend to be formed, they will tend to be more mobile and be looking for higher-standard accommodation. Demand is stimulated by lower taxes and tax allowances, and subsidies on property, and discouraged by high taxes and rates and rating of empty properties. The timing of taxes can also be important to the developer: taxing imputed gain before the property is sold raises costs, increases capital requirements and adds to the risks.

3.12   DEVELOPERS' EXPENDITURE AND REVENUE

Developers' costs include those for market research, site investigation, land, planning and design, site clearance, development and construction, marketing, fees, administration, interest and taxes. If, in addition to developing property, they also retain it as an investment, they incur further management costs and possibly running costs, fees, interest and taxation on the building.

Market research informs developers about the variables in the market within which they propose to operate. Developers need to estimate the total demand for property of the type they propose to develop in the areas they are considering, the current supply and the extent to which other developers are likely to meet the demand. Market transactions need to be studied to estimate the likely price profile. This depends not only on the size and standard of the building but on the location, the importance of which was discussed earlier. It is also necessary to investigate clients' preference and likely basis of evaluation.

Site investigation is necessary to establish both the site's physical attributes and likely planning potential. Physical attributes of importance include access for people and goods, vehicle access for parking and loading, access and storage during construction, load-bearing characteristics (particularly important for redevelopment sites), size, shape and gradient, existing construction and rights of light. Planning potential depends not just on zoning and planning density but on the likely flexibility of the official planners and the price that may be demanded in terms of land for public use and the development of public amenity. It is also necessary to check the availability of water, drainage, power and telephone lines.

Sites may be purchased or leased. Leases for development land are generally for periods comparable with the likely life of the development but the ground rent may be fixed for a much shorter period. Where the development is likely to be particularly speculative only a peppercorn rent may be charged in the early years, in order to encourage development. This policy is often followed by landowners trying to revive a run-down area or open up a new one, for example, local authorities attempting to upgrade a part of the inner city or a town development corporation opening up a town centre. It is a way of subsidizing costs and a recognition of the time it is likely to take to attract sufficient activity to raise values and hence rents to a level sufficient to cover costs and normal profits. If land is leased, developers require less capital but the profits on sale will be less in total.

Planning and design is carried out by a professional in-house team or by consultants or sometimes under contract for designing and building. Generally an in-house team prepares a brief based on clients' preferences as indicated by market research. The form, standard and style of the development depends on the anticipated cost and price. A development likely to give the best return on the capital employed tends to be unique to that site. Selecting the best solution requires information, experience and judgement. Planning and design costs are likely to be substantial, generally 10–15% of construction costs.

Site clearance and construction are generally put out to tender, except where the developer is himself the contractor. Average costs of constructing the most common types of building are available from price books [5]. Costs per unit of floor space vary considerably. Site clearance and services are very variable in cost, tending to be particularly costly on redevelopment sites. Underbuilding costs can also be high on disturbed land. Some previously used sites are cluttered with utility services and may even have chemical pollution which can be expensive to neutralize. Access to sites in built-up areas can be difficult; often the costs are difficult to estimate until work actually begins. Contracts usually contain a rise and fall clause, especially where work is likely to take several years. Over such periods it is difficult to forecast the likely extent of inflation.

Credit costs depend on the shape and length of the stream of credit required to finance the development. This has a cost whether the credit (capital) is borrowed from a finance house or is supplied in-house. Development may take several years and a substantial amount of capital may be tied up from the beginning. Site acquisition may take a number of years, especially where land has to be purchased piecemeal from a number of owners, with the developer waiting several years for leases to fall in before development can commence, or having to buy out leases. Obtaining planning consent and the redevelopment of roads and services can also adsorb much time, as can the development work itself. When the development is complete the economic climate may have changed, for better or worse. If demand has fallen it may be difficult to let or sell the property to an occupier and a sale to an investor may be at a heavily discounted price.

Management and selling costs can be considerable. Management costs are incurred throughout the period of development. Fees arise for valuation of the site and for selling, as well as for planning and design. Usually developers engage estate agents to find clients, whether aiming to sell or lease the property. Their fees and those of solicitors to draw up the contracts are usually substantial.

With so many separate operations uncertainty is unavoidable, but timing and phasing are important both to complete the development when market demand is at its highest and to minimize the capital outstanding and the costs of credit. It is desirable to complete the development as rapidly as possible, providing that unacceptable additional development costs are not incurred as a result and to postpone large items of expenditure as long as possible. Aims include avoiding delays between the various phases and completing phases which bring in a revenue as soon as possible. In some cases it may pay to split the development into sections which can be used on their own and hence let or sold in advance of total completion. The phasing will generally be worked out using critical path analysis or some similar technique, with adjustments to the programme if development gets out of the planned phasing [6].

Developers' capital is generally limited relative to the volume of development they wish to undertake, especially when demand is high. It may be possible to borrow at an initial rate of interest lower than the expected return on their capital. The more finance the developer borrows the greater the possible profits but the greater the risk of losses from changes in market conditions. Generally developers borrow short-time credit from banks and longer-term credit from insurance and pension funds. The availability of loan finance depends both on the security the borrower can provide and the conditions in the credit market. Rates of interest can vary widely over short periods, in part reflecting government action. If financial conditions become difficult banks may call in their loans. This often occurs when business confidence is low and credit to possible purchasers tight and expensive, so that sales and lettings are difficult except at uneconomic prices. In such circumstances a developer who has borrowed heavily in the short term in relation to his capital may incur losses and even become insolvent.

3.13 PROPERTY INVESTORS

Property investment is a different type of business from development, although some investors also develop their properties. Development is a relatively short-term, complex and high-risk operation, whereas the investor is looking for a reliable long-term income, with rising revenues to at least offset inflation. Much of property investment is undertaken by financial institutions such as life assurance and pension offices, pension funds, unit trusts and other savings institutions. Their preference is for property let on long leases to firms and institutions of good standing who will remain over the life of the property and be unlikely to default on their rent. They prefer to let properties as a whole with the tenant accepting responsibility for maintenance and insurance. Well established firms in a stable line of business such as chain stores, banks and multinational firms are preferred. If developers can secure such tenants, the opportunities for an early sale are greatly increased. If leases can be arranged before completion, or even before starting construction, a sale may follow with sale proceeds immediately on completion. The earlier this can be arranged, the more secure the developer's line of credit and the cheaper it is likely to be. However, such investors require property in prime positions, raising site costs and reducing developers' interest in sites in other positions, in particular in run-down areas where redevelopment might be more desirable from a social point of view. The extent to which investors wish to purchase developments depends, in addition, on property occupiers' confidence and financial ability to lease new properties and hence on the buoyancy of the economy, and on the flow of savings to the investment institutions. If developers have failed to forecast movements in the economy correctly or failed to complete on schedule, there may be a surplus or, less often, a shortage of new property available to meet market demand.

Property values depend on rents and the rate at which these are discounted. Rents tend to be unique to each property reflecting the demand for its type, size, quality and position. As explained earlier, position is particularly important. While some statistical data on rents are published by estate agents, they are not very useful for estimating the likely rent of a particular property. This is generally estimated by an estate agent in relation to other rents in the area. The capitalized value of the rents will depend on expectations of interest rates, life of the property, future rents and so on. The lower the rate of interest and the higher the expectations about future rents, the higher the multiplier applied to the current rent to find the capital value. For a property with a long life expectation, the capital value would be about three times as great if the rate of interest was 4% than if it was 15% (Fig. 3.3). For a property with a shorter life, about 20 years, the difference would be about twofold.

Initial yields on the capital costs of property, that is the rate at which rents are discounted, are much lower than the rate of interest payable by borrowers and vary with rates of interest and other market factors. Despite current high rates of interest an initial yield of 4% would probably be acceptable for first class shop and office premises. For good class property acceptable yields would be higher, perhaps up to 6% for office property and up to 9% for secondary shop property and offices, and for good factory and warehouse property. Yields on poorer property or property subject to high risks would be in excess of 10%. Thus, currently, capital values of most property lie between 10 and 25 times initial rents.

3.14 COST ANALYSIS

Rents are determined by the market, by the interplay and bargaining of owners and clients. Clients estimate what they can afford to pay in relation to their revenues and other expenditure; this will vary to some extent from property to property. Their assessment of a reasonable rent may be based on comparing the rents of properties known to them or it may take the form of a costs-in-use analysis in relation to their proposed operations in the property [1]. In the commercial world the analysis might start with a comparison of the estimated revenue from their operations against expected expenses and an allowance for reasonable profits. Expenditure on the property includes maintenance, cleaning, lighting, heating and ventilation, labour and fuel for them, other services, management, rent and rates; allowance might also be made for other operation costs, taxation and so on. Property costs might be estimated on the lines indicated in Table 3.1.

Investors compare estimated revenue against expected expenditure and reasonable profits to determine whether the proposed investment is likely to be worthwhile. Generally, investors prefer to let on the basis of a full repairing lease under which the tenant is responsible for all the outgoings on the property. They can then capitalize rent at the desired rate of yield to estimate a reasonable price to pay for the building. However, in some cases, especially where the building is let to a large number of tenants, the landlord provides all the services and may include the rates with the rent. His balance sheet is then more like that for a tenant with a full repairing lease or an owner-occupier (Table 3.1). Because the developer is catering for investors, tenants and other occupiers, he needs to take account of their expenditure and revenues in considering the economics of proposed developments (Table 3.1 and 3.2).

Example 3.1

The kind of balance sheet a developer might prepare is illustrated (Tables 3.1 and 3.2). The considerations would be much the same whether he was developing as an owner or for sale. In order to illustrate the importance of rent levels and site costs the example considers two properties providing similar accommodation in different locations.

Property A might be a high class office block in the centre of a business district commanding a high rent, while property B might be located on the periphery of the town or in a local business district. Running costs might not differ very much except for rates and insurance which would be related to rents and capital value. It is the net rents that would be capitalized to give the development value, the price the investor could afford to pay for the development. A higher yield might be required on secondary property. The developer must meet all his expenditure and profits from the capitalized value.

Gross revenue (rent) is fixed by the market; rates reflect the estimated annual value and local levels of taxation; other running costs are to some extent dependent on design (Chapter 11). Again site costs are determined by

Table 3.1 Investors' balance sheet for two properties

	Property A	Property B
Gross revenue per 1000 m (£)	200 000	100 000
Expenditure (£) Maintenance	7 000	6 000
Cleaning	7 000	6 000
Utilities	10 000	9 000
Management and service staff	13 000	11 000
Rates, insurance	22 000	9 000
Rent (balance to be capitalized)	141 000	59 000

Table 3.2 Developers' balance sheet for two properties

	Property A	Property B
Capitalized value (£)	2 420 000	888 000
Expenditure (£) Site	320 000	30 000
Fees, management	300 000	70 000
Interest	400 000	90 000
Profit and contingencies	400 000	130 000
Construction, site clearance	1 000 000	568 000

the market, while other development expenditure is to some extent within the control of the developer. Economic design can produce savings on the costs of construction and on building running costs, while effective management can reduce the time taken to carry out the project and hence interest and management costs. Developers can reduce profit margins and contingency allowances, but even so, many proposed projects prove to be financially unsound: the probable rent may be too low in relation to the cost of the site and other expenses. Construction costs vary much less than the rent and the cost of the site. Most of the difference in costs in the example would probably arise from site differences – higher costs of building on a redevelopment site in a congested area and of building high rather than wide. Other development expenditure would be lower for the peripheral site because of a possible shorter development time, lower building costs and values, and lower capital outlay. Rents, site costs and development costs are, however, all linked. Rent will depend on the location and quality of the building. To secure a high rent it is necessary to have a good location which will command a high site value and a good quality building implying high construction and design costs.

Development project analysis aims to balance revenue and expenditure. If the site proves to be too expensive in relation to probable rents, it might be possible to find a site at a cost which the development could bear or to obtain planning consent for a higher density of development and hence secure a larger rent. Another possibility would be to develop a building of a higher quality which could command a higher rent, even though this would generally put up other costs. In the longer run economic and financial conditions may change and enable revenue and expenditures to be balanced. If demand for a class of properties rises relative to supply rents may rise more than site prices, at least in the short run. Rates of interest might fall and with them expected yields, resulting in a relatively higher capitalized value and reducing the cost of interest during development. Thus the volume of worthwhile developments changes with economic conditions.

3.15   PROPERTY OWNERSHIP AND RETURNS

Property is a form of investment as well as an envelope for housing social and business operations. It can provide a revenue either directly through being leased or indirectly through saving the rent of a property which would otherwise need to be leased. Generally, property is considered to provide a more stable revenue and to retain its value in real terms better than most other forms of investment. For individuals, ownership of their dwelling provides an asset which tends to have a stable real value and is less subject to market fluctuations than most other investments. Often its value as an investment is increased as a result of tax legislation. Commercial and other occupiers owning their buildings sometimes find their properties provide a better investment than the operations they house. Finance houses such as life assurance offices and pension funds also favour some investment in good class property because of its reliability as a source of income and its stable real value. If however, technology, fashions and demand change and a building cannot easily be adapted, or the building is allowed to deteriorate physically its real value may fall. The price of property tends to reflect the value given to it as a superior investment. Prices for some classes of property tend to increase at times faster than the prices of other assets and draw in additional capital to property development.

3.16   PUBLIC PROVISION OF BUILT ENVIRONMENT

As indicated earlier, public sector development can be divided into development for the market, for example, public housing, development for public occupiers producing goods and services for the market, development for public occupiers generating public services and development of built facilities for direct public use, such as roads. Consideration has already been given to the first two classes of development.

Social services include education, health, social and municipal services of all types, the costs of which are met from taxation rather than a direct charge for the services sufficient to meet their costs of provision. Development decisions arise from political decisions about the provision of services. These give rise to demands for the necessary built facilities to house them. Political decisions are also made in respect of built facilities for direct public use such as highways and outdoor recreation facilities. Central government directly or indirectly funds much of such development and exercises control over decisions (Chapter 14).

Central government controls the overall expenditure on public built facilities (Fig. 3.4). It exercises such control in relation partly to financial policy and partly to economic policy. When the economy and tax revenue are buoyant and inflation is not a problem, central government generally encour-

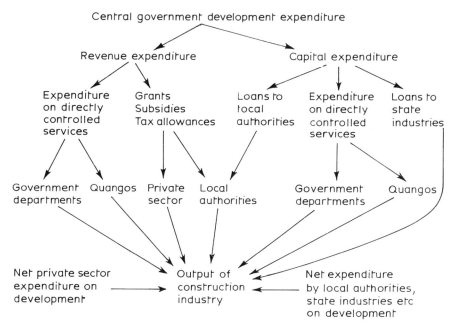

Figure 3.4   Central government and other finance for construction.

ages all types of urban development. In the past, when inflationary forces were weak, governments often stimulated development expenditure during periods of business decline in order to stimulate the economy (Chapter 2).

Public expenditure on development can be controlled by central government directly in the case of its departments and quangos, and indirectly through controlling subsidies, grants and investment programmes for local authorities and by controls on credit to nationalized boards (Fig. 3.4). In addition, central government can set targets for expenditure on individual built facilities (Chapter 14).

Elected members and administrators of public organizations decide their development programmes and the design and cost of each facility in relation to need and the resources at their disposal. Need is largely determined by the administrators of the services and their professional staff. Consultation with members of the community who will use the services and directly or indirectly meet their cost is difficult to organize and usually limited in scope. In the absence of a market guide it is difficult for the public developers to determine what scale and standard of facilities to provide. Generally they have little information on the users' priorities and relative values or often of the techniques for determining value for money and little incentive to use them. Often capital and running costs are charged to different accounts and administered by different groups and the decision-takers do not know or suffer the total costs or enjoy the total benefits (Chapter 14).

REFERENCES

1. Stone, P. A. (1980) *Building Design Evaluation–Costs-in-use*, 3rd edn, E. & F. N. Spon, London.
2. Anstey, B. (1965) Changes in Land Values in the London Area 1950–64 – *Land values*, Sweet and Maxwell, London.
3. Stone, P. A. (1965) The Prices of Building Sites in Britain – *Land Values*, Sweet and Maxwell, London.
4. Stone, P. A. (1973) The structure Size and Costs of Urban Settlements, National Institute for Economic and Social Research, Cambridge University Press, London.
5. Davies, Belfield, and Everest (eds) *Spon's Architects' and Builders' Price Book*, E. & F. N. Spon, London.
6. Stone, P. A. (1983) *Building Economy*, 3rd edn, Pergamon Press, Oxford.

4

Measuring the planning context

4.1 QUANTITATIVE DATA

The major source of quantitative data are government statistics [1]. Most government departments publish regular statistics obtained either from the administrative processes of the department or collected for information purposes. The primary publications usually provide detailed information on the methods of data collection and analysis, information necessary for an adequate understanding of the data and their interpretation. The more important data are also published in statistical abstracts, trend reports and digests.

Generally, official statistics published by the Government Statistical Services are free from bias and more reliable than most other sources. Those wholly based on census data usually have only small margins of error but some census information is based on samples from a census and is subject to sampling error. All sample data are subject to statistical errors which increase as the size of the sample falls, and as the variability of the items increases.

In interpreting data it is necessary to take into account how they were collected and analysed. Some data only relate to a part of the population under examination. For example, data on national income relate to the visible part of the economy; incomes and output generated by the unofficial economy and by private households doing things for themselves are not included. Again, unemployment figures relate to those registered, while job vacancies relate to vacancies reported to the job centres, about two-thirds being unrecorded. Often assumptions are made in order to produce the estimates required. For example, results obtained from the larger firms in an industry may be scaled up to allow for the output of numerous small firms. In some cases output is estimated by multiplying the number employed by an average output per person employed. The method of estimation may preclude some further manipulations of the data.

Errors in survey data arise not only from random effects but also from a lack of balance in the sampling frame. For example, lists of electors and rate-payers do not provide completely comprehensive coverage of adults or households: not all adults are on the electoral register and not all households pay rates. Whether the use of such sampling frames results in biased information depends on the type of information required and whether statistical correction of bias is possible. Frequently historical series of data are required. Compiling such series is not always easy because of changes in definition, in coverage, breaks in series and the revision of methods of collection and analysis.

The need to study the way the data are compiled is particularly important in projections, frequently necessary in town planning. Projections of population scale, structure and location are particularly prone to error. Population growth depends on births, deaths, immigration and emigration. Births depend partly on the decision of individuals to have children and partly on the number of women of childbearing age. Both, particularly the former, can be variable and the two may not move in a related way. Similarly, deaths depend both on age structure and on the incidence of death at any age, but mortality tends to be more stable than fertility. Migration tends to be relatively limited at the national level, but assumes more and more importance with the reduction in the size of the area for which population is to be projected.

The simple assumption that past and present trends will continue unchanged, ignores the underlying changes, and the effect of past performances on the future. For example, in the case of durable goods, such as cars and houses a rapid increase in supply might soon outpace demand because the commodities produced in the past may continue to be available to meet future demand.

Data from non-government sources are generally not as reliable and useful as those from government sources. Often academic workers cannot afford to collect census data or data from large samples and their results may relate only to limited areas. While data from political sources, and industrial and other pressure groups may be reliable, consideration needs to be given to how they were collected, analysed and reported.

Data from secondary sources are generally less reliable than from primary sources. Often the method of data compilation is unknown and errors can arise from misinterpretation of the data, copying and printers errors. Such data can, however often be useful for illuminating qualitative aspects of the subject.

4.2 PROJECTIONS AND PLANNING DATA

Planning projects can range from a development for a whole country or region, down to planning and designing a single building. At one extreme the valid context includes projections for future population, economic, social and technological change, while at the other extreme it may only be necessary to consider the likely future of the immediate location, the potential of the site, and the future needs of the proposed occupier and users.

As explained in Chapter 3, development and planning are for the long-term future. The future cannot be known, the best that can be achieved is to narrow the possibilities. Using past and present data it is possible to project the bounds of likely future contexts.

The further ahead projections are pushed, the wider such bounds will inevitably be. For example, the adults to be catered for in the next decade and a half have already been born, although adjustments will need to be made for deaths and migration, whereas the number of children to be catered for in fifteen years' time can only be projected on the basis of past experience. Household projections have to be based on population projections together with information on household formation. The longer the period of projection, the greater the likelihood that the underlying determinants will change. The scale of the errors made in projecting population in the last few decades indicates how hazardous the process can be [2].

The behaviour of the economy is important in the context of development and planning, both on the supply and demand sides. It affects the volume of human, physical and financial resources available to carry out development and the scale, nature and location of demand. Even short-term economic projections are subject to large-scale errors. Social change, such as behaviour patterns and lifestyles interact with changes in the economy to affect both the supply of resources and the demand for the built environment. Technological change again affects not only the means by which consumer preferences are met, but the preferences themselves. For example, television has not only created the need for new electronic industries and reduced the demand for cinemas and transport, it has stimulated home-based entertainment, changed eating and drinking habits, created new demand for consumer goods and services, new patterns of news dissemination and some would feel it has even been instrumental in changing the moral basis of society.

Developments themselves change the future patterns of life: for example, roads and other developments (even projected ones) can affect location preferences. Green belts, by limiting development within their boundaries, may reduce population growth in the region, lead to a higher density of development in adjacent areas or additional development elsewhere in the country or abroad. Planning control can prevent development in one place but not ensure that it takes place at a chosen location. Because statutory plans influence the amount of development within an area, account is taken of them in some projections, for example, projections of local housing demand and land requirements. However, while plans may be to some extent self-fulfilling, the influence of demand cannot be ignored.

4.3 SURVEYING THE STOCK

The amount of data available about the stock of the built environment varies considerably from one class of development to another [3]. Generally the availability of data is more comprehensive at the national than at the regional level, with even less available at the local level. Some of the information is based on estimates which are only sufficiently accurate at the national level. Much of the information is more concerned with quantity than quality.

It may seem paradoxical that historical data are useful in planning and development, which are concerned with the future; however, they are of value in the way they throw light on what exists and its future potential. The need is usually for information on the volume and capacity of useful stock and on its condition, so that estimates can be obtained on probable needs for new construction, maintenance, servicing and conversion. There is a shortage of data on the condition and potential of the stock. Special surveys are often necessary; these can be expensive and often are only practical for small samples and at the local level.

Information about land use is very limited, even at the broadest level and there is practically no information about the potential of land. The Census of Population provides information about the number of households. The Department of the Environment estimates information about the stock of dwellings. National and regional data are available about the age distribution of dwellings. Broad information about condition is available from occasional House Condition Surveys [4]. For other types of buildings floorspace data are available on a national and regional basis, and rateable value data are available for most property at district level. Some idea of the rate at which the built environment has been stocked up at national level can be obtained from estimates of Gross Domestic Fixed Capital Formation. Data are available on the mileage of roads, railways, telephone cables, water mains and public sewers.

Data published by the Government Statistical Service can often be obtained for much smaller areas than available from published sources. Local authorities and public corporations also have small area data. Some data can be obtained from secondary sources such as the NEDC paper on infrastructure [5]. A general guide to statistical sources for housing and construction is given by Fleming [3].

While existing data are often adequate to provide a general estimate of potential and need, a local survey is usually necessary as a prelude to development. Stocks of the built environment tend to vary widely in condition and potential even over a small part of a town; in some small areas the stock may be of a uniform, good standard with potential for a long useful life, while in other areas standards and potential may be low. Generally it would be more efficient to use a multi-stage survey. A broad first stage survey could aim at determining the boundaries of areas with property of broadly different standards and potential. A second stage could concentrate on properties in those areas revealed to require early rehabilitation or redevelopment. The earlier stages might be on a sample basis but ultimately a detailed survey of every property needing attention may be necessary.

4.4 MEASURING CONSUMER DEMAND

It is necessary to distinguish between economic and social demand. Economic demand is backed by a willingness to pay the market price. Information on consumers' demand schedules may be obtained by studying market prices in relation to particular commodities, and by studying lifestyles, behaviour patterns and preferences of potential customers. Social demand implies demand for which market prices are not offered. This includes not only demand for goods and services for which no direct charge is made, such as roads and public open space but demand for subsidized services, such as local authority housing for which the charge is not related to the costs of supply. There is often a much greater consumer demand for goods and services for which there is no direct charge or only a nominal one than for those for which a market price is demanded. For example, the demand for public health services is practically unlimited. Demand is influenced by political pressure instead of the purse. If large-scale waste is to be avoided, the preferences and needs of consumers for social goods and services need to be studied as much as the commercial ones.

  The preferences of potential consumers can be ascertained from sample surveys, to find out their current patterns of use and preferences and the basic motivation behind their lifestyles and the way they are influenced by economic, social and technological forces. Such surveys can be used to measure probable future preferences. Framing the questions requires considerable skill and experience to avoid suggesting a system of values and solutions based on current experience. While open-ended questions are more trouble to code and analyse, they may provide a more accurate picture than ones with prescribed alternative answers.

4.5 COMMERCIAL AND INDUSTRIAL DEMAND

Commercial and industrial demand generally implies market demand, the study of which usually starts by examining the potential demand for the goods and services themselves. This information provides a basis for estimating the space requirements for their production and distribution: industrial and shopping space, for example. It is also necessary to examine the probable prices or rents which occupiers are likely to be able to afford in the future and how these compare with the costs-in-use of providing and service the space (Chapters 3, 11 and 12).

4.6 DEMAND FOR TRANSPORT INFRASTRUCTURE

Most transport infrastructure is supplied either without a direct charge or at a charge not directly related to cost. User demand is expressed through political pressure on government bodies who have to meet the cost. The scale and quality of transport infrastructure has a considerable effect both on the business sector and the private sector, affecting both costs and convenience. In the business sector transport costs work their way into both home and export prices and hence affect national output. Governments raise the finance to meet the costs of the development and maintenance of transport infrastructure through taxes or borrowing, and these in turn have consequences for gross national demand (Chapter 2). Governments therefore need to weigh up the effects of transport infrastructure provision and the finance necessary on national well-being. They also need to consider the cost–benefits of each individual development as a guide to the most cost effective plan (Chapter 14).

Movements of goods and people on land is increasingly by road (Chapter 8). The future demand for goods transport may be projected through estimates of future production, methods of distribution and modes of handling. The projection of future private traffic will need to take into account the effects of growing affluence, propensity to travel, car ownership and so on. Despite extensive studies of the demand for road transport and the development of sophisticated methods of projection, demand has frequently been underestimated. As a consequence road and bridge construction have tended to lag behind demand and to lack the capacity to stand up to the volume and weight of traffic.

Many studies have been made of the behaviour of road users. Extensive studies have been carried out by the Road Research Laboratory and other bodies which provide a basis for estimating such factors as modal split (i.e. the proportion travelling by car, bus, bicycle, on foot etc.), peaking, drivers' time evaluation and other factors taken into account in estimating traffic flow. The estimates of road capacity requirements tend naturally to be more reliable where land uses are predetermined. The larger the area for which road uses are planned, the more alternative routes and the greater the possibilities of changing land uses, the more likely that additional traffic will be attracted and capacity requirements underestimated.

The demand for goods and passenger rail transport is declining and rail networks are being reduced (Chapter 8). Projections of demand for rail transport are necessary as a basis for rationalizing rail networks, electrification schemes, linkages to airports and additional networks within cities. Railways are competing with road and air transport and traffic projection is strongly influenced by price and convenience considerations.

The demand for air transport is increasing but not always as rapidly as past projections have suggested. Factors taken into account in projecting demand by passengers include changes in lifestyles, prices and convenience, as well as population.

4.7 DEMAND FOR PUBLIC UTILITIES

Utilities such as electricity, gas, sewerage, telephone and water supplies are only partly subject to market pressures. They are all monopolies with either no or limited competition. Prices tend to be determined largely in relation to supply cost and often government policy. For sewerage and, generally, for water, price is not related to consumption, but to a measure of ability to pay. Demand per head or per unit of building tends therefore to be determined by consumer patterns of behaviour and technological change. In the case of the other utilities, while price is a factor, so are the state of the economy, technology and lifestyles. Demands for public utility networks are primarily local, and are affected by the development and demolition of the built environment, and the intensity of local use. The local demands in turn create the demands for trunk networks and generation and other terminal plants.

4.8 PLANNING MODELS

A planning model is merely a mechanism for bringing together the demand and supply factors affecting the scale, form and quality of a proposed development. The factors to be considered depend on the nature of the plan. At the broadest and largest scale the plan may be expressed only in the broadest land use terms, with perhaps some indication of the scale of the planned land use capacities. A plan for a settlement would be expressed in more precise land use terms, possibly with proposed densities and include a road network. At a lower level a plan for site development would be likely to include ground plans of buildings, access and perhaps public utility services.

  In developing a model, account is likely to be taken of the numbers and activities of each type of occupant to obtain estimates of building, land and service demands [6]. The model needs to include estimates of space requirements for users for each type of activity, factors of demand for services, traffic generation factors and so on. The projection of the built environment may be developed on a sector basis and be applied to a range of possible land use patterns and road networks. The estimates of total demand can then be related to the potential capacities of land, buildings, roads and services already available in order to obtain a measure of additional development and its feasibility. Costs may be introduced to provide estimates of the financial resources required and the cash flow. These may be compared with estimates of revenue. The model may incorporate measures of social benefit. Depending on the design of the model it may be possible to obtain specifications and costs of a large range of solutions or the model may include criteria for finding optimum solutions.

The scale and type of planning model depends on the scale and complexity of the proposed development. For a small development with limited ramifications on land uses and services outside the site, a simple manual model may be adequate. It may involve little more than finding the best building design to meet the needs of the proposed occupants, given the site characteristics. For a large development, there may be many options and many factors to take into account. A mathematical model to be run on a computer may be the only feasible way to develop and evaluate the possible solutions.

A mathematical model carries out the arithmetic, it does not eliminate the thought process; the solutions and evaluations it produces depend entirely on the way it is constructed and the values written into it. Even a large computer model cannot handle every possible solution, nor deal with every detail. Simplifications and approximations are necessary. There is inevitably some pre-judgement of the solutions. Many of the factors introduced will be assumptions. This is likely to be equally true whether the model is for planning development or for projecting a context for a plan in terms of populations, scale and structure and the level of economic activity.

REFERENCES

1. Government Statistical Service (1986) *Guide to Official Statistics*, HMSO, London.
2. Stone, P. A. (1970) *Urban Development in Britain*, National Institute for Economic and Social Research, Cambridge University Press, London.
3. Fleming, M. C. (1986) *Spon's Guide to Housing, Construction and Property Market Statistics*, E. & F. N. Spon, London.
4. English House Condition Survey (1982/3) *Parts 1 and 2, 1981*, HMSO, London; Welsh House Condition Survey (1982) *1981 Survey*, Welsh Office, Cardiff.
5. National Economic Development Council (1985) *Investment in the Public Sector Built Infrastructure*, NEDC, London.
6. Stone, P. A. (1973) *The Structure Size and Costs of Urban Settlements*, National Institute for Economic and Social Research, Cambridge University Press, London.

PART TWO

The context

5

Development and resources

5.1 NATIONAL INVESTMENT

National investment is measured in national accounting as gross domestic fixed capital formation (GDFCF) [1]. The total includes ships, vehicles, aircraft, machinery of all kinds, and dwellings, and other buildings and works. The latter items, broadly part of the built environment, account for about half of the total and consume about one-twelfth of the UK Gross Domestic Product [1].

Public investment used to contribute about one-third of capital formation but has declined; in 1985 it contributed only just over one-fifth [1]. About half of public investment arises from the public corporations, a large slice from local authorities and the smallest slice from direct central government expenditure. The central government provides most of the finance for investment by both the public corporations and the local authorities, and sets limits to their expenditure (Chapters 3 and 14).

Capital expenditure is only a small part of total government expenditure, about one-tenth. A large part of revenue expenditure consists of transfer payments to citizens through social security, expenditure on health, defence, education and other services, grants to local authorities, and subsidies to public corporations.

Governments find it difficult to control public expenditure. Once services have been established and staff appointed, it is very difficult to withdraw them. Even in real terms, i.e. in volume, UK government expenditure has tended to increase year by year and to take a larger and larger proportion of the national income. Over the last 20 years, the expenditure has nearly doubled, having grown much faster than national income and now taking over 40% of it, one-quarter more than 20 years ago [2]. Capital expenditure is incurred mainly through contracts let to the private sector for works and goods. It is easier for public authorities to withhold such contracts or even cancel them, than to reduce services and staff, especially those for new

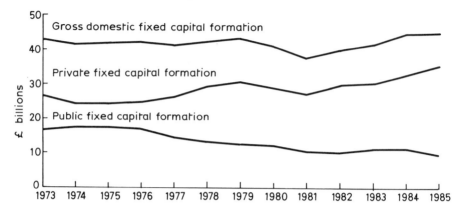

Figure 5.1 UK gross domestic fixed capital formation at 1980 prices. Source: Government Statistical Service (1986) *Annual Abstract of Statistics*, HMSO, London.

buildings and works, and for maintenance work. Real expenditure on public sector capital works was cut back in 1977 and has continued to decline (Fig. 5.1). Over the last decade the reduction in public GDFCF has more than offset the rise in private expenditure, and GDFCF has taken a declining proportion of gross national product (GNP).

5.2   RESOURCES FOR THE BUILT ENVIRONMENT

The built environment is developed and maintained by the combined forces of the construction industry: contracting, materials manufacture and professional services operating on land. In real terms the measured output of the construction industry increased from a low level in the late 1940s to peak in the late 1960s and early 1970s at levels nearly twice as high [3]. Since then it has fluctuated with a low in 1981 at just over three-quarters of the earlier peaks; the size of the labour force fell broadly proportionally [2, 3]. In 1984, the total measured value of construction work was about £26 billion (Table 5.1). Construction work represents about one-tenth of the GDP as against nearer one-eighth in the late 1960s [2]. Currently there is a large amount of unused capacity in the construction industry.

The official measured output is not the total output of construction work. The unofficial economy is believed to be particularly active in construction work, especially housing repair and maintenance work, which includes alteration and small extentions. 'Do it yourself (DIY)' work also contributes in these fields. Unofficial estimates suggest that the unofficial economy carries out £3–4 billions of repair and home improvements work per year [4].

A measure of the types of work carried out is provided by the official estimates. These indicate that, in 1984, new work accounted for 54% of the

Table 5.1 Value of construction output – Great Britain
(1984)*

Type of work		£ billions
New work		
Housing		
public	1.077	
private	3.831	
Total		4.908
Other		
public	3.833	
private – industrial	2.342	
– commercial	3.110	9.285
Total new work		14.192
Repair and maintenance		
Housing	6.251	
Other		
public	3.746	
private	2.014	
Total		12.011
Total all work		26.203

*Current prices and rounding off errors
Source: Government Statistical Service (1986) *Annual Abstract of
Statistics*, HMSO, London

total output of the construction industry, of which new housing was about
one-third, but housing accounted for over half of the maintenance work
(Table 5.1). For new housing work the public sector accounted for under
one-quarter compared with half in the late 1960s, while for all new work the
public sector share fell from over half in the 1960s to about one-third [2].

A more detailed picture of the types of new work being carried out can be
obtained by examining the value of new orders (Table 5.2). In addition to
building housing, mainly a local authority function, the public sector builds for
education and health purposes, and offices and other buildings in which to
carry out its own operations; nearly two-thirds of the work, however, is for
transport infrastructure, public utilities, energy and so on. The private sector
is mainly concerned with buildings for housing and commerce.

Interpreting maintenance figures is difficult, not only because of the lack of
a detailed breakdown but also because of the way the work is defined. In the
case of housing work, repairs and maintenance include improvements, con-

Table 5.2   Value of new construction orders – Great Britain (1984)*

Type of construction	£ billions	
Housing		
Public	0.876	
Private	4.001	
Total		4.877
Other public works		
Energy	0.161	
Rail and air	0.222	
Schools	0.338	
Universities	0.031	
Health	0.619	
Offices and facilities	0.750	
Roads	0.849	
Harbours	0.100	
Water	0.117	
Sewerage	0.256	
Other	0.706	
Total		4.150
Other private		
Industrial	2.203	
Commercial		
offices	1.601	
shops	0.702	
entertainment	0.564	
garages	0.171	
schools and colleges	0.065	
other	0.296	
Total	3.400	
Total		5.603
Total all work		14.630

*Current prices and rounding off errors
Source: Government Statistical Services (1986), *Annual Abstract of Statistics*, HMSO, London

versions, extensions, alterations and redecorations as well. In contrast, for non-housing work, extensions, major alterations and improvements are included in new work. There is also the problem of the work of the unofficial economy and DIY work discussed earlier. Given that there were about 21.7 million dwellings in 1984, the figures suggest that about £290 was spent on average in maintaining and upgrading each dwelling, just over 1% of the average construction price of a new dwelling [2, 3]. To this figure should be added an allowance for work carried out in the non-official economy and occupiers. It is difficult to equate the value of housing and non-housing stock; such evidence as there is (gross capital stock (GCS) figures) suggests that the value of the stock of non-housing is twice as great as for housing, implying an even lower level of maintenance. Information on the condition of the stock of the built environment, to be discussed later, suggests considerable under-maintenance and a large backlog of maintenance work.

5.3 COSTS AND PRICES OF CONSTRUCTION WORK

Measures of change in the price of construction work are not very reliable. It is difficult to measure changes in both costs and volume of construction work. Construction contracts vary widely with differences in specification and in the physical conditions under which the work is carried out. Estimates of work content and costings are not very accurate [5]. It is only possible to aggregate construction work in money terms, and as a result estimates of changes in prices and output are not independent.

Over the last three or four decades construction prices do not appear to have moved much out of line with general price levels. Construction prices appear to have increased slightly less than general prices, reflecting some improvement in productivity or reduced profit margins [2, 3]. International comparisons of prices are even more difficult. Such evidence as is available suggests that construction prices in Great Britain rose faster than in some parts of Europe, no doubt reflecting higher levels of inflation but also that British price levels may still be comparatively low [6].

5.4 BUILT STOCK

There are a number of measures indicative of the built stock but none which provide an accurate base for estimating the total quantity and quality of the stock and hence for projecting potential demand for building work. The main indicators available are gross capital stock (GCS), floor space estimates for commercial and industrial buildings, rateable values, numbers of dwellings and lengths of roads and other transport facilities and public utility infrastructure. The indicators which provide the most complete coverage are GCS and rateable values. The former provides a measure of the value of the built environment [2], while the latter provides aggregates of net annual value at the date of the last valuation.

5.5 HOUSING

The stock of dwellings in Great Britain has increased from 13.9 million in 1950 to 21.7 million in 1984, an increase of over 50% [2, 3]. Annual output

Table 5.3 Age of dwelling stock in Great
Britain (1984)

Date of construction	Percentage
Pre–1890	15.1
1891–1918	13.4
1919–1944	20.6
1945–1970	33.8
Post–1970	17.0

Source: Government Statistical Service (1986)
Social Trends, Construction Statistics 1974–84,
HMSO, London

has varied from 200 thousand to over 400 thousand dwellings and there have been other small gains from conversions. Losses from slum clearance and other causes have varied from about 30 thousand to well over 100 thousand a year. By 1984, about half the dwellings were of post-war construction but nearly one-sixth were over 90 years old (Table 5.3).

If the current housing supply is compared with the projections for 2001 (which underestimate housing demand, since no allowance has been made for vacancies and second homes) it seems somewhat uneven (Table 5.4). The number of additional dwellings needed to provide one dwelling for each projected household is relatively lower in the conurbations, (in some cases negative i.e. a surplus of dwellings over households) and in other areas with a declining population than in the areas of growth. The additional numbers that would be required indicate the effects of migration and the areas in which additional dwellings are likely to be needed. Note that the total required is about 10% greater if estimated from the sum of the areas shown than from the GB total. The actual figures based on the sum of districts would be considerably higher. While the largest number of additional dwellings will be needed in the areas to which population is migrating, the declining areas are likely to have the oldest and poorest housing and need a large programme of replacements.

The age of a dwelling is only a crude indicator of likely replacement needs. Some older dwellings have better standards of construction and more space than newer ones and, if inadequately maintained, may be worth rehabilitating (Chapter 12). The practice of complete clearance and redevelopment following the war has now been abandoned in favour of rehabilitation, on both economic and social grounds. The problem of missing services such as inside WCs, hot water systems and fixed baths has now been largely overcome: less than half a million dwellings remain to be improved. More important are the numbers which need extensive repairs, and the design and construction failures of industrialized system built houses and flats, together with tenant reaction against them and against high-rise flatted developments.

The gains in dwellings over the decade 1973–1983 indicate that the number of additional dwellings has been related to population changes. Gains are least in the conurbations, higher in the rest of those regions and higher still in the rural regions to which population has been migrating (Table 5.4). The regional age distributions reflect rates of replacement as well as additional building. There are a greater proportion of older dwellings in the rural regions of East Anglia, the southwest and Wales (Table 5.4).

Nearly one-third of existing dwellings are over 60 years old (Tables 5.3 and 5.4). Most have a longer potential lifespan than this provided they are adequately maintained and their services and fittings are replaced as standards and fashions change. Housing standards have risen markedly, particularly over the last three decades. People are no longer satisfied just with internal toilets, fixed baths and constant hot water, or even partial room heating. Demands now include full central heating, multiple sinks and basins, and tiled bathrooms and kitchens. As a result there is a demand for rehabilitating dwellings built only in the last few decades. Many owner-occupiers have spent, and appear likely to continue to spend, considerable sums to meet the rising standards for fixtures, fittings and equipment, and many have been assisted by government grants. Despite government grants less has been achieved in private rented housing, for many of which rents have been too low to cover even adequate maintenance. It is generally more economical to rehabilitate dwellings than replace them, even those classified as slums (Chapter 12).

A substantial proportion of post-war public housing has been developed on the basis of industrialized system building; at times something of the order of one-third of such housing was built by non-traditional methods [2]. System building was used both for houses and low and high flatted blocks. Many of these systems have failed to a greater or lesser extent and some blocks, particularly of high-rise flats, need extensive repair; some require demolition.

A recent survey of their own dwellings, carried out by the local housing authorities in England for the Department of the Environment, has produced an estimate for making good arrears of maintenance and renovation of £18 844 million (Table 5.5). It is estimated that 84% of the stock of 4.564 million need attention at an average cost of about £5000 each. The proportions needing attention by age group and average costs are difficult to interpret because there is no information on work already carried out. Nevertheless, as would be expected, average costs per dwelling decline with age (Table 5.5). The average costs per dwelling are highest for the unspecified dwellings, suggesting perhaps that these are particularly old and have been purchased from other forms of tenancy. The figures indicate that the work specified and costed covers much more than repairs; the costs for interior

Table 5.4 Housing and population*

Regions	Stock of dwellings 1984 (000s)	Decadal increase 1973–1983 (000s)	Per-centage gain	Dwelling stock built (percentages)					Household projection 2001 (000s)	Apparent shortfall/surplus (households compared with 1984 stock)† (000s)
				Pre-1891	1891–1918	1919–1944	1940–1970	Post 1970		
Northern	1 233			12	15	20	36	17	1 192	−41
Tyne and Wear	461	25	5						430	−31 }
Rest of region	772	71	9						763	−9 }
Yorks and Humberside	1 934			14	16	22	34	15	1 978	+44
South Yorks	509	32	6						521	+12
West Yorks	809	50	6						824	+15 }
Rest of region	616	64	11						633	+17 }
East midlands	1 526	177	12	14	12	20	34	20	1 657	+131
East Anglia	785	139	18	21	8	14	34	23	863	+78
South-east	6 798			15	13	23	33	16	7 273	+475
Greater London	2 782	158	6						2 800	+18
Rest of region	4 016	574	14						4 473	+462
South-west	1 799	245	14	21	10	17	33	19	1 960	+161
West midlands	1 988			12	12	23	37	16	2 083	+95
Conurbations	1 105	63	6						1 009	−6 }
Rest of region	973	129	13						1 074	+101 }
North-west	2 511			15	15	23	32	16	2 474	−37
Merseyside	571	18	3						532	−39 }
S.E. Lanc Conurbations	1 024	28	3						1 005	−19 }
Rest of region	916	86	9						936	+20 }
Wales	1 112	111	10	22	18	14	31	16	1 116	+4
Scotland	2 028	161	8	11	16	17	38	18	2 028	0
Great Britain	21 694	2 079	10	15	14	21	34	17	22 625	+931

* Rounding off errors
† Negative figures indicate an excess of dwellings over households
Sources: Government Statistical Service (1984), *Housing and Constructions Statistics 1973–83*, HMSO, London
Government Statistical Service (1985), *Regional Trends* HMSO, London

Table 5.5 Estimated costs of repairs and renovations of L.A. Housing – England (1985)*

Percentage of expenditure	Date of construction				
	Pre-1919	1919–1944	1945–1964	Post-1964	Un-specified
Repairs to structure etc.	46	37	38	43	
Rewiring and plumbing	10	11	8	4	
Asbestos, fire protection	neg	neg	2	3	
Heating, insulation etc	13	18	23	27	
Kitchens, bathrooms etc	19	29	21	6	
Conversions and adaptations	8	1	1	4	
Common parts and environment	3	4	7	13	
Demolition	neg	neg	neg	neg	
Total (£ millions)	758	5 171	8 072	3 641	1 202
No. of dwellings (000s)	115	977	1 787	1 530	155
Average cost per dwelling (£000s)	6.6	5.3	4.5	2.4	7.8
No. of dwellings needing attention (000s)	83	794	1 650	1 185	125
Average cost of those needing attention (£000s)	9.1	6.5	4.9	3.1	9.6

* Rounding off errors
Source: Department of the Environment (1985) *An inquiry into the conditions of the local authority housing stock in England 1985*, D.O.E., London

work are of the same order as for the structure and include upgrading (Table 5.5). The costs for demolition are higher on average for the youngest group of dwellings but still very small, especially in relation to the number of system built blocks reported in the past as in need of demolition.

An analysis of the average costs per dwelling by type and age indicates, with one exception, an expected fall in costs from older to younger dwellings and lower costs for traditional rather than non-traditional dwellings (Table 5.6). The exception is for non-traditional high-rise flats 1945–1964.

Other, higher estimates of the likely cost of repairing and rehabilitating local authority dwellings have been published but none of the estimates appear to have been based on detailed costings by each authority. Since the authorities would anticipate that the central government would use them at some time as a basis for determining approved expenditure plans and making grants, it is unlikely that they would intentionally underestimate the costs. These figures are probably the most reliable currently available.

These estimates only cover dwellings in England. The state of dwellings in Wales and Scotland are unlikely to be any better. The costs of repairing and rehabilitating local authority dwellings in Great Britain on a grossed up basis might therefore be of the order of £25 billion. On the basis of these figures about another £12 billion might be needed for private and other rented housing which are probably no better than the local authority dwellings.

Table 5.6 Average costs (000s) per dwelling needing attention – L.A. Housing, England (1985)

Type of dwelling	Date of construction			
	Pre-1919	1919–1944	1945–1964	Post-1964
Houses				
Traditional	8.0	6.3	3.9	2.0
Non-traditional		9.5	7.2	3.5
Flats				
Traditional	13.6			
Low-rise flats				
Traditional		8.2	5.5	2.8
Non-traditional			6.0	5.4
High-rise flats				
Traditional		14.2	7.5	4.7
Non-traditional			4.0	5.6

Source: Department of Environment (1985) *An inquiry into the condition of the local authority housing stock in England 1985*, D.O.E., London

Owner-occupied housing is probably in better condition, on average, than other housing. Estimates made by the contractors, materials' manufacturers and retailers of building materials suggest that probably as much work is carried out by unregistered contractors and DIY householders as by registered contractors. Perhaps one-fifth of owner-occupied dwellings, those owned by the poor elderly, are neglected. If they need as much attention as the local authority traditional dwellings, they might cost another £12 billion to repair and rehabilitate. Thus, very roughly the current arrears of repairs and maintenance might be of the order of £50 billion. This is probably about five times the annual total of work carried out even including non-registered contractors and DIY. The current amount of repair and maintenance work is unlikely to be sufficient to prevent its backlog from increasing. Thus the volume of such work may need to be increased by one-quarter over the next two decades.

The Housing Research Foundation (HRF) estimates a need for about three times as many new dwellings as implied by comparing 1984 stock with projected households. They estimate 200 000 to 220 000 dwellings need to be constructed annually until 1991 (145 000 for new households and 60 000 to 80 000 to replace demolitions) and 200 000 annually from 1992 to 2000, providing 100 000 for new households, 40 000 to 50 000 for geographical shifts, second homes and better standard dwellings, and 40 000 to 50 000 for replacements [7]. Such a programme would probably cost £5.5–6 billion a year at current costs. Even at the current low level of output the total that would be built would not fall all that short of the HRF estimate of need. At its peak the industry produced nearly twice as many dwellings per year.

While the annual output of new dwellings is below need, the main shortfall for housing is in repairs and maintenance, including upgrading. Figures published by the National Federation of Housing Associations indicates that the UK invests a smaller proportion of GDP in housing than most other western countries, about two-thirds of the EEC average [8].

5.6   OTHER PUBLIC SECTOR DEVELOPMENT

Non-housing public development includes building for government services, local government and public corporations. As well as building it includes infrastructure such as roads, sewerage and water. The estimates for the value of the work carried out and new orders in 1984 were given earlier (Tables 5.1 and 5.2). In that year new construction orders were estimated at £4.150 billion and about £3.746 billions of maintenance and repairs were carried out.

A study by NEDC considered public housing, roads and bridges, water mains and sewers, the National Health Service Estate, School building and the PSA estate [9]. It found evidence of arrears of maintenance and replacement, and additional building need in all these services and was critical, not only of the funding provided but of the basis of decision which it considered produced poor value for money (Chapter 14). Much of the infrastructure is said to be very old and have only a few years of life left before total collapse is expected. For example, roads were not designed to carry current traffic loads, many water mains are so faulty that a large proportion of processed water pumped through them escapes, while many sewers similarly are inadequate for current loads. Problems are not, however, confined to old stock. Much of the post-war development is considered to be unsatisfactory. Motorways built only two decades ago have to be rebuilt, considerable repairs have been necessary to the Severn bridge and other long-span bridges and it is reported that many concrete road bridges suffer from structural deterioration. Many school and university buildings, and some health, office and other public service buildings were constructed on the basis of industrialized systems not dissimilar from those used for flatted blocks and houses. Some of these are already displaying defects and some may need to be demolished.

Only a few public organizations publish statistical information on the scale yet alone condition of their stock. Estimates of the backlog of maintenance brought together by Simon [10] include £4 billion for trunk roads [11], £1.7 billion for sewers [12], £0.5 billion for secondary schools [13] and £1.7 billion for hospitals. Even these four sectors have estimated arrears of maintenance greater than the value of public non-housing maintenance and new work in 1984 (Table 5.1).

5.7   OTHER PRIVATE SECTOR DEVELOPMENT

Private sector development consists mainly of buildings and works on private property, together with estate roads and services; the major part of the infrastructure is provided by the public sector. The value of new orders for industrial buildings in 1984 was £2.2 billion, and for commercial buildings, which includes all the other categories, £3.4 billion, giving a total of £5.6 billions (Table 5.2). Maintenance expenditure in 1984 was valued at £2.0 billion (Table 5.1). There does not appear to be any information on backlogs of repairs and maintenance for this sector but as will be argued later, any arrears are likely to be on a smaller scale than in the public sector (Chapter 14).

The shift in employment from manufacturing to services does not imply a decline in demand for industrial buildings. Output is not falling relative to the numbers employed. Moreover changes in the types of manufacture, in types of plant and machinery used, and in location create a large demand for new buildings. Further, distribution patterns and techniques are changing, creating a demand for new warehouses. Office development has been considerable as more people have been absorbed into office employment and offices have been relocated. While shopping floorspace has declined as more intensive retailing techniques have been developed, the new techniques have required newly developed floorspace; much of the new location has been outside the town centres; shop styles tend to be changed at short intervals creating a demand for additional shop-fitting. The growth of leisure pursuits has created a large demand for entertainment and other leisure buildings and works.

5.8   CONVERSION AND REPLACEMENT OF BUILDING STOCK

Building obsolescence is initially more likely to arise from financial or functional considerations than from physical obsolescence. Financial obsolescence arises when the site has a more valuable use than its current use. This is likely to lead, subject to planning consent, to alteration or adaptation to a more valuable new use or to redevelopment. Functional obsolescence arises from changes in demand for some types of buildings, from changes in the technology of the activity for which the building has been used and from inefficiencies arising from the plan and design of the building. If there is insufficient demand for buildings and sites in an area, buildings become redundant (Chapter 10).

Buildings cannot always be adapted economically to meet new requirements. New modes of building have not always been as efficient as earlier modes. In some cases maintenance costs per unit area are higher and energy efficiency lower. Information from a survey of office buildings by Henley Management College indicates that the energy efficiency of office buildings built a decade ago are particularly poor and service costs compare unfavourably with those built more recently and at an earlier date. It has been suggested that many buildings from the 1960s and 1970s will need to be rebuilt, partly because ceiling heights are too low to allow new service requirements to be met.

5.9   FUTURE NEEDS FOR BUILDING RESOURCES

The evidence given in this chapter suggests that there is likely to be a continuing large demand for new construction, depending on the buoyancy of the economy. There would appear to be a growing backlog of desirable construction work in the public sector generally and in private housing, with a growing need for replacement, conversion, maintenance, and rehabilitation of existing buildings. The greater the delay in meeting their needs, the more urgent they will tend to become and the greater the scale of building work which will be required. The delay in making good the existing infrastructure is largely because of government attempts to limit expenditure where it is easiest by reducing contracts for building work, and to a lesser extent because many private persons lack the financial ability to exert economic demand or the financial incentive to have building work carried out.

The construction industry is now operating about one-fifth below the peak it reached in 1973; the size of the labour force has declined even more. The manufacturers of building materials and the professional firms have similarly cut back their operations. These industries could be built up again to produce much more output but this would take time. Many of the workers made redundant are likely to have been the older and the less skilled. Many new workers would have to be trained if the labour force was to be increased to its former level. Similarly new plant would need to be brought into use to replace that discarded. If demand was increased too rapidly it would lead to inefficiencies and inflated costs, and to the use of untested technology and design.

Since construction currently accounts for only about one-twelfth of the GDP, increasing the output of construction (for example by one-quarter) would only increase the GDP by about 2%, other things being equal. In practice increasing the demand for construction would probably be accompanied by increasing demand in other fields, such as for furniture and equipment used in buildings. Increasing demand would also arise from the multiplier effect of the additional incomes generated by the rise in construction employment (Chapter 2). If there was concentration on improvements to the built environment which produce comparable savings elsewhere, unit costs in the economy might be reduced, resulting in the economy becoming more competitive and growing from a larger home market and increasing exports.

A study of the economic effects of increasing public expenditure on the built environment indicates that an increase of £1 billion a year for 5 years would increase employment by between 70 and 100 thousand at an average cost of about £8000 per job per annum [14]. The net increase in public borrowing would be about half the cost of the spending programme. There would be an inflationary effect of about 0.5% per year and some increase in imported materials, mainly timber.

REFERENCES

1. Government Statistical Service (July 1986) *Economic Trends*, HMSO, London.
2. Government Statistical Service (1986) *Annual Abstract of Statistics*, HMSO, London.
3. Government Statistical Service (1985) *Housing and Construction Statistics*, 1974–84, HMSO, London.
4. Building Employers Federation (3/3/1986) *The Times*, London.
5. Stone, P. A. (1983) *Building Economy*, 3rd edn, Pergamon Press, Oxford.
6. Davis, Belfield, and Everest, (1987) *Spons Architects' and Builders' Price Book*, 112th edn, E. & F. N. Spon, London.
7. Housing Research Foundation (1984) *Housing and Land 1984–1991, 1991–2000*, HRF, London.
8. National Federation of Housing Associations (1985) *Inquiry into British Housing: The Evidence*, NFHA, London.
9. National Economic Development Office (1985) *Investment in the Public Sector Built Infrastructure*, NEDO, London.
10. Simon, D. (May 1986) Investing in the Infrastructure in *National Westminster Bank Quarterly Review*, London.
11. Policy Studies Institute (1984) Rebuilding the Infrastructure, PSI, London.
12. Water Research Centre, London, 1984.
13. Audit Commission (1985) *Capital Expenditure Controls in Local Government in England*, HMSO, London.
14. Ormerod, P. (1984) *The Economic Impact of Increased Public Spending on Construction*, National Council of Building Materials Producers, London.

6

Economic, social and technological factors affecting demand for the built environment

6.1   DURABILITY OF THE BUILT ENVIRONMENT

As pointed out earlier, the built environment has a long potential life, obsolescence arising as much from technical and financial limitations as from physical ones. It is often more economical to maintain the built environment in a sound state and to adapt to new requirements than to rebuild (Chapter 12). To reduce the incidence of technical and financial obsolescence it is necessary to think about the long-term future when planning and developing buildings and infrastructure. This involves a consideration of future changes in economic, social and technological contexts and how this will affect future changes in the scale and distribution of population, household formation, employment, lifestyles, consumer preferences and so on.

6.2   POPULATION

Population lies at the heart of projections of future contexts of the demand for the built environment. A reasonably accurate picture of the scale and structure of population in the recent past can be built up from survey and census data. For example, the 1981 Census of Population indicated a population in Great Britain of about 54.7 million people [1]. This was officially projected to rise to 56.4 million by 2001 [1], now revised down to 56.1 million [2]. The size and demographical structure of population depends on births and deaths, and inward and outward migration. The main difficulty in projecting population at the national level tends to lie in projecting rates of birth. Over the last hundred years crude birth rates per 1000 population have varied between 13 and 35 [3]. Projected birth rates can have a large effect on population projections – in 1964 the Registrars General were projecting a population in 2004 of 72 million [3]. Reasonable assumptions of possible variations in the factors to be considered gave boundary figures of 56 and 85 million [3]: it is the lower boundary figure which is closest to current projections. (Death rates are far less volatile than birth rates).

Birth rates tend to have fallen throughout the western world. In the European community only Ireland had a crude birth rate above a common level in 1981 of 10–15 per 1000 population [1]. Crude death rates ranged in 1981 from about 8–12 per 1000 population. As a result the net rate of population change has been small for some years, 1.3 per 1000 for the UK, reaching negative values for some members of the European Community [1]. Net migration in the UK has tended to be small and negative but against low rates of natural increase it is likely to have more significance than in the past [2].

Even if there are no dramatic changes in female fertility, the number of births is likely to fluctuate because of changes in the number of births in the 1950s and 1960s, and hence the number of women of child-bearing age. It is projected that birth rates will decline in the near future but increase again towards the end of the century. This has implications for services for young children, including primary education and teacher training [4].

The number of people of working age has increased over the last ten years as a result of the baby boom of the sixties. In early 1980s the tendency to an increased working population was offset by the retirement of people born in the baby boom of the twenties, but this effect is now fading [5]. Later, in the early 1990s, the number of potential young workers will decline reflecting the decline in birth rates in the mid-1970s [4].

Assuming no catastrophies and no dramatic changes in migration the projected numbers in the post-school age groups by the end of the century (Table 6.1) should not be subject to large margins of error. The numbers of people of working age and total pensioners appear likely to be much the same at the end of the century as today [2]. In the next century, the number of people of pensionable age is expected to rise steeply, while the number of workers falls [2]. By the end of the century a 40% rise in people over 75 is expected [2]. Such changes will have considerable implications for demand by the different age groups, for services to the old, for output and resources.

6.3 SPATIAL DISTRIBUTION OF POPULATION

The demand for the built environment arises more from local than national needs: inter-regional movement can be far more important than external migration. Over two decades a quarter or more of the population may migrate

Table 6.1 Projected population – Great Britain (2001)

Age group	Population (000s)
0–4	3 863
5–14	7 961
15–44	22 817
45–retirement	11 741
Retired	10 052
Total	56 434

Source: Government Statistical Service (1984)
Regional Trends, HMSO, London

into or out of a region (Table 6.2). As a result projected regional population is likely to have a wider margin of error than projected national population. It is necessary to consider not just past trends but the current and future strengths of the factors encouraging migration and the potential availability of development resources in each area. The scale of regional migration over the period 1961–1981 was quite large and it is projected to continue to be large in the period 1981–2001 (Table 6.2).

Population is moving south and particulary to the south-east and the rural regions of East Anglia, the south-west and the east midlands (Table 6.2). Intra-regional movements may be as important as inter-regional ones. Most conurbations are expected to loose and some have lost population, while the largest gains have and are expected to be by the non-conurbation parts of the regions (Table 6.3). An analysis of the 1971–1981 population change by district confirms the decline in population in Scotland and the north, and particularly in conurbations and cities (Table 6.4). Apart from the new towns, population has increased to the largest extent outside the cities in small urban and even rural districts. In England and Wales an estimated net population increase of 262 thousand is estimated to be made up of gains of 1768 thousand and losses of 1506 thousand, while in Scotland an estimated net loss of 98 thousand consisted of estimated losses of 281 thousand and gains of 183 thousand. The probability is that the scale of movement was even greater than this: the extent could be revealed by an area analysis within districts.

The above conclusions are reinforced by a study of functional areas, that is areas defined in terms of commuting, employment and retailing patterns [6]. This analysis, based on revised rather than preliminary census figures, indicates that population losses in Great Britain, 1971–1981, were concentrated in the core zones of dominant functional regions, broadly the conurbations, the centres of 20 metropolitan regions, which are estimated to have lost 9.7%

Table 6.2   Regional population change – Great Britain*

Standard region	Population (millions)			Inter-regional movement (millions) 20 yrs at 1982 rates		% Change in population (projected)	
	1961	1981	Pro-jected 2001	To region	From region	1961–1981	1981–2001
Great Britain	51.4	54.7	56.4			6.6	3.1
North	3.1	3.1	3.0	0.84	0.92	0.2	−4.1
Yorkshire and Humberside	4.7	4.9	5.0	1.42	1.52	5.2	1.2
East midlands	3.3	3.9	4.1	1.56	1.50	16.8	7.5
East Anglia	1.5	1.9	2.2	1.14	0.86	27.3	15.3
South-east	16.1	17.0	17.9			5.8	5.3
Greater London				3.14	3.82		
Rest of south-east				5.20	4.44		
South-west	3.7	4.4	4.8	2.30	1.78	18.0	8.9
West midlands	4.8	5.2	5.3	1.42	1.68	8.9	2.9
North-west	6.4	6.5	6.3	1.50	1.92	0.8	−2.7
Wales	2.6	2.8	2.9	0.92	0.88	6.8	1.9
Scotland	5.2	5.2	5.0	0.88	1.00	−0.7	−2.6

*Absolute figures have been rounded off and will not yield the rates calculated from the original figures
Source: Government Statistical Service (1984) *Regional Trends*, HMSO, London

of their population. The largest gains in population are estimated to have occurred in freestanding functional regions; that is areas outside the Metropolitan Regions, those in the rings around the cores gained 10.6%, those in outer rings 10.2% and those in rural zones 9.4%. It is estimated that the cores as a whole lost 1466 thousand people and the other three types of zone gained 1763 thousand people. This figure is six times as large as the net population increase in Great Britain over that period and would require approximately six times the amount of new built environment than would have been required without the migration.

The four types of zone each have distinctive age distribution patterns, although there is less difference between the outer and rural zones than the others [6]. Broadly, the outer and rural zones appear to have a higher proportion of people of retirement age, about the same proportion of middle aged but less younger people than the other zones. The core zones have the lowest proportion of young people aged 0–15, but a younger labour force than the ring zones. These figures confirm the attraction of core zones for the

Table 6.3 Population changes within regions – Great Britain 1961–2001*

Conurbations and other areas	Population (millions)			% Change in population	
	1961	1981	Projected 2001	1961–1981	1981–2001
Tyne and Wear†	1.2	1.2	1.0	−6.9	−6.9
Rest of north	1.9	2.0	2.0	4.8	0.4
South Yorkshire†	1.3	1.3	1.3	1.5	−0.1
West Yorkshire†	2.0	2.1	2.1	3.2	1.6
Rest of Yorkshire and Humberside	1.4	1.5	1.6	11.5	1.3
Greater London†	8.0	6.8	6.8	−14.7	−0.8
Rest of south-east	8.1	10.2	11.1	26.1	9.2
West midland conurbation†	2.7	2.7	2.6	−1.8	−3.1
Rest of west midlands	2.0	2.5	2.7	23.4	9.1
Greater Manchester†	2.7	2.6	2.5	−3.4	−4.1
Merseyside†	1.7	1.5	1.4	−11.1	−11.2
Rest of north-west	2.0	2.3	2.4	16.7	4.2
Central Clydeside†	1.8	1.7	–	1.4	–
Rest of Scotland	3.4	3.4	–	1.4	–

* Absolute figures have been rounded off and will not yield the ratios calculated from the original figures
† Conurbations
Source: Government Statistical Service (1984) *Regional Trends*, HMSO, London

school leavers, the ring zones for families and the outer zones for retirement. As would be expected dependency ratios, children and elderly compared with persons of working age, are higher in the outer and rural zones, than in the cores and rings. Economic dependency ratios, the proportion of non-economically active to economically active follow a similar pattern to the dependency ratios. Regionally the lowest ratios are for the London region and nearly the highest are for the rest of the south. They are high in the heavily populated areas of the midlands and the north, where unemployment is high but higher still in the northern peripheral zones.

Such changes in population scale and structure indicate significant problems for the local economies and for planning and development. A falling population and declining proportion of economically active points to a lack of adequate demand and revenue to sustain redevelopment and a redundancy of buildings in the core zones. The rise of population in the ring, outer ring and rural zones points to rising demands for land and buildings in these zones on a scale much greater than in the country as a whole. It will be necessary later

Table 6.4   Population change by type of district 1971–1981 – Great Britain

Type of district	Population change (000s)	Percentages
Great Britain	+164	+0.3
England and Wales	+262	+0.5
London and Metropolitan regions	−1302	−17.7
Inner London	−535	−17.7
Outer London	−221	−5.0
Metropolitan districts	−546	−4.6
Principal cities	−386	−10.0
Other districts	−160	−2.0
Non-Metropolitan regions	+1564	+5.3
Large cities	−149	−5.1
Smaller cities	−55	−3.2
Industrial districts		
Wales and three northern regions	+42	+1.3
Rest of England	+158	+5.0
Districts that include new towns	+283	+15.1
Resorts, seaside and retirement areas	+156	+4.9
Other urban and urban–rural districts		
Outside south-east	+307	+8.8
In south-east	+354	+6.7
Remoter, rural districts	+468	+10.3
Scotland	−98	−1.9
Glasgow city	−216	−22.0
Other large cities	−65	−7.4
Other urban	+98	+3.8
Rural and islands	+91	+10.0

Source: Government Statistical Service (1984) *Regional Trends*, HMSO, London

(Chapters 7 and 10) to consider the economic and social implications of these changes.

6.4   HOUSEHOLD FORMATION

Household structure has been changing faster than population. The average size of households has declined since 1961 by about 15%. This, coupled with an increase in population, has resulted in an increase in the number of households of about 20%, over 3.3 million in Great Britain [7]. As a result the number of households has been increasing about five times as fast as the increase in population. Compared with the scale of population decline in the core zones, the number of households did not decline appreciably, so that housing choice in the older and less well endowed areas did not greatly increase [6]. In areas of rising population, housing demand increased relative to household formation and supply increased to meet demand. Average household size generally declined most in the largest cities and least in free-standing urban regions and rural areas [6].

As would be expected, overcrowding in terms of persons per room declined between 1971 and 1981 from an estimated 7.1% to 4.3% of all private households in Great Britain, the number of people affected declining from about 7.4 to 4.6 million [6]. However, overcrowding is four times as high in Scotland as in England and Wales and worse in the core zones in both countries [6]. In England and Wales overcrowding was highest in London, the north, north west and west midlands.

In 1983, there were about 19.5 million households in Great Britain [7]. About one-third were of two persons, much the same as 20 years before but now there are far more one person households, nearly one-quarter, and less larger households [7]. Whereas there were nearly 21.5 million dwellings in 1983, two million more than households, even this statistical excess may have disappeared by the end of the century [3]. Moreover, many of these dwellings, even if fit, are the wrong size and in the wrong place, a tendency likely to increase as the end of the century approaches.

6.5 LABOUR MARKET

As indicated earlier the number of people of working age in Great Britain has been increasing, particulary over the last two decades, while the number available for economic activity has increased even faster, from 24.9 million in 1965 to 26.3 million in 1984 [7]. During that period the number actually employed and self-employed declined by over one million, while the number registered as unemployed rose by over 2.5 million [7]. It is projected that the labour force – the number available for economic activity – will rise by nearly another million by 1991 [8].

The increase in the number available for economic activity results not just from increases in the number of people of working age but from changes in activity rates. These have declined for men because of longer education and earlier retirement but risen for women because of a large increase in the proportion of wives working – from 22% in 1951 to 58% now – although the rates for unmarried women have declined [7]. As a result the number of married women in the labour force has increased by 75% since 1961; even so, economically active men still outnumber women, and whereas men are mainly full-time workers, half the married women are part-time workers.

There are a number of reasons for this switch in employment between men and women, partly arising from demand and partly from supply. On the de- mand side the principal reasons are the run-down of manufacturing industry and reduction of labour force arising from increased productivity, where the number of jobs, mainly for men, declined by 2.3 million in the 10 years 1973–1983 [7], and the growth in service employment of 1.1 million over that period, mainly jobs for women and much of it part-time. On the supply side, as a result of changes in tax and social security arrangements, part-time employment for the wives of men in work has become well worthwhile and part-time women have become less expensive to employ than full-time workers. At the same time there have been, for example, changes in average child-bearing age, and changes in school arrangements, such as children staying at school for lunch, the provision of pre-school attendance centres, and the provision of child-care at the place of employment; changes which have eased the problems of mothers of young children taking up employment. As a result of these changes the proportion of people of working age in jobs in this country is much higher than in other EEC countries, despite the level of unemployment and longer working hours.

Labour statistics are notoriously difficult to interpret. For example, as indicated earlier, only about one-third of vacancies are reported to Job Centres, so that total vacancies are about three times the published figure. More recent evidence from the Department of Employment, based on a Labour Force Survey carried out in 1984, indicates that of the nearly 3 million claimant unemployed only just over 2 million were looking for work, whereas there were nearly 0.9 million non-claimants who would take a job were it offered; over two-thirds of these were women [9]. These figures do not provide any measure of the number of claimant unemployed who operate in the unofficial economy. Estimates of its size vary from about 8 to 14% of the officially measured labour force. Even the higher figure is less than half the level estimated for Italy. Of course, not all the people who work in the unofficial economy are claimants; many will be self-employed who keep registered earnings below the thresholds for value added tax (VAT) and income tax, and some will be registered employed who do a second unregistered job. Some downward adjustment to the number of claimant unemployed is necessary to obtain a true measure of unemployment and a substantial adjustment upwards is necessary to the number registered as working.

Clearly the active labour force is larger than official statistics imply and there is a substantial pool of labour which could be drawn into the active work force given effective demand. Demand for labour depends not only on the strength of demand for goods and services at home and abroad but also on labour productivity and the costs of employing labour. Labour costs depend to an important extent on taxation and social payments, and on labour regulations, as well as on wage rates and labour productivity. Demand side factors will be considered later.

The reduction in jobs over the decade 1971–1981 has been greatest in London and other conurbations; there have been gains in independent towns and rural areas [6]. The south had an estimated overall gain of jobs over the decade of over 100 000, while the north had overall job losses, particularly in the metropolitan areas [6]. Again the greatest job losses were in the cores. Long-term unemployment increased relative to all unemployment, particularly in the north relative to the south and in conurbations.

6.6 CHANGES IN NATIONAL OUTPUT AND RESOURCES

The satisfaction of demand for goods and services, and ultimately for the built environment depends on national output. More economic activity increases the demand for the built environment both through increasing the demand for environment facilities to support production and distribution, and through increased consumer demand for housing and other amenities for living.

It is difficult to appreciate the extent to which the gross domestic product, GDP, has increased over recent decades and the transformation in the standard of living and life styles which it has made possible. Even at the slow rate of increase in GDP experienced in Great Britain, an average of about 2.25% per year over 35 years, GDP has more than doubled [10]. During the 1950s and early 1960s the rate of increase was running at a somewhat higher level. The overall rate of increase of GDP has been slower than the rate in many other western countries: as a result Great Britain's GDP per capita fell from being one of the highest to one of the lowest in the EEC with a level only about two-thirds that of the leading country, West Germany [11].

Even if GDP continued to increase at only 2.25% per year, however, it would increase by one-quarter in 10 years and be nearly doubled in just over 30 years. Many countries have achieved an average increase of 3% or better, with a doubling in 25 years (Table 6.5). At such rates of increase GDP could increase over four times in 50 years, a period well within the potential physical life of the built environment now being developed. It is difficult to

Table 6.5. Possible growth in gross domestic product in real terms

Possible average annual rates of growth in GDP (percentages)	Periods of growth (years)			
	5	15	25	50
1	1.05	1.16	1.28	1.64
2	1.10	1.35	1.64	2.69
3	1.16	1.56	2.09	4.38
4	1.22	1.80	2.67	7.10
5	1.28	2.08	3.39	11.47

imagine how lifestyles would change given these levels of wealth and what demands would be made on the built environment.

If the potential active labour force increases as projected to 1991 and reasonably full employment is achieved (in the early 1960s there were only about 300 000 persons unemployed) GDP could rise 10% or more for these reasons alone, that is without further increases in productivity. Offsetting such rises and those from increased productivity, could be losses from shorter hours of work, longer holidays, longer periods of education, earlier retirement and the withdrawal of married women from the labour market. There might be some interaction between these factors and productivity, offsetting some of the potential loss.

Fears that increasing output would lead to satiation and lack of demand have always proved groundless: needs are insatiable, as soon as one is satisfied another appears. In the last century output increased sixfold and it was all absorbed [12]. Only a few decades ago few households had central heating, refrigerators, telephones, televisions or washing machines and many lacked hot water and a fixed bath. Most households now possess all these things and nearly half have cars [13].

The factors affecting the level of aggregate national demand have been discussed earlier (Chapter 2). It was explained that while the forces operating on the various phenomena in the macro-economy are broadly understood, there is little agreement about how the total economic system operates. Because the economy is in a constant state of change, it is difficult to isolate the effect of changes in any factor, difficult to produce reliable statistics and certainly difficult to produce them in time to provide a basis for decisions to support correcting action. Reliable projections of the economy in the short term are difficult enough; reliable long-term projections of GDP are subject to unacceptably large errors. It is only feasible to consider the consequences of possible levels and patterns of growth.

6.7   CHANGES IN REGIONAL OUTPUT AND ECONOMIC WELL-BEING

Statistics are available for regions but not comprehensively for functional zones. It was mentioned earlier that reductions in job levels were greatest in the conurbations and in the cores; job levels rose in independent towns and in rural areas. This pattern is likely to be similar for per capita GDP and personal incomes. Per capita GDP has remained greatest in the south east probably because its economy is strongly orientated to those services for which added value is higher than for manufacture (Table 6.6). Broadly speaking, the regions with extensive conurbations, except for the south east, have lower GDP per capita than the more rural regions. Of particular significance is the decline in relative GDP per capita for the west midlands

Table 6.6 Per capita GDP and unemployment in regions expressed as percentages

Region	Per capita GDP at factor cost			Unemployment[1]		
	1966[1]	1974[1]	1981[2]	1965	1975	1985
United Kingdom	100	100	100	100	100	100 %
North	84.1	90.1	94.5	179	144	141
Yorkshire and Humberside	96.7	93.0	92.4	79	98	112
East midlands	96.5	95.6	95.5	64	88	96
East Anglia	96.0	93.4	96.9	93	83	80
South-east	114.7	116.6	115.9	57	68	74
South-west	92.0	93.1	95.3	107	115	92
West midlands	108.2	99.3	90.3	50	100	116
North-west	95.7	94.5	95.1	114	129	122
Wales	84.2	83.9	84.6	77	137	128
Scotland	89.1	93.4	98.4	207	127	118

Sources: 1. Kemp Smith D. & Hartley E. (1976) *United Kingdom Accounts – Economic Trends No. 277*, HMSO, London
2. Government Statistical Services (1966–86) *Regional Trends*, HMSO, London

and the relative gain for Scotland. The west midlands was until recently excluded from assisted area benefits and subject to industrial development certificate (IDC) controls (Chapter 7).

While unemployment has increased everywhere, regional differences are less than in 1965 (Table 6.6). Again, while the south-east has the lowest rates, generally the highest rates are in regions with conurbations. There is again a marked relative rise in unemployment rates in the west midlands and a relative decline in Scotland.

Personal income per head varies broadly as GDP per capita (Tables 6.6 and 6.7). Again as would be expected, social security benefits per head tend to vary inversely to income per head (Table 6.7). Average house prices generally follow incomes, except in Wales where house prices are relatively lower.

If these figures are compared with those for population movements, it will be seen that migration was to areas enjoying the higher levels of affluence. This will need to be considered in relation to regional policy (Chapter 7).

6.8 SOCIAL CHANGE

As indicated above, while couples still comprise the majority of households, more single person households and less large households are being formed. In 1983 in Great Britain 23% of households were single person ones and 32% were households of two persons [7]. Two-thirds of the single person house-

Table 6.7 Regional differences in economic well-being expressed as percentages

Region	Personal income per head [1]	Social security benefit per head [2]	Average house price [2]
United Kingdom	100	100	100 %
North	94	111	91
Yorkshire and			
Humberside	93	102	85
East midlands	95	92	91
East Anglia	96	86	91
South-east	114	94	119
South-west	98	99	100
West midlands	92	97	93
North-west	95	109	93
Wales	89	111	102
Scotland	97	106	100

Sources: 1. Government Statistical Services (1984) *Regional Trends*, HMSO, London
2. Government Statistical Services (1985) *Regional Trends*, HMSO, London

holds contained people over 60 as did over half the two person households [13]. Only about one-tenth of the households contain five or more people [7]. The size of dwellings in terms of number of rooms are large relative to household size. Although fewer people are now marrying, they still tend to form households of a conventional size.

The decreasing size of households results not only in the number of households increasing faster than population but raises the demand for dwellings, their furnishings and fittings. The ageing of the population increases the demand for specially designed domestic facilities and housing, and mobile home services.

6.9   LIFESTYLES AND CONSUMER PREFERENCES

The increase in the proportion of married women taking paid employment instead of being full-time housewives has a number of important implications. In a period when the demand for labour is comparatively low it tends to reduce the demand for young men and women as well as older men and unmarried women. Unless labour demand increases sufficiently to employ a much larger proportion of the population than it does at present at conventional working periods, either there will be substantial pools of people unemployed or there will need to be smaller average work periods and hence more leisure time. The situation would be modified if more women taking paid employment employed people to carry out their home duties, especially looking after children; the latter is gradually being provided for through schools and day nurseries. However, if married women work as well as their husbands they enjoy larger incomes and a higher level of consumption, creating a larger demand for some types of goods and services; higher unemployment would tend to reduce demand.

Increases in leisure time will tend to increase the demand for leisure facilities. Already in recent years expenditure on such facilities has greatly increased, both for those within the home and those outside it. In some directions leisure activities tend to be increasingly home based, many being centred around electronic apparatus and DIY activities. Both tend to increase the demand for goods rather than services: for example, a decline in cinema attendances but more demand for television sets, videos, computers and their sundries, and a comparatively lower demand for building craftsmen but a larger demand for builders' materials. Outside the home demand is increasing for eating houses, sports' centres, travel and places to visit. These create demands for additional labour but to a large extent labour working unsociable hours.

Consumption patterns change with the levels of incomes and retail prices [7]. As income increases a smaller proportion of it is necessary to satisfy demands for basic goods and services and more is available for higher quality and additional goods and services. In the last few decades the proportion of expenditure on food has dropped despite a change to higher quality and more expensive foods. A larger proportion of income is spent on housing, heating and lighting, clothing, transport and leisure. Goods such as clothes and furnishings tend to be regarded as disposables to be replaced as fashions change. More people go on holiday, for longer periods and travel further. They take more of their meals away from home. There is an increasing demand for social and health services. Public officials tend to be taking over services once provided by members of the extended family.

6.10 TECHNOLOGICAL CHANGE

Technological change leads to improvements in existing goods and services, the creation of new ones, increases in productivity and changes in market conditions, with changes in the demand and prices for existing goods and services. It makes possible higher standards of living and new life styles, and creates a demand for new and converted buildings and works.

Projecting technological change is difficult. In the short term it is possible to review current new technological developments and speculate on which will be successfully exploited and accepted by the market. In the longer term it is difficult even to guess the nature of new technological developments. In this chapter it is only possible to examine and speculate on technological change in a few fields. These will be limited to areas in which buildings and infrastructure are likely to be substantially affected.

The field in which technological innovations appear most likely to have the greatest consequences for the built environment in the foreseeable future is electronics, particularly in information handling. Computer control of machinery offers greater accuracy and speed of production with economies in both labour and materials including energy, while applied to stock control and goods handling it offers ways of reducing stocks, handling and transport both in production and distribution. It is expected that in future computers will be generally applied both to processes and the integration of manufacture resulting in changes in the organization of industry. Applied to controlling internal environments it offers greater comfort and economies in energy consumption. The most dramatic effects of electronics may be in relation to face to face contacts, both in business and in leisure. It offers convenient ways, not only of transferring data and pictures over any distance but the remote control of analysis, recording and instructing machinery of many kinds, reducing the need to meet for discussions, shopping, financial transactions, plant control, education, training and passive entertainment. The result may be a future in which those servicing people and animals, transporting people and goods, and constructing and servicing buildings and plant need to be on the spot, while most others might be able to operate from home. It is not possible to know how soon and to what extent such innovations might be practical and economically viable.

Technological innovation in building design has had mixed results. As indicated earlier, system building of housing, education and other buildings has left behind many building failures; failures are also reported from new systems of road construction and bridge design. The extensive use of glass and light claddings in offices and similar buildings has tended to result in buildings inefficient in the use of energy and expensive to run. Computers offer opportunities of much more detailed analysis of building performance and design evaluation which could assist in designing structures which would function more economically and effectively, making better use of the properties of the raw materials, including natural heat and light. New types of contractors plant have increased the practical size and range of buildings and the feasibility of engineering structures but innovations in managing construction have probably been as effective in increasing efficiency [13].

Technological improvements in extracting heat and power from sources of energy and in extracting minerals have considerably extended the apparent availability of energy resources. Even so mineral energy resources are finite, although reserves of workable coal are large. Technological innovations are being developed for various types of renewable energy such as wind, wave, tidal, solar, geothermal and biomess power but not all the technologies appear to be economically viable under current conditions. Only water and nuclear power have won a place in conventional energy generation beside the use of fossil fuels. Both conventional and unconventional sources of energy have environmental consequences. Most make large demands on land and water and, generally the plant is intrusive, while some create pollution, ecological disturbance or health hazards. On the other hand, the creation of water sources for water power, as for storage purposes, can often be combined with the creation of water facilities for sports and other amenities, and transport infrastructure, but may still have extensive environmental consequences.

In the past there have been major innovations in surface transport, most of which have been exploited. Changes in railways in the near future include further electrification with greater speed and comfort. The application of computers to signalling and train control might assist in increasing the intensity of track use with greater safety and faster journeys. Magnetic levitation offers a new type of tracted transport. Improvements to the internal combustion engine probably also largely rest on computer control to increase energy efficiency and the reduction of pollution. The alternative of electric propulsion for road vehicles is held up by difficulties in developing a suitable battery. Ships are getting larger; innovations in powering them indicate a wider possible choice with possibilities of a return to solid fuel, and even wind, at least as supplementary power, and nuclear power.

Innovations in plant and animal breeding and in methods of husbandry have enabled farmers to respond to government price incentives and produce far more food from much the same area of land. Productivity has increased rapidly to the point of excess (Chapter 8). Related innovations may develop plants and animals requiring lower inputs without proportional losses of output and with less ecological disturbance. Considerable advances are being made in biology and chemistry with the development of biotechnology in industry, in particular the use of microorganisms to manufacture chemicals, drugs, food and fuel. This development is likely to create a demand for new industrial buildings and may reduce the advantages of the existing centres of the chemical industry.

Contemporary society produces large quantities of waste arising partly from inefficient processes and partly from wasteful consumption. The former arises from conflicts between material and labour efficiency; the more expensive labour tends to be relative to materials, the more likely it is that materials will be wasted in maximizing the economic use of labour. The latter arises from the growing wealth of society, from rising labour costs for maintenance relative to manufacture and from an increasing tendency to replace goods on grounds of fashion rather than because they are worn out. Other causes include increasingly elaborate packaging which is not reusable and in particular the growing use of paper. In the absence of new technology to create economic recycling, the use of raw materials and energy in manufacturing and distribution increases and with it the volume of refuse to be handled and disposed, creating further demands on land, and environmental and pollution hazards. Innovation in information handling may reduce the use of paper, computer control of production may reduce industrial waste, while innovation in materials may equate the life of materials closer to the life of the product and reduce the difficulties of waste disposal.

6.11 DEVELOPMENT AND PLANNING CONTEXTS

Clearly it is impossible to be exhaustive within the confines of one short section on the contexts for development and planning. It is only possible to suggest the types of parameter to bear in mind and to indicate some of the factors which may be important.

Because birth rates are currently low both in Great Britain and western Europe, population is expected to rise only slowly to the end of the century and the numbers of people of working and pensionable age appear likely to remain fairly stable. Changes in birth rates would initially affect the number of children, having consequences for other groups as time passes. Unless there are dramatic changes in lifetime hours of work, the volume of potential labour appears unlikely to change much in the foreseeable future.

The national demand for new built environment depends on the sum of local changes in population and activities. Future changes in demand are likely to depend much more on migration of people and activities than on changes in national population. Local population changes resulting from inter-regional movement from north and west to south and east, and from intra-regional movements from inner cities and metropolitan regions to smaller towns and villages, and the activities of the people migrating, appear likely to create the major needs for new development.

Households are increasing in number much faster than population, increasing both the demand for dwellings and dwellings of different sizes. At the same time the rise in incomes and changes in lifestyles result in a demand for dwellings offering higher standards and changed amenities.

The geographical distribution of jobs is broadly parallel to that for population. The demand for new buildings and infrastructure in areas of growth adds to the demand arising from changing activities and changing technological demands. To the demands for new development to meet the consequences of growth, migration and technological, social and economic change must be added new development and rehabilitation arising from past neglect of buildings and infrastructure.

REFERENCES

1. Government Statistical Service (1984) *Regional Trends*, HMSO, London.
2. Government Statistical Service (1986) *Social Trends*, HMSO, London.

3. Stone, P. A. (1970) *Urban Development in Britain*, National Institute for Economic and Social Research, Cambridge University Press, London.
4. Ermisch, J. (1983) *The Political Economy of Demographic Change*, Policy Studies Institute/Heinemann, London.
5. Department of Employment (July 1984) *Employment Gazette* D.O.E., London.
6. Centre for Urban and Regional Development *Functional Regions 1983/4*, University of Newcastle Upon Tyne.
7. Government Statistical Service (1985) *Social Trends*, HMSO, London.
8. Department of Employment (July 1985) Employment Gazette D.O.E., London.
9. Department of Employment (October 1985) Employment Gazette D.O.E., London.
10. Government Statistical Service (1950–1986) *Annual Abstracts of Statistics*, HMSO, London.
11. Statistical Office of the European Community (1984) Euro stat.
12. Brittan, S. (May 1985) Back to Full Employment; The Economic Aspect. *National Westminster Bank Quarterly Review*, London.
13. Government Statistical Service (1986) *General Household Survey 1984*, HMSO, London.
14. Stone, P. A. (1983) *Building Economy*, 3rd edn, Pergamon Press, Oxford.

PART THREE

Developing the built environment

7

National and regional development

THE NATIONAL ECONOMY AND SPATIAL DISTRIBUTION

The conditions necessary for a high level of economic activity tend to vary from region to region, from settlement to settlement, and within settlements. The pattern of distribution varies from one time period to another.

Throughout recorded history the economies of countries, regions and settlements have had changes in fortune as the conditions making for a successful economy and the local balance of advantages have changed. Deposits of minerals, forests and fertility have been exhausted; natural changes such as the sea receding or encroaching, rivers silting-up and more or less favourable climate have enhanced or removed the comparative advantages of one place over another; changes in demand, technology and skills have created or destroyed local economies. Conditions have changed as a result of political and other human action. Such changes in conditions have increased or reduced local employment opportunities, enhanced or reduced the value of local skills and changed the levels of local affluence. As a consequence population has migrated; some settlements and regions have declined and others have grown.

7.2 CHANGING DISTRIBUTION OF LOCAL ADVANTAGES IN GREAT BRITAIN

In the nineteenth century industrial location was often determined by a supply of energy, either water power from fast rivers or coal for steam power. Now most power is provided by electricity, gas or oil which are available more or less universally. Even coal can easily be transported long distances. The special climatic conditions needed for such industries as cotton spinning can now easily be reproduced artificially. Proximity to raw materials is also now much less important, partly because of improved and reduced real costs of transport and partly because many of the local supplies of raw materials, once available in this country, have been exhausted and now have to be imported from overseas. Further, the industries which used to need large supplies of heavy and bulky materials are now mostly in decline.

Automation, other tools and the subdivision of operations are reducing the need for traditional skills. Labour can often be trained in a short time to the less exacting level of skills now required for many industrial operations. Many of the old industries have lost out to third world countries where the labour force, far less expensive than in this country, can easily be trained to carry out the techniques now used. As a result many of the old skills are no longer required.

Again, because of the lower costs in real terms of transport, nearness to the market is less important. At the same time the trading partners of Great Britain have changed with much more trade across the North Sea to Europe, reducing the advantages of the north and west and increasing those of the east and south. As transport becomes easier and cheaper, and communication links multiply, local markets become more open to competition from other areas, internationally as well as nationally and regionally. Nevertheless, some specialized industries, concentrated in particular areas, still flourish. Many consumer goods still tend to be manufactured near their main markets, the large concentrations of population. Most service industry is concentrated in the market area.

Unless the advantages of proximity to local markets are important, firms in the same trade tend to locate in the same area of the country, in order to enjoy the services of a pool of skilled labour and subcontractors which develops around a cluster of firms with similar requirements. Unless local disadvantages have developed, the chosen locality is often the one which had initial advantages such as local raw materials, particularly if they were heavy and bulky, labour with the appropriate skill and aptitude, scientific and entrepreneurial expertise, markets or ports. There appears to be a great deal of new industry which in theory could operate in many places but which concentrates in certain areas rather than spreading across the country. Initially location may depend on local loyalties of the entrepreneur but once a location is established it becomes attractive to other firms in the same trade. Plants set up in other areas tend to be secondary and the first to be closed if trade declines.

7.3 REGIONAL DISTRIBUTION OF INDUSTRY

The newer and expanding industries tend to concentrate in the south and east of Great Britain to the neglect of the north and west. There are some exceptions, for example, the development of electronic industries in Scotland.

The decline of economic activity in the north and west is not just because new industries are not developing in those areas but also because of the decline of industries traditional to them. It is notable that the decline of economic activity in the north and west is concentrated much more in the conurbations, the centres of the dying industries, than in the rest of the regions. This suggests that the aftermath of these industries, the run-down environment and the concentration of skills and aptitudes relevant to the declining industries, do little to attract development there. The new industries usually require clean air and buildings, very different from those left behind by the firms which have closed. Incoming firms generally would need to bring in skilled labour and management, not easily attracted without the attractive housing, consumer facilities and services available in the areas from which they would need to be attracted and would need to re-train local labour.

While population movement out of the conurbations and cities is general over the country, it is greater in the north than elsewhere (Chapter 6). Locational advantages have shifted from the north and west to the south and east. The problem of the distribution of industry appears to be both inter-regional and intra-regional.

7.4 INVESTMENT FACTORS

A large number of factors determining the success of an enterprise depend on its management and on its ability to determine accurately the market, the design of the product, where and how to promote sales, purchasing policy, the extent to which work should be subcontracted, the training and organization of labour, credit policy and so on. There are also the external factors to be considered, some of which have already been discussed.

Confidence is important in encouraging investment. Firms may be reluctant to invest in an area, even where external conditions are satisfactory, if they are not confident about the quality of some of these factors. Failures of enterprises in an area, strikes, civil strife, a reputation for a poor work ethos, high rates and a poor local government image, however undeserved, all tend to undermine confidence. While local government and other organizations can do something to correct an undeserved poor image, it is difficult to create confidence in an area with a poor reputation.

Negative factors also discourage migration into an area of the management and skilled labour generally necessary to set up a new enterprise. Such people are also reluctant to move to an area with a poor infrastructure, an unattractive climate and a lack of satisfactory facilities for education, health, sports and other leisure pursuits. Apart from climate, such amenities are either directly under the control of local government or can be influenced by them.

A major difficulty for areas with unsatisfactory external factors lies in the strength of competition from successful areas which usually have the amenities sought by firms and people. A ban on development in attractive areas may not lead to the frustrated development going to other areas but to a reduced level of national development, leading to below optimum levels of employment, output and income. This reduces the national resources available to assist the less buoyant areas to upgrade and improve their physical and industrial environment.

7.5   THE CASE FOR REGIONAL DEVELOPMENT POLICY

The case for differential regional policy rests largely on the argument that each region should have as near full employment as possible; this it is claimed would make the best use of national resources and promote the highest level of national output.

Whether governments can usefully take action to increase the uniformity of the spread of employment and affluence, and what types of action are most economic and effective is open to question. Most governments have such objectives but success is by no means uniform. There are also differences of opinion as to whether there is a conflict between maximizing national affluence and achieving a more even geographical spread of affluence. Some argue that if economic activities are allowed to develop where they find conditions most favourable, output and resources would be maximized, providing a surplus for investing in less favoured areas. Others argue that if development is not controlled, it will concentrate in the most favoured areas until eventually growing congestion and local shortages will reduce the advantages below the level of other areas. While in the end the formerly less favoured areas may be stimulated it may be only after resources have been wasted in the formerly more favourable ones.

The criteria of success applied by individual enterprises are different to those applied by governments. Individual enterprises, whether public or private, are concerned with using their own resources to the best advantage, generally to maximize the return on the capital they employ. They have no means of working out the economic and social optimum national distribution of resources and no way of influencing others to conform to a national plan. In the long run the resulting competition between enterprises for scarce local resources and growing congestion will tend to reduce the expected advantages of a location. The complexity and scale of activities is probably too great for an optimum distribution of enterprise to be planned. Even governments tend to lack both adequate information and the skills to produce and implement an optimum plan for national enterprise.

Clearly, past development has created a considerable amount of built environment, much of it sound and with potential for a long future life, or at least with the potential to justify rehabilitation. If population and activities move out of an area, much of the built environment there will become redundant and its equivalent will need to be developed elsewhere using additional national resources.

There are social costs as well as economic ones. People develop roots with family ties and friends, and many are reluctant to move very far. Households in rented dwellings, particularly public authority dwellings, cannot easily transfer to accommodation in other towns, and not at such favourable rents. Differences in the purchase price of houses often impede the migration of owner-occupiers. Those who do migrate tend to be those with skills in particular demand, who are looking for better opportunities for employment, housing and environment. This process tends to leave behind in the depressed areas those without the skills now in demand; generally they will be less easy to employ in the absence of the more skilled.

A decline in the local economy and growing unemployment reduces the real revenue to both public and private enterprises. As a result the marginal ones tend to close, creating more unemployment and reducing services, and reducing further the ability of firms and public undertakings to rebuild and rehabilitate the built environment and raise the standards of the area. These problems will be considered later in looking at the problems of declining settlements (Chapter 10).

7.6 NATIONAL DEVELOPMENT POLICIES

The exercise of planning powers can permit or prevent development but cannot enforce development. Particular developments may be encouraged through financial or planning incentives and sometimes by discouraging or preventing development elsewhere. To achieve more, government needs to support planning by sponsoring development, but sponsored development will only be of use, if there is an adequate market demand for the goods and services produced in such built development. The policies of central government for physical planning tend to be confused with those for regional development. In this country there are no comprehensive national or regional plans for physical development.

The major policies for spatial distribution have been concerned as much with reducing congestion in the conurbations and protecting the countryside from development as with guiding development to the less favoured areas. The Green Belt policy is concerned with controlling the spread of conurbations by creating large areas around them in which development is discouraged, except for infilling in existing towns and villages. Congestion within the conurbations of the south and midlands, in particular London, has been handled by rationing the development of industrial and office buildings. While such development has been rationed generally in the south and midlands, although to a lesser extent outside the conurbations, development has been encouraged in designated new towns and expansion towns outside the Green

Belts. These policies have limited development in the areas most favoured by developers, but encouraged development within acceptable areas favoured by government and reduced pressure in the conurbations of the south and midlands. The controls have been gradually relaxed as the areas in which development was rationed, particularly in the inner cities, have lost their economic buoyancy. Pressure has built up in new locations in the south, for example, along the routes of the newly created motorways, particularly along the M4 corridor between Reading and Bristol. Thus development frustrated in locations of developers' first choice could still find accommodation without developing in areas unattractive to them. The balance of cost and benefit varies with the enterprise and the optimum conditions for its success.

The designated new towns and expansion towns were in areas potentially attractive to industry and commerce but lacking development. Their growth depended, not just on the existence of the availability of planning consents but on active promotion by public bodies, by the development by the public sector of infrastructure, services and a nucleus of housing, industrial and commercial properties, and by incentives to people and firms to migrate to them. The government financed the development of new towns directly and expansion towns indirectly through local authorities.

The promotion of new and expanded settlements in the north and west where demand was less buoyant, has been less successful. In such areas, demand has been more from people and firms within the region looking for a location more attractive than the existing industrial towns and conurbations, than from people and firms from other regions. To persuade people and firms to migrate to areas not favoured further incentives are required.

7.7   REGIONAL DEVELOPMENT POLICIES

Regional policies for industry were based on the principle of taking work to areas with unemployed labour, as distinct from taking labour to areas with excess demand for it, by lowering the costs to firms setting up and operating in them. When these policies were first conceived, in the 1960s, the national rate of unemployment was very low (Chapter 6). There were labour shortages in the more buoyant regions, particularly in the south-east and midlands. It was thought that employment potential could be transferred to areas with unemployed resources to the benefit of both them and the buoyant areas, bringing employment to the former and reducing inflationary pressure and congestion to the latter. By the time the policies were put into practise unemployment was rising everywhere, confidence had declined and there were fewer entrepreneurs willing to risk expansion, particulary in areas with relatively poor industrial and physical environment.

For the purposes of regional policy, Great Britain and Northern Ireland have been divided into 'assisted' and 'non-assisted' areas. Broadly the south-east and midlands were non-assisted areas, while the west and north were assisted areas. The latter were divided into intermediate areas, development areas and special development areas, with an ascending order of government assistance. The areas were defined on the basis of travel to work areas, but their composition has varied from time to time as economic conditions and the level of unemployment have changed. For most of the period during which the policy has been applied, Scotland, Wales, northern England and the south-west have been development areas, with special development area status for some of the heavily built-up old industrial areas in the north and Northern Ireland. Yorkshire and Lancashire were generally intermediate areas, although Merseyside was a special development area.

In the last few years the extent of assisted areas has been greatly reduced. In 1979 they still covered 44% of the work force but by 1982 the figure had

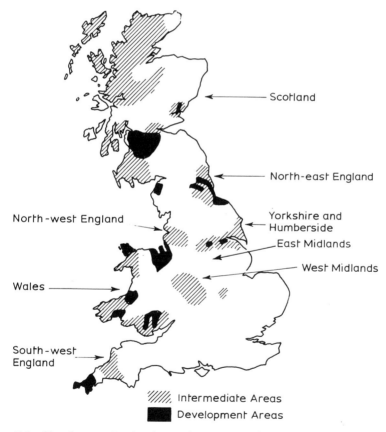

Figure 7.1   Sketch map of assisted areas in Great Britain, from November 29th 1984.

fallen to 27%. Further important changes were made in 1984. The system was revised to cover two types of assisted areas: development areas containing 15% of the working population, and intermediate areas. It is now mainly the old heavily built-up industrial areas which are development areas but the west midlands has now been made an assisted area with intermediate area status (Fig. 7.1).

The form of assistance has varied over time with the emphasis on reducing capital costs either by grants or through tax relief; assistance with labour costs in the form of training allowances or directly with labour costs has, at times, been provided. Overall the result has tended to be to attract capital intensive plants rather than labour intensive ones. Many of the plants which have been attracted have been oil and heavy chemical plants which would have been likely to have set up in the assisted areas in any case.

Other countries have followed somewhat similar policies, as a result of which international firms have been able to obtain competitive offers of grants from different governments. The European Commission makes grants, mainly to industrial and infrastructural projects in the Community's less favoured regions. Clearly governments have had to form a judgement on the viability of projects so as to avoid subsidizing those where there was little hope of success even with grants. Making such judgements is difficult, especially for government officers who generally lack the appropriate business experience. Many of the projects, which have been aided, have failed. Often they have been branch plants and closed, as marginal, when trade declined.

At the time of writing only in the development areas are grants, now 15%, automatic; in intermediate areas financial assistance is selective. Capital grants are limited to £10 000 per job as against average costs at 1982 prices of four times as much for jobs created in the 1960s and 1970s [1].

7.8 CONGESTION POLICY

In addition to the positive encouragements to development in selected areas, negative action has been taken against development in areas considered particularly buoyant, and liable to congestion, principally the south-east and west midlands. It was considered that these areas generated so much industrial and office development, that limiting development would not affect their prosperity. Development disallowed in these regions would, it was hoped, take place in the assisted areas.

Industrial development certificates (IDCs) were introduced in 1947 [2]. At one time IDCs were necessary for developments or redevelopments of industrial space in excess of 5000 square feet (about 470 m^2), sufficient space for only 10 to 20 workers. Gradually controls were relaxed for smaller developments, particularly outside the south-east, until 1981, when the regulations were revoked. The need to obtain government permission to erect or extend a factory would in itself have discouraged development. It is claimed that the rise of unemployment in the west midlands was at least in part the result of this policy.

Office development was also controlled. For a short time in 1964 office development was banned in London. The ban was replaced in early 1965 by regulations limiting the size of developments which could be undertaken without an office development permit (ODP) [2]. Development areas were exempt from this control on development. The control on office development was not operated as restrictively as the control on industrial development; exempt floorspace areas were generally greater and were gradually increased and the number of areas in which restrictions applied were successively reduced until this control was also revoked.

7.9 OTHER SPATIAL POLICIES

Regional policy has been assisted by other means as well as by planning regulations. In 1963, the Location of Offices Bureau was set up to encourage office firms to move their operations from London, particularly central London, to development areas. This policy was designed both to reduce congestion in London and to assist the spread of economic activities. Later, in view of the problems of economic decline in inner London, it promoted office development in such areas as well as outside London. The Bureau has now been abolished. Further policies to help assisted areas included the dispersal of government offices from London to such areas and the encouragement of government departments to place contracts with firms in these areas. Policies have not always differentiated between the conurbations and the rest of the less affluent regions. As indicated earlier (Chapter 6), it is the conurbations and particularly their inner areas in which economic and social decline has been concentrated. More recent policies have been directed to the inner areas, for example, the enterprise zone policy and the inner city partnership programmes and urban development corporations (Chapter 10).

The Government has introduced the concept of enterprise zones (*Local Government, Planning and Land Act, 1980*). The zones have been conceived as small areas in economically depressed districts to test whether industrial and commercial activities could be encouraged by the removal or streamlining of the administration of certain statutory and administrative controls. Certain local authorities were invited to prepare schemes for zones. These offered planning permission to most developers (hazardous and certain undesirable uses were excluded) while IDCs were to be waved. Once a scheme was accepted by the Secretary for State, financial inducements were to be made available such as exemption from development land tax, rates, training board levies and government requests for information, a possible 100% first year allowance for capital expenditure on industrial and commercial building to be set against income and corporation tax, and priority treatment and relaxation of normal criteria for custom-free warehousing [3]. The exemptions and the zone status were to last for 10 years. Twenty five zones have been established. Fears have been expressed that the zones would draw in development which might otherwise have taken place outside them. There is some evidence that most of the firms setting up in such zones are local and that comparatively few new jobs are created.

Another proposal to encourage industrial development is the concept of 'freeports'. This concept has been used to a limited extent in other countries, for example, USA, Holland and Ireland. Within the area of the freeport goods can be imported for processing without payment of customs or excise duty. Such duties are only levied on goods taken into the home market. The government has set up six freeports but their attraction has been much reduced in practise because duties have to be paid initially. The reduction in cash flow and the cost of credit until the duties are eventually repaid adds considerably to costs compared with freeports elsewhere.

The urban programme initiative was set up in 1968. It was an early attempt to assist the inner city. In 1977 the inner city partnership and programmes initiative was set up. Fifteen districts have been designated, mainly in assisted areas but some in London [4]. The partnerships bring together central government and local authorities with the aim of bending main programmes to favour the inner city. They are concerned with social, economic and environmental problems with the emphasis on reducing economic decline and environmental decay.

Urban development corporations, as with new town corporations, are funded directly by the government, have planning and development powers broadly comparable with those of local authorities, but operate more like private developers. They have wide powers and the finance necessary to reclaim land and provide infrastructure as a preliminary to the private development of industry, commerce and housing. They can bring properties into new uses, improve the environment and organize the provision of social facilities. Initially urban development corporations were set up to redevelop London docklands and Merseyside docklands. Following their success in these areas, four more are being set up for areas in Greater Manchester, Teeside, the black country and Tyne and Wear.

Other agencies of regional policy have been created such as the Scottish and Welsh Development Agencies and the English Industrial Estates Corporation. The former have powers to intervene in regional industry. They took over the work of the Scottish and Welsh Industrial Estate Corporations. Northern Ireland also has a development agency. Assistance in creating enterprises is also provided by the Development Commission and the Council for Small Industries in Rural Areas, by the voluntary enterprise boards such as those for London and the west midlands, and by some of the activities of the Manpower Services Commission [5].

REFERENCES

1. Study carried out by the University of Cambridge for the Department of Trade and Industry.
2. McCallum, J. D. (1979) The Development of British Regional Policy *Regional Policy*, Martin Robertson, Oxford.
3. Department of the Environment (1980) Consultation Document *Enterprise Zones*, HMSO, London.
4. Policy Review Section (1985) *Regional Studies*, Vol. **19**, No. 1, Journal of Regional Studies Association.
5. Lawless, B. (1981) The role of some central government agencies in urban economic regeneration in Regional Studies, Vol. **15**, No. 1, (J. RSA) Journal of Regional Studies Association.

8

Other national development and planning issues

8.1 DEVELOPMENT IN TOWN AND COUNTRY

Great Britain is one of the more densely inhabited countries, but most of the land is rural rather than urban. It has been estimated that in 1971 just over 8% of the land was used for all urban purposes, including towns, villages, isolated dwellings, farmhouses and transport facilities [1]. The distribution of the various types of use is very uneven. The heavy concentrations of urban development, the urban heartlands, are in the south-east around London, and northwestwards in a band through the west midlands to the north-west and around Glasgow. The least intensively used land, mostly uplands used for rough grazing and forestry are in the west and north, especially in Wales and Scotland. The regions are differentiated as much physically as economically.

The planning problems for both town and country differ considerably from one region to another. In the urban heartlands the main concerns are the prevention of congestion and further urban spread, preserving open land around the settlements and urban renewal. The latter in its widest sense includes economic as well as physical renewal. As indicated earlier, concern is with the concentration of physical and economic development in the south-east and the economic and physical decline in the north and west (Chapter 7). In the countryside the concerns are with limiting the spread of urban development, especially around the large urban centres, the conurbations; maintaining the viability of country towns and villages, and preserving the areas of special interest. More recently concern has been expressed at the effect of agricultural and forestry policy on the appearance and physical condition of the countryside. Other major concerns include the provision of suitable transport networks to meet the needs of people and goods, roads, rail, ports and airports, the exploitation of minerals and the generation of energy.

As indicated earlier two of the main policies in national planning have been aimed at spreading economic and social well-being more evenly over the country and reducing congestion in the south-east and west midlands, especially in the conurbations (Chapter 7). The control of the development of industrial and office buildings in London and Birmingham were to contribute to congestion policy as well as to support the assisted area policy in spreading economic development to the north and west (Chapter 7). Protecting the countryside around the conurbations and cities has been largely promoted through the Green Belt policy and by siphoning off development to the new and expanding towns. The Green Belts largely lie across the country most favoured for development. Development has been limited, not only around the conurbations and cities but also around most small settlements, generally only infilling has been allowed. Other areas have been protected by designating them as Areas of Outstanding Natural Beauty, National Parks, Heritage Coasts and Conservation Areas. Major new development has taken place in the new and expansion towns, and along new transport facilities, particularly in the south.

8.2   EXISTING URBAN SETTLEMENTS AND OBSOLESCENCE

Inevitably settlements are in a constant state of change. Buildings and infrastructure age and tend towards financial, functional and physical obsolescence and require increasing maintenance, adaptation and alteration, and eventually replacement. The rate of such obsolescence depends to a large extent on the prosperity of the firms and households who occupy the buildings and contribute to the revenue of public bodies. In settlements with a prosperous economy there is generally both the finance and the demand to maintain and adapt the built environment. Obsolescence in such conditions is often financial, leading to the clearance of physically sound property to allow a more profitable development. In a settlement old activities decline, new ones develop. If the parent settlement cannot adapt to provide appropriate facilities such as good access, attractive environment and skilled labour, new development may take place at the periphery or move to other settlements.

The oldest activities and buildings are generally in the inner city and this is generally the first area to become obsolete and the most difficult and expensive in which to provide facilities and environment to meet current demands. Firms close and move out, new ones often employ less workers. Those with more skill, education and training tend to leave, while the less skilled, for whom there is little work tend to remain. With fewer activities, there is less demand and resources to rehabilitate or redevelop. Replacing the old industrial and commercial properties with housing is of limited economic or social value, unless there are adequate employment opportunities (Chapter 10).

8.3 CITY EXPANSION AND MIGRATION

Large scale city expansion depends on cheap and frequent transport to bring in daily supplies of food, other commodities and people to work, and to convey from the city its output, waste products and its workers to their homes. The extension of transport systems and reductions in transport costs have reduced the need for high density residential development and increased the possible viable size of cities. It enables more people to enjoy living near the countryside. The possibilities of cheaper development at the periphery encouraged developers to provide properties to meet the demand. Each successive wave of development destroys some of the advantages of earlier ones, engulfs villages and small towns, and threatens that further settlements may be joined into continuous built-up areas with consequences for the costs and benefits of the settlement (Chapter 10).

Attempts to hold the boundaries of cities by Green Belts and other planning devices, and the growing preference for life in small towns and villages, made possible by improved and cheaper transport, especially the private car, have encouraged migration from the cities to smaller settlements within their hinterland. New towns have been created and nominated small towns expanded beyond the boundaries of the Green Belts. As electronic communications improve, the need to attend large work centres may be reduced and life in small settlements may be viable for many more people. In the favoured areas of the country some small towns have expanded considerably, others may follow and new small towns may be built. How far there might be expansion to villages depends on the local provision of services and employment opportunities, and environmental quality.

Over recent decades employment opportunities and services have often declined in small towns and (especially) villages beyond the daily reach of large centres. The number of jobs in agriculture has decreased markedly and agricultural services, such as the distribution of inputs, i.e. fertilizers, feeds and so on, and processing and marketing farm produce is now dealt with on a larger scale in the larger centres. Small towns and villages have lost activities and jobs in this way. Further activities and employment opportunities have been lost with the decline in the number of retail outlets, and often their concentration in larger settlements. The possibilities of the empty premises being used for small industrial and commercial enterprises do not appear to have been realized. An increasing number of workers from the smaller settlements have had to look to the more substantial towns for employment opportunities. This may involve journeys to work of 20 to 30 miles or moving to the centres of job availability. The extension of electronic communications appears more likely to encourage migrants to reside in small settlements rather than to provide jobs for those displaced by other changes.

Particularly attractive small settlements with local attractions and reasonable communications attract both the retired and tourists. While the latter may create some additional employment, both tend to reduce the supply of housing available for the young villagers forming households for the first time. However, the migrants tend to bring wealth and drive, and improve the built environment. Old industrial villages, such as mining ones, and those which are remote are unlikely to obtain relief from either tourism or migration and tend to decline (Chapter 10).

The more car ownership grows, the greater the tendency of public transport to lose its viability. Services are cut, reducing convenience and encouraging more potential passengers to use private transport, so further reducing viability and services until they are withdrawn, trapping those without private transport in the small towns and villages. This occurs in conditions under which more journeys to larger settlements tend to be necessary to obtain the services and jobs no longer available in the villages. As transport, jobs and services decline, villages become even less viable. If they are not to continue to decline or become dormitories for those with private transport, it will be necessary to find some form of viable public transport and to achieve greater success in encouraging small businesses to set up within them. Currently it is uncertain whether the deregulation of buses will encourage entrepreneurs to provide more convenient and better designed services for small towns and villages, or whether it will lead to marginal traditional services being withdrawn without new forms of services being provided.

8.4 TOWNS, TRAFFIC AND SERVICES

While the network of roads in the countryside is generally more than sufficient to handle current levels of traffic, road capacity tends to be less adequate at the approach to towns and within towns. The narrowness of roads in old towns leads to considerable traffic congestion at peak periods, which is exacerbated by unloading and parking. Generally the layout of existing shopping, warehousing and small industry does not provide for adequate off-the-street unloading bays or parking, and the problem has been exacerbated through the increasing use of very large delivery vehicles. Delivery in quiet periods appears difficult to arrange.

Parking facilities in most towns are inadequate and expensive, encouraging street parking despite prohibitions. The inadequacies and cost of parking tends to discourage the use of town amenities such as shopping, eating places and places of entertainment. This reduces the attractiveness of such towns to visitors and as a place to reside, reduces trade and employment, and public and private revenues, and consequently the resources to maintain the built environment to an adequate standard (Chapter 10).

All of these factors, together with a lack of sites sufficiently large to accommodate customers' cars and other facilities now required, high land costs and rates, encourage developers to seek out-of-town sites, the development of which tends to take trade away from established town centres. Reductions in the number of shops selling necessities such as food, clothes, electrical goods and others, especially those offering a wide range of goods at competitive prices, tends to reduce the number of shoppers patronizing town centres. Those with their own means of transport tend to transfer their patronage to out-of-town centres, leaving behind the patronage of those without their own means of transport and generally with less purchasing power generating a vicious circle and increasing economic decline. Often the specialist shops with slower turnovers such as bookshops, handicraft shops and haberdashers close and are not replaced in new shopping centres, where rents tend to be too high for such businesses and where their best selling lines are appropriated by the chain stores.

Out-of-town shopping centres are usually built where the road networks provide good access. Given the quality of the access and the convenience provided by the centre, the areas around, other things being equal, will tend to become attractive places to live, with perhaps growing pressure to develop housing there. Residential development creates a demand for other amenities and facilities, and provides a pool of labour for industrial and commercial enterprises. Hence out-of-town shopping centres may be potential new settlements which, in due course, might grow and coalesce with the parent settlement (Chapter 9).

The problems of inadequate car parking for shoppers often arises particularly in towns enjoying economic growth, generally from the growth of its office sector. Offices draw their staff from a wide hinterland; many of the workers cannot conveniently use public transport or may need cars for visiting clients and arrive in individual cars. Since they arrive before the shoppers, in the absence of private parking provisions, they tend to take over car parking needed by shoppers and consumers of other services. Keeping the parking closed until too late to be of use to the office workers is only a limited solution, since without suitable parking facilities the offices might have difficulty in recruiting sufficient staff.

In many existing towns there is not sufficient land in the central area to meet the combined needs of shopping, other consumer services and offices and the parking they generate. Often central area roads have inadequate capacity and parking is limited to reduce traffic loads. Widening and supplementing roads in town centres is expensive both in resources and in terms of environment. Building high to obtain greater densities is not only costly but generally creates the potential for yet more floorspace and hence parking demand, without increasing road capacity. Multistorey car-parking is also expensive (Chapter 9).

Some towns have or are considering developing office centres away from their town centres. A distinction must be made between retail and wholesale offices. Retail offices imply service centres which deal with the public over the counter such as banks, building societies and insurance brokers, together with professional and medical centres. Such offices need to be located conveniently for their clients. Wholesale offices imply head offices and regional offices of commercial and industrial firms which generally do not deal with the public except by post and telephone. The argument for the need for face-to-face transactions appears to have little weight for such offices in provincial towns. Usually companies leave a small office in the national or provincial capital, moving the routine operations which do not deal face-to-face with the public to the smaller provincial towns. However, with a developing network of electronic communications, face-to-face contact and hence location is becoming less important.

The main need for centrality for offices appears to arise from the need to be convenient for staff access and lunchtime staff amenities such as shopping and restaurants. In some cases such amenities and facilities are being provided in areas away from the centre, where it is easier and cheaper to provide adequate parking. Travelling by public transport to such centres is less convenient than to the town centre. Public transport might need to be reorganized and road capacity increased. However costs of land and development are less at the periphery of the town or in the inner areas.

8.5 RESIDENTIAL DEVELOPMENT

Additional housing is needed not only in areas in which population is increasing but also where it is stable. As households divide and decline in size more dwellings are needed. Land for development of housing and other urban amenities could be made available on derelict and under-used land within cities and towns, at the periphery of existing towns, and in new areas between settlements.

The government's official figure for registered unused land in England was in 1982 115 000 acres (about 46 000 hectares) [2]. This was on 11 500 sites, 60% of which were owned by local authorities and most of the balance by nationalized industries. While not all of this land is suitable for housing and some may not be of physical or economic value for industrial or commercial uses, it is considered that a good deal of it could be used to reduce the demand for undeveloped land [2].

While there is some pressure for development on rural land in most places, particularly in areas around the conurbations and cities, this pressure is much greater in the south than in the north, with the greatest pressure in the south-east. Additional housing needs to be sited where employment is available. Generally, pressure for industrial and commercial development is also much greater in the south east, particularly in the home counties.

Consumers usually prefer housing adjacent to the countryside or open space, overlooking rivers, lakes or the sea, or within existing areas of attractive housing. Locations within inner areas adjacent to run-down housing, large local authority housing development, industry and commerce especially if run-down, are not favoured by purchasers of housing or hence by developers.

Private housing developers build for the market and look for areas for which demand is high, where they can achieve rapid sales at high prices and where land is cheap to purchase and develop in relation to the value of the finished properties. Virgin land on the outskirts of settlements or in the countryside is particularly attractive since such areas offer sites large enough to secure economies of scale. The prices they can offer far exceed the value of the land for a rural use. Large lightly developed sites in good housing areas are also favoured. There is a reluctance to redevelop derelict and vacant industrial and commercial land in the inner city where demand is weak and land expensive to develop. Some developers are prepared to build villages or small towns within the countryside. For example, Consortium Developments Ltd wish to build towns of about 15 000 people and propose to provide open space and sports facilities. Their first proposal is for a development in the London Green Belt.

8.6 TRANSPORT AND DEVELOPMENT

Policies relating to transport can have a profound effect on spatial distribution, and on economic and social well-being. Transport policies appear to be aimed more at meeting industrial and commercial demand than directly supporting regional and planning aims.

The decline of heavy industry, the dispersion of production and distribution facilities, changes in distribution and goods handling, and the growth in size of road vehicles, together with the increasing comparative costs of rail over road transport, have brought about the decline of rail and the growth of road transport. Steps to reduce the costs of the rail system, by closing branch lines and consolidating goods handling in fewer larger depots, have reduced the value of rail transport to many of its potential customers and further encouraged a switch to road transport.

The national road network has been improved by the creation of motorways, the widening, usually with dual carriageways, of other trunk roads and bypassing towns and villages astride them. Initially improvements were made to the network between London and the provincial cities. This was followed by links between the principal towns and cities, and between them and the ports, particularly those on the east coast.

Changes in the relative importance of the different types of goods entering into overseas trade and the countries with which the UK trades, together with consequential changes in shipping and goods handling, have had a profound effect on the growth and decline of ports. The growth in the size of ships and the development of new types, large tankers, bulk carriers, container and roll-on/roll-off ships, together with a demand for speedy loading and unloading, has been to the advantage of modern ports with deep water, large areas of uncluttered space, modern handling equipment, a flexible labour force and good road communications. The growth of trade with Europe has given east coast ports an advantage over those on the west coast. The old ports, such as those of London, Liverpool, Bristol and Glasgow have declined to the gain of ports such as Felixstowe and Dover, creating a demand for trunk road improvement from them to London and the provincial cities. Except for short sea crossings, as much for cars as for passengers, international passenger traffic is now by air rather than sea.

Airport policy has concentrated development on the government-owned London airports, Heathrow and Gatwick, with a long running attempt (now being implemented) to expand Stansted to a national airport. The provincial airports are mainly municipal and have been restricted largely to local and feeder services and package tour operations rather than international services. Lightweight valuable cargo is increasingly sent overseas by air. Internal air services are limited; most people and goods travel by road to the international airports, increasing traffic loads, particularly near them.

While considerable progress has been made in developing intercity roads, policy for city roads has been less certain. Until the 1960s city road policy appeared to be aimed at increasing traffic capacity and the speed of the traffic flow. The Buchanan Report [3] drew attention to the financial and environmental costs of developing adequate capacity for traffic in large towns and cities, costs already experienced by those cities which had started to develop urban motorways. London abandoned its ringway and radial system so that the motorways and other trunk roads coming into London deposit their traffic largely on an unimproved road system. One consequence has been that the M25, which encircles London, is already overloaded, although the last link has only just been completed at the time of writing. A similar situation exists in many of the provincial cities. Even where city networks were developed they tend to provide efficient through passage rather than efficient access to the traffic generators within the city, particulary in the centre. Current policy appears to be more concerned with limiting traffic to existing capacity and keeping it moving than in providing access to the terminals and adequate parking space.

8.7 OTHER LARGE LAND USERS

Mineral workings and energy generators are amongst the most demanding and obtrusive of land users. There is a large scattering of abandoned mineral workings and spoil heaps, disused power generators and other plant. These occur both adjacent to settlements and in the countryside. In some cases spoil heaps have been landscaped and flooded workings converted to leisure facilities but there remain many areas of dereliction untreated, probably the most difficult to handle [2]. Some old energy generators and industrial workings are being tidied up as historical monuments or to meet interest in industrial archaeology. There are continuing demands on land for energy plant such as oil workings, conventional and nuclear electric power stations, hydroelectric and non-conventional generators, using wind and water power for example, and new coal mines. All require large areas of land, often land designated for preservation in its existing state because of its special attractions.

Other large users of land include water storage and the armed forces. Water storage often involves very large scale changes to rivers and lakes, and the loss of farmland, forestry and settlements. In the long run the changes may be acceptable and contribute to leisure facilities. Of course, the largest users of land are agriculture and forestry. Both are subject to criticism for the way they use land. Agriculture is censured not only for producing agricultural produce in excess of demand at considerable cost to the consumer and tax payer, but for erecting obtrusive buildings, while leaving existing ones to become derelict, and for grubbing hedges and trees, draining marshes and clearing historic woodlands. The agricultural industry has been largely left free from the planning regulations which control other forms of development. The impact of such large scale developments as power generators, and water collecting and storage facilities can be widespread and complex. The direct costs of development and operation and the value of output are often the least difficult to evaluate. It is often difficult to foresee all the ramifications of such developments.

Most power generators are obtrusive, create pollution and carry risks from malfunctioning. The extent of pollution and risks to health and life are generally not appreciated until long after the facility has been commissioned. The consequences of power generation tend to be international as indicated by the distribution of acid rain and the consequences of the nuclear accident at Chernobyl. There is little agreement on the risks or the environmental impact of power generation. Most of the expert opinion is within the generating industry. Increasing evidence of plant failure and unsuspected pollution has reduced public confidence, particularly in nuclear generation. Risks are uncertain and difficult to evaluate; widespread damage is possible if not very probable. Developing power generators at a distance from areas of power use only partly reduces the level of risks to the majority of the population and still leaves many people and environments exposed to the associated risks, while requiring long transmission links. The longer these are, the greater the environmental impact and risks, the more costly the construction and the greater the loss of power in transmission. There are also costs for the disposal of mineral and nuclear waste.

Developing water facilities whether for water supply or as a basis of power generation can also have large scale consequences. Large areas of land may be taken from other uses with loss of agricultural production, forests, homes and work places and natural habitats. The drainage of land around may be altered, and estuaries and coasts scoured or silted up. Other areas may be affected by quarrying for material with which to build dams and embankments.

8.8   GREEN BELTS AND OTHER OPEN LAND

Interest in the use of the countryside has grown, particularly in the last few decades. Concern has extended from limiting urban spread to reducing and controlling the use of land in the countryside for public utilities, mineral workings, transport, agriculture and forestry. Legislation has been introduced and public bodies set up to protect land of special interest and beauty.

Green Belts were introduced by an Act in 1938 which laid emphasis on the preservation of land from development in order to enhance amenities and preserve health. Later they were seen as a way to prevent urban spread such as ribbon development, extended development around favoured settlements and the growth of settlements into each other, and to preserve wedges of open country between the arms of developed areas. Green Belts have been drawn around the major conurbations and large cities to a depth of several miles. While much of the area is open country, existing settlements, some quite large, have been included.

Generally development plans allow enough land for limited expansion, mainly for rounding off settlements within the Green Belts. Not all the open land is agricultural or forest; some is current or worked out mineral land and some is derelict. It is often argued that derelict land provides no amenity and might as well be developed, particularly where it is adjacent to development. Farming on the periphery of settlements is difficult in some cases because of interference and damage by trespassers. Land affected in this way may cease to be cultivated. The difference in value between land with and without planning permission for development can be of the order of one hundredfold. There is a temptation to allow land to become derelict to increase the likelihood of obtaining planning permission for development. The attraction of Green Belt land to developers lies in the high level of demand usual in such areas. Particularly in the London Green Belt the land offers a high level of amenity in an area of buoyant economy and affluence. Further, development on green fields is generally much cheaper than on previously developed land. Moreover, Green Belt land potentially offers large sites and an easy way for developers to build up land banks. Preserving Green Belt land by reducing development opportunities on green field sites, is thought to enhance the attraction of redevelopment sites within settlements. Nevertheless Green Belt land is taken extensively for public development of roads, public utilities and other purposes.

Current government policy for Green Belts is that once approved they should be altered only in exceptional circumstances but earlier drafts of the latest Department of Environment circular [4] were less firm on preserving the Green Belts and there can be no certainty that this line will be maintained especially when considered in relation to other government policy circulars.

Since Green Belts already contain a considerable amount of urban development, including towns and villages, they are vulnerable to the further potential development that they generate. In some places further development would soon result in cohesive development from the present periphery of the cities adding several additional kilometers to their size and further reducing the limited amount of open space available for leisure purposes within them.

Settlements developed within daily travelling distance of conurbations and other large existing settlements tend to be commuter dormitory settlements and themselves add to the pressures for further development and the expansion of transport networks. The New Town programme was intended to avoid this situation by creating self-contained settlements outside the hinterland of the conurbations. Some of the early New Towns were developed only just outside the Green Belt. While most, particularly those in the south, have been successful in attracting enterprise and population, some too successful in relation to the planned capacity of the surrounding area, some have nevertheless become in part commuter towns.

In some areas, particularly in the south east, it is already difficult to find any sizeable gaps between existing settlements into which further settlements could be sited without creating new or extending existing conurbations. Motorways with their good communication links between major settlements and the ports are particularly attractive to both industry and commerce. There is likely to be considerable future pressure for planning consents along their corridors (already the M4 corridor is attracting much industry and commerce). The Channel Tunnel is likely to enhance the attractions of the M20 corridor and the south-east generally relative to other parts of the country. The M25 runs close to the London periphery and is likely to be particularly attractive for development, probably stimulating growth of those settlements close to the interchanges. There is a particular danger of pressure to infill undeveloped areas between the London periphery and the motorway, creating a demand to develop Green Belt and other open land.

The motorways have already attracted considerably more traffic than was expected when they were planned. Development around them would add yet further traffic and bring forward the date of saturation, especially at the intersections around growth points. As a result costs to users of motorways would rise and there would be pressure for widening and building supplementary ones.

The importance given to rural spaces between settlements is not confined to

Green Belts. Local planning authorities often apply criteria to the countryside comparable to the criteria applied to Green Belt land. Often development outside existing settlements, except for designated new and expanding towns, is discouraged. Pressure for land for development is met by increasing densities in existing developments. Developers claim that insufficient land for development is being made available, particularly for housing; and themselves tend to press for higher densities, especially on land they have acquired. This both reduces land cost per dwelling and increases the number of dwellings they can build and from which they can generate profits. As a consequence housing densities are rising to levels associated with Victorian low-cost housing – levels once condemned. Some of the space about the buildings is taken for garaging and parking, reducing the size of gardens to little more than outdoor rooms. Some question whether sufficient space is being provided to meet the needs of increasing leisure and more home-based activities. If it is not, it needs to be considered whether technical and social obsolescence is being built into such high density development as it was with high density flatted development.

Despite the policy of protecting rural spaces there is considerable industrial and commercial development outside the built-up areas. For developers and users the generally lower costs of peripheral over inner area development and the availability of spacious sites with easy access are considerable attractions. One of the planning safeguards in protecting rural spaces from development was the official presumption that agricultural land should not normally be developed because of its value in that use. From February 1987 this presumption has been dropped, reducing the level of protection against development afforded agricultural land.

The development of motorways and other trunk road bypasses takes trade as well as traffic out of existing towns astride the old routes and reduces their attraction for commerce and industry relative to potential areas along the new routes with better access and ample space for development. The pressures on rural land for development along the trunk routes are particularly great in growth areas such as those around London and in the south of England generally.

The purposes of protecting the countryside include the preservation of open space and areas of beauty, archaeological and ecological interest. For these areas to be enjoyed access is necessary. Densities of use of such areas often do not need to rise very high before their attractions start to be destroyed. Destruction of rural amenity results not only from excessive traffic, parking, caravan and camping sites but also from an excess of pedestrians in relation to the loads paths and grass can tolerate, and an excess of various types of users of water facilities.

Changes in the way land is used occur all the time. Initially the changes are on a small scale and do not appear to have much consequence, but often their scale increases rapidly, endangering treasured amenities. While land uses cannot be frozen and planning needs to be flexible, planners have to envisage the way patterns of use are likely to change and their likely consequences, and to make appropriate allowances in their planning proposals.

8.9 AGRICULTURE AND FORESTRY

British agriculture has been achieving increasing yields per hectare and increasing efficiency per man employed for several decades. This was occurring long before Great Britain joined the European Economic Community (EEC), with prices guaranteed above world levels for the main types of produce; prices which are fixed for the total output, whether or not it exceeds demand. In fact output here and in the rest of the EEC has increasingly been above demand levels. As efficiency continues to rise, annual surpluses (subject to fluctuations in the weather) and stocks grow larger. Surplus produce can only be sold ouside the EEC and at prices much below those at which the produce is purchased from the farmers. Great Britain is now an exporter of its most important agricultural products and is self-sufficient in most others.

The agricultural industry has achieved its outstanding increase in productivity, about 3% per year on average over the last 33 years, by adopting new strains of crops and breeds of animals, and by using much more fertilizer – a sevenfold increase in nitrogen alone [5]. Farming patterns have changed to enable the new strains and breeds to be fully exploited. Grasslands have been drained and ploughed up to provide additional land for cereals. Straw is burnt on the fields to enable winter wheat to be sown early. Cattle and poultry are reared indoors to fatten them rapidly and obtain large yields of eggs. Trees and hedges have been removed to provide larger fields to enable a more economic use of larger and more sophisticated farm machinery.

There has been an economic and environmental price to pay for this increased productivity. Not only does the EEC need to find large funds and hence set high taxes to meet the difference between the prices at which it buys and sells, and the costs of storage, but the consumer has to pay higher taxes and higher market prices for the food than would be necessary if it was purchased on world markets. Farmers have been paid not only guaranteed prices but have received grants for ploughing up grassland, for drainage and for buildings, subsidies for some of their inputs and free research and advisory services, and are exempted from rates. Estimates suggest that about a half of the value of farm output is contributed by the public through higher prices, price supports, subsidies and grants [5]. Farming has become a high yield business but also high cost and energy intensive. It is a large user of energy both directly as a fuel and indirectly as a feed stock for agricultural chemicals.

The removal of hedges and trees, the drainage of meadows and the ploughing up of pastures is changing the rural face of the land, from the pattern of small hedged fields with a wide variety of herbage and wild flowers, to one of large open fields with a single crop. Far fewer animals are seen in the fields and industrial complexes of steel and concrete replace clusters of small buildings in local materials. Natural habitats for flora and fauna have been lost with the new methods of husbandry. It is perhaps ironic that what has been lost is a form of development created by the agricultural industry as the most satisfactory solution to the needs of an earlier age but it is that form of development which the community values rather than the more efficient current form.

Doubt has been expressed as to how long the present methods of husbandry are sustainable. Monoculture tends to exhaust the soil's natural properties. Without the use of natural manures and a balanced rotation of crops the soil tends to lose its natural fertility and its humus, and the top soil tends to blow off and be eroded by rain. This has occurred in many countries where monoculture has been practised. Nearly half the arable land in Britain is said to be threatened by erosion [6]. Clouds of soil already blow off the fields in East Anglia, but water induced erosion is said to be the greater danger especially on thin soils such as on the South Downs [6]. Further, many of the fertilizers, herbicides, fungicides and pesticides now used in increasing quantities destroy the flora and fauna now valued, as well as washing through the ground into rivers and lakes, where they destroy water life, and pollute the public water system.

The increases in agricultural output have been achieved on a reducing area of farmland. Farmland is being lost steadily to urban development, forestry and other uses. In England and Wales the percentage of land under agricultural use declined from 80.5% in 1951 to 76.9% in 1971 and is projected to fall to 72.6% by 2001 [1], a decline of 10% over 50 years. The projected change allowed for an increase in urban land from 8.9% in 1951 to 11.0% in 1971 and 14.1% in 2001, with increases in land under forestry from 6.5 to 7.5 to 8.7% over a similar time period. In Scotland only about 3% of the land is used for urban development and about 90% for agriculture [1].

About one-third of the land in Great Britain is of low grade, much of it is in the north, Wales and Scotland in the form of rough grazing supporting only a few sheep; in Scotland where the major part is to be found, much of it consists of deer forest. Rough grazings account for well over one-quarter of the land surface of Great Britain. The balance of agricultural land is divided mainly between cropland and permanent grass. Since 1939 in England and Wales the former area has increased by over a half at the expense of the latter [1]. Much of the cropland taken from permanent grass was Grade III land.

With agricultural productivity per hectare increasing and output already in excess of demand, it is feared that equating supply and demand may entail a rapid decline in the area of land under agriculture. To what extent this might occur and how the pattern of land use might change will depend on the policies pursued. For example, lowering guaranteed prices tends to result in marginal land going out of production, but it might further stimulate the use of nitrates on better land, since they are cheap in relation to the value of the additional yield they make possible. It would appear to be the hill and other low grade land which is at greater risk of going out of production. Much of the land in the heavily populated areas, is the more fertile land, some of it is Grade I, upon which agricultural production would be most likely to continue. Land taken out of cultivation would not necessarily return to land of acceptable ecological interest and beauty. Steps would need to be taken to stimulate appropriate husbandry.

The Country Landowners Association appears to advocate a general diversification of farming activities to include forestry, tourism and small rural industries, with the price support funds being redistributed to encourage non-intensive farming practises compatible with conservation [7]. Other suggestions include finding new demands such as more organically grown food, more home-grown fruit and vegetables, special crops like evening primrose and import substitutes such as oats and cashmere wool. Such developments would depend on the acceptability of quality and price, and might not make a large demand on agricultural land.

More land might be used for forestry of which Great Britain has comparatively little, while world supplies of timber are declining and demand increasing. New varieties of deciduous trees are being bred to mature rapidly. If mineral energy sources become scarce more effort might be put into energy saving and production from plant sources. Suggestions include the use of nitrogen fixing and green manure crops, planting for vegetable oils, coppicing and culture for biomass.

Some commentators expect farmers to become more than agriculturalists. They suggest that land might be developed as much for amenity as food production, with areas of woods and scrub to produce timber and other products, with farmers catering for tourists and leisure pursuits such as fishing, shooting and camping, and some producing other rural products.

It does not follow that a reduction in farm output would necessarily entail large areas of land going out of cultivation. An alternative scenario, following recent commentaries might be for a gradual reduction in the amount of lower grade land used for cereals together with changes in husbandry. If this land were returned to permanent pasture it might be used for grazing animals now kept in sheds, reducing both the output of cereals and beef. Both cereals and grass yields would decline if less nitrogen was used. Again if monoculture of cereals was reduced and cereal production was included in a balanced rotation of crops, cereal output would be reduced and the quality of the soil improved. Such changes in farming practise would involve the use of strains and breeds suitable to a different type of husbandry. At the same time some additional land would be likely to be required for urban development and forestry.

Clearly to achieve a smooth change in agriculture the EEC and national governments would need to work out appropriate policies for the pricing of agricultural output, fertilizers and other chemicals, for grants and for social payments to marginal farmers. Policies would need to be tailor-made to meet the very different situations which would arise for different types of farmers in different parts of the country, and they would need to be phased with feasible rates of change in farming practise to avoid damaging the industry.

Our present official thinking both in the EEC as a whole and in this country appears to be more interested in limiting output by setting aside some of the land, than in adopting a policy of low input–low output. Land set aside would revert to unkempt scrub unless put to some other use. The British government appears to favour forestry as the major use of land set aside. It is proposing limited schemes of grants to farmers to plant trees, to carry out environmental farming in designated environmentally sensitive areas and undertake ancillary activities and it proposes to encourage the planting of novel crops and to give greater freedom to convert redundant farm buildings to new uses [8]. These proposals would not appear to go very far in meeting the need to reduce output. Planting trees is not very attractive to farmers, because it produces little income from the land and they cannot usually afford to wait for the long delayed capital return.

REFERENCES

1. Best, R. H. (1976) The Changing Land-use Structure of Britain. *Town and Country Planning*, 43(3).
2. Department of the Environment (1986) *Transforming our Wasteland*, HMSO, London.
3. Buchanan, C. D. (1964) *Traffic in Towns*, HMSO, London.
4. Department of the Environment and Welsh Office (1984) *Circular 14/84*, HMSO, London.
5. The Economist (2/11/1985) London.
6. Hodges, R. D. and Arden, C. (1986) *Soil Erosion in Britain*, The Soil Association Ltd, Bristol.
7. Country Land Association (1985) The Gretton Report – *Maintaining Income from Land*, CLA, London.
8. The Times (11/2/1987) *Commons Statement by Minister of Agriculture Fisheries and Food*, London.

9

Settlement structure

9.1 CHARACTERISTICS OF SETTLEMENTS

Settlements can be freestanding independent units or interdependent and related clusters forming either a single urban complex, a city region or coalesced into a conurbation.

Individual settlements can be highly centralized (the traditional pattern) with a concentration of economic activities and hence jobs in the centre, and with residential facilities spread around. Alternatively, most economic activities can be decentralized into subcentres with employment areas and their related residential areas around them (i.e. district settlements) or the employment areas can be distributed amongst smaller neighbourhood residential areas.

While the shape of most settlements is distorted by local topographical features, most tend to be broadly circular. This is the most compact shape, with the minimum perimeter and the shortest distances from the centre. Fingers of development into the countryside bring more people in contact with open land but increase distances to the centre. A settlement developed systematically with fingers of development is known as star shaped. If a settlement is elongated it becomes linear or elliptical. An extreme form of such a settlement is a thin band of development, which can be bent to form a circle or oval, or even crossed to form a figure of eight.

The range of size of settlements is almost infinite, ranging from hamlets of less than a hundred people to cities of several millions. At one extreme the settlement may occupy only a hectare or two of land and at the other several thousand hectares. The larger the settlement the greater the possible range of employment and services but the greater the distances between homes and jobs, the more traffic generated per head of population.

Densities of development in a settlement can also vary widely, reducing or increasing the land area per head. At one extreme each building may be set in spacious grounds and blocks of development separated by extensive open space, while at the other extreme most of the ground may be covered by buildings of many storeys. Generally density is highest in the middle of a settlement, the central area, and declines as the distance from the centre increases. Density is generally measured either in terms of people, units of accommodation or floor space per unit area. The measures are related through space standards; the higher these are the lower is population density to building density. Building density depends on a number of factors such as the function of the building, the required standards of internal space and environment, and local climatic conditions. It is necessary to differentiate between site density, the density of neighbourhoods and districts, and settlement density.

The net density of housing areas can vary from less than a habitable room per hectare to several hundreds. The usual range for houses with private gardens is generally within 40 to 300 habitable rooms per hectare, while if multistorey flatted blocks are used the net residential densities can rise to 500 habitable rooms per hectare, or even more [1]. At such high densities the space about buildings declines to less than 20 m^2 per habitable room within which provision is generally required for access roads, footpaths, parking, play areas, garden and other facilities and amenities. The requirements depend on the lifestyle of the inhabitants. If these are limited and the inhabitants do not have private cars, very high densities can be obtained, as for example in Hong Kong. Where private cars are normal, storage for them and other large consumer goods may have to be provided underground if high densities are to be achieved.

Office areas can be built to very high densities. Frequently the site is completely covered with buildings, which can be, exceptionally, 80 to 100 storeys high. Gross densities of a commercial district will depend on the provision of space for people and their vehicles, that is on space for roads, paths, car parking and incidental open space. Often in town centres tall multistorey blocks are erected where two or three storey ones used to be, greatly increasing the scale of traffic and pedestrians, and causing considerable congestion. Sometimes some space is left under the buildings for pedestrians but often the ground floor is used for shopping arcades, as in downtown Sydney, increasing traffic generation even further. Very high gross densities can result, particularly if little provision is made for vehicle transport and parking, or for open space.

Generally shopping facilities are provided on one floor at access level, although department stores are often on several levels. Usually, except for central areas in large cities, shoppers will expect to be able to use their private vehicles, particularly where they have to carry away large amounts of heavy goods, such as for the weekly shopping. In such cases a considerable amount of land will usually be required for access roads and parking.

Industrial development is generally far less dense than office development, partly because most industrial development is single storeyed, particularly for heavy industry, and partly because a large amount of space is generally necessary about the buildings for parking, loading and open air storage, although with the development of the fork-lift truck storage tends to be vertical rather than horizontal to an increasing extent.

While dense development results in the use of less land for buildings, large areas of land are usually still required for roads, parking and open space. In recent typical new towns in Great Britain something of the order of 2300 hectares were required for each 100 000 persons (Table 9.1). This amount is not all that different in total from the average for established settlements such as County Boroughs [1]. Of the 2300 hectares about two-fifths was for housing, nearly one-fifth for open space and one-sixth for roads (Table 9.1).

In countries nearer the tropics buildings can be closer together without sacrificing natural light; the consequential loss of sunshine may be an advan-

Table 9.1 The use of land in a typical new settlement. From [2]

Function	Type of area (hectares per 100 000 persons)				
	Residential	Central	Industrial	Other	Total
Housing					
Dwellings	955				955
Roads	138				138
Commercial					
Buildings		69			69
Roads and public parking		45			45
Social					
Buildings		31			31
Roads		22			22
Industrial					
Buildings			113		113
Roads			32		32
Schools and colleges	53			113	166
Hospitals				28	28
Main roads				150	150
Public utilities		4	85		89
Parks and gardens		20		28	48
Playing fields	150		73	52	275
Other open space	40	11	40		91
Total	1336	202	343	371	2252

tage where temperatures are very high. The environment can be affected by the way buildings are laid out, even at the same density. Buildings developed along the side of open spaces, water fronts, railway lines and so on enjoy more light than those which are part of a continuous built-up development, even if nominally at the same densities. Continuous development at the same densities will generally enjoy less light than broken tower developments but the areas away from the street will tend to be protected from street noise by the continuous block of building.

Settlement size is largely limited by communications. The more rapid and cheaper it is to convey goods and people, the larger settlements can become, the lower the practical densities and the wider possible spread. Most settlements were intially unplanned. Generally they were broadly circular, subject to natural topography, were developed around route crossings, road, river and sea, and had workplaces and residences combined. As they grew and specialization developed, homes and workplaces tended to be separated, with the latter in the centre. Successful settlements continued to grow with additions at their periphery and by redevelopment with greater specialization by district and greater density. Forms became distorted as properties were developed and by limits in direction of growth imposed by natural topography. Equally, the form of planned settlements is distorted with subsequent growth and redevelopment.

9.2 CAPITAL COSTS OF CONSTRUCTING A SETTLEMENT

As explained earlier (Chapter 5) movements in construction prices are difficult to measure. Some studies of the costs of settlement construction were made some time ago when there was a considerable interest in the development of new settlements. The estimates of settlement costs [2] were based on 1967 prices. Since then construction prices appear to have risen about sixfold [3]. Absolute costs are less important than relative costs. Adjusting prices to current levels would suggest a level of accuracy which would have little foundation. Hence absolute costs will be given in 1967 prices, without adjustment for inflation.

Capital costs of constructing a new town to provide all the facilities normal in 1967 were found to be about £2400 per head of the population (Table 9.2). This figure includes the costs of construction, fees, interest and land. The major factors affecting costs were density and land prices. Form, shape and size mainly affected costs through those of the main road system but this in itself only accounted for about 5% of the cost.

Housing construction accounted for about 40% of the cost. Trebling the density from those comfortably achievable with houses to those for which flatted blocks would be needed, mostly high rise, would have added about 50% to the construction costs, while reducing the land area and its costs by

Table 9.2 Capital costs of a new settlement. From [2]

Settlement development	£s per head (1967 prices)	
Buildings		
Housing	973	
Shops and retail services	102	
Other commercial	114	
Factories	210	
Other buildings	183	
Total buildings		1582
Civil engineering		
Residential development	97	
Non-residential development	87	
Main roads	115	
Public utilities	158	
Total civil engineering		457
Total construction		2039
Fees and interest		204
Land		123
Total capital cost		2366

two-thirds, but would have left total costs a third higher. The increase in the construction costs from using multistorey rather than single storey for large buildings such as factories would have been about 20% [4]. Multistorey parking would have cost 10 times as much as ground level parking, while decked parking would have cost 6 times as much [2]. Open shopping decks would have cost 5 to 6 times as much as ground level shopping precincts [2]. Elevated motorways would have cost 8–9 times as much as roads on the ground, cut-and-cover about 15 times as much and bored tunnels 50 to 60 times as much [5]. Hence increasing densities would have added considerably to the costs but saved very little land; the main saving of land would have been from high density housing development.

9.3 CAPITAL COSTS OF MAIN ROADS

The size, shape and form of settlement affected the capital costs of the main road network [2]. The range of capital costs over alternative size, shapes and forms studied were estimated at from £60 to £126 per head of population, using 1967 prices. Capital costs were found to increase about 23% when the size of settlement was increased from 50 000 to 100 000 persons and by about 49% when the size was increased from 50 000 to 250 000 persons (Fig. 9.1).

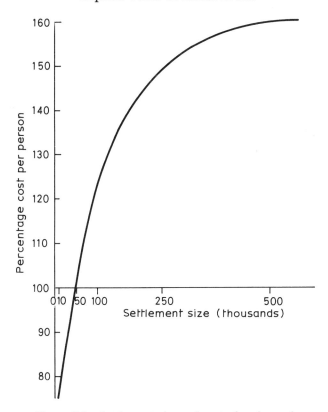

Figure 9.1   Settlement size and cost of main roads.

Projecting the figures further suggested that the costs would continue to rise with size but at a reducing rate; for a settlement of 500 000 persons road costs might be about 60% higher than those for a settlement of 50 000. For a settlement of 10 000 persons costs might have been only 75% of those for a 50 000 person settlement. Shape had rather less effect on main road costs: on average, rectangular settlements were found to have the lowest main road costs; those for linear ones would have been 14% higher and for star shaped ones 17% higher. The effect of form on main road costs was also limited; decentralized settlements had the lowest costs, with costs increasing as centralization increased, with fully centralized ones costing 19% more than decentralized ones. Interactions are found between size, shape and form. For example, the additional main road costs for large settlements were found to be least in the linear form. Main road costs were slightly increased when residential density was reduced but the increase was small relative to the reduction in the costs for housing. Costs of main roads were also affected by the extent to which distance deterred long journeys to work, by the modal split and by the level of peaking during the main times of travel. The maximum difference was about 10%.

Consideration was also given to the cost consequences of developing a 250 000 person settlement as a cluster of 5 smaller settlements. Clearly, the more dispersed the settlements, the longer the average journey to work and the more costly the main road system unless distance was a deterrent to travelling. It was found that if distance was not a deterrent to travelling to another settlement in the cluster for work, the cost of the main road system for a cluster of settlements would be 20 to 30% greater than for a single settlement of the same size. For the cluster settlements it was found that the least costly arrangement was to arrange the five small settlements in the form of a cross. On the other hand, if distance was considered a deterrent to travelling, there appeared to be little difference in capital costs for the main road network as between cluster and single settlements of the same size. In this case there would be less choice of jobs in the cluster than in the single settlement. Clearly the higher the deterrent effect, the less effect the plan had on the costs of the road network.

9.4   EXPANDING SETTLEMENTS

It is unusual to find a suitable site for a new settlement which contains no development at all within its curtilage. There may be only scattered houses and farm buildings but there may be villages or even a small town. The advantages and disadvantages of developments within the curtilage of a new settlement depend on the size, form and condition and how they can be integrated into the new settlement. The social and economic advantages of villages and small towns during the early stages of development can be quite considerable but in the long run construction and land costs will generally be higher. Suitable existing development can provide services for the early migrants and reduce the rawness and discomforts which generally accompany a new development under construction. Towns and villages within the curtilage of the site usually have some facilities with spare capacity which can be used to serve the needs of the early migrants, reducing the urgency for the construction of a whole range of built facilities. On the other hand, the presence of the existing built development on the site can result in difficulties in achieving the most economic form of development for the new settlement. Often existing settlements cannot easily be adapted to meet current needs. For example, the main roads of an old country town may be very narrow and there may be little space for parking. Shops and other facilities may be unsuitable for current methods of retailing and need eventually to be altered or redeveloped. Land in and around and the existing settlement tends to be more expensive than agricultural land, while development on disturbed land, moving services and so on adds to the costs of development.

The additional costs of incorporating existing settlements or expanding them in developing a new or expanded town depend on their size, on the scale of existing development and on the way it is incorporated into the new development. Estimates were prepared on the basis of existing development for 50 000 people being incorporated into a new town with a total population of 250 000 persons [2]. The closer the integration the more it appears to cost. For example, if the existing settlement is kept as a separate free standing one only additional road connections might be necessary at a cost of perhaps £10 million (1967 prices). If, however, the existing settlement is incorporated as a district of the new town, capital costs might be five times as great, and six to eight times as great if incorporated as the centre of the new settlement. While total costs depend more on the size of the existing settlement than the new one, costs per head are greater if the total expansion is smaller. A large proportion of the additional costs arise from the higher costs of acquiring land: from the point of view of the community the land cost would be a transfer cost rather than a real one.

9.5   ECONOMIES OF SCALE IN SETTLEMENT DEVELOPMENT

It is unlikely that the forms of development would be the same in larger settlements as in smaller ones. In particular the central area of a centralized settlement of 250 000 people might be spread over an area of some 500 hectares with central car parking of some 70 hectares (Table 9.1). In order to make the commercial centre more compact and convenient to the users, it might be developed on a deck with roads and parking underneath, or at least the car parking might be below ground or multistorey, solutions which would increase the costs of the commercial centre as indicated earlier. The larger the settlement the more likely that some housing would be high density with multistorey flatted blocks which again would raise costs. As indicated earlier, main road networks increase in size with the size of settlement and costs per head rise giving diseconomies of scale.

At the smaller end of the size range there may be some economies of scale. These may be exhausted by the time the 50 000 population level is reached. Some economies of scale have been indicated for some public utilities such as drainage, sewerage treatment works and water supply [6]. There may be economies of scale for local power supplies and telephones. Some confirmation of the economies and diseconomies of scale as settlement size increases is provided by work in Italy. This work suggests that the capital costs of the infrastructure of a settlement are U-shaped, costs declining up to a settlement of 50 000 population and then increasing (Table 9.3). Svimez's figures

Table 9.3   Relation of infrastructure costs to settlement size.

Settlement size in persons (000s)	Percentage infrastructure costs per head of population
Up to 5	128
5–20	102
20–50	100
50–100	105
100–250	111
250–600	120
600 and above	140

Source: Svimez (1968) quoted in *Regional Policy in the European Free Trade Area*, EFTA.

indicate greater increases in costs with size of settlement than British figures but they may allow for higher densities as the size increases.

9.6   COSTS-IN-USE OF JOURNEYS TO WORK

Annual travelling costs per head for journeys to work were estimated from the model settlement study to average at about £51 (1967 prices) [2]. While this is only half the capital cost of the network, it is more important, because being incurred every year its equivalent capital cost is perhaps ten times as great as the construction costs, the ratio depending on the rate of discount. On average the travelling costs per head were found to be nearly twice as high for a 250 000 person settlement as for one of 50 000.

The travelling costs for a linear settlement were nearly one-quarter more than for a rectangular settlement, with the costs for a star shaped one lying in between. The degree of centralization did not appear to make very much difference. Again moderate increases in density appeared to have only a marginal effect on travelling costs. Travelling costs varied, of course, according to the deterrent effect of distance, modal split (the division of journeys between different forms of transport) and peaking.

Travelling costs vary much less than the capital costs of main roads for different forms of cluster settlement, or between individual and cluster settlements but the rectangular decentralized form had the lowest costs, with the cross marginally the lowest of the cluster ones [2]. Clearly the greater the deterrent effect of distance the more travelling declines in the cluster settlements relative to the single ones. When the deterrent effect is high costs vary little from one form of settlement to another. A high deterrent effect on travelling in cluster settlements means that most workers seek jobs within their own settlement so that the range of job opportunities does not increase much in practise.

If it is assumed that settlements are constructed with the same types of building units whatever the size, the cost consequences of size tend to be mainly limited to the capital costs for the main road networks and for journeys on them. Amortizing the capital costs at a net real rate of discount of 5% and adding them to travelling costs indicates annual costs-in-use per head difference between a 50 000 and a 100 000 person settlement of about £12, with a difference between a 100 000 and 250 000 person settlement of about £24. To these differences must be added the additional cost differences of other types of journey and the costs of maintaining, cleaning and lighting the road network.

Double-decker buses can carry about 50 times as many people as the average car, while occupying only about three times as much road space. Clearly if workers travelled to work by bus instead of car the road capacity required would be much less. In such a situation road capacity might depend more on demand for other types of journey and at least some of the network might need to be of no more than two lanes. It was estimated that if the proportion of workers using cars for journeys to work fell from 80 to 25%, the capital costs of the main road network would fall 30 to 40% with savings per head of £20 to £50 (1967 prices), for 50 000 and 250 000 person settlements respectively [2]. This assumed that distance did not deter travelling to work within the settlement, the greater the deterrent effect the less the savings. There would also be some savings from the reduction in the size of car parks in industrial and commercial areas. Theoretically such savings were estimated to be of the order of £20 per head. It was estimated that bus-only roads to provide a faster and more attractive service would cost about £40 per head.

The equivalent annual savings on the main road network by a greater use of buses were quite small. Even after allowing for maintaining and servicing roads and parking the equivalent annual savings, by busing people to work appeared to be only of the order of £3 to £5 per head (1967 prices). In comparing travelling costs by bus against car, the value placed on travelling time is important, because walking to bus stops and waiting for the bus increases journey time by bus over that by car. If a low value is placed on travelling time, the real costs of journeys to work by bus and car appear to be much the same, while at market prices, with average subsidies on buses, car travel is generally more expensive. The higher travelling time is valued, the more bus costs rise relative to car costs. In practise workers generally have a car for domestic purposes and are concerned only with the running costs of cars for the journey to work. On that basis the costs of the journey to work are less by car than by bus whether market or factor (real) costs are considered [2]. If bus-only roads were added the costs of the bus alternative would be raised further.

Of course, the situation in an established settlement might be very different. If much more traffic is generated than the road network or parking facilities can handle, it could be more economic to provide buses than meet the costs of increasing the size of the road network and parking facilities, because of the high costs of demolition and redevelopment, and possible environmental damage. In such cases it might be economical to subsidize the bus service to bring the charge below the marginal costs of using the family car for journeys to work.

Attempts to compare the costs-in-use of rail and car journeys to work were made for the 250 000 person settlement [2]. Again it was found, assuming travelling time was costed at half average earnings, that the rail option would be cheaper only if cars had to be purchased solely for the journey to work.

9.7 OTHER FACTORS AFFECTING COSTS-IN-USE OF SETTLEMENTS

As the density of housing rises above a moderate density, running costs tend to rise as well as capital costs. Increasing the height of buildings tends to add to costs of maintenance as all external work becomes more difficult and lifts and other vertical features have to be serviced. In the case of housing less of the work can be left to the tenants in high blocks than in the case of one and two storey housing. It was estimated that maintenance and servicing costs would rise a little faster than capital costs as density was increased by using high blocks. Current experience suggests that as a result of technical failures and abuse by occupiers, maintenance and servicing is considerably more expensive for high rise blocks than for housing. In the case of high density housing most of the space about the buildings becomes public space and further adds to the costs-in-use. Current evidence suggests that the estimates that costs-in-use would be something over 50% more for high rise flatted estates as compared with low rise housing are likely to have been considerably underestimated. The higher costs-in-use do not appear to be justified by occupiers' preferences. The evidence suggests considerable dissatisfaction with high rise estates, some of which can no longer be let and a few of which have been demolished. While less heat is lost through the surfaces of compact blocks than separate houses, exposure in high blocks is greater and can result in a greater rate of heat loss per unit area (Chapter 11).

Industry is not likely to be much affected by the form and shape of a settlement. Its main concern is usually that the road network is adequate for the traffic and free of congestion and that there is enough space on the site for parking, loading and external storage. Planned settlements usually provide these conditions. Manufacturers usually favour sites large enough to take single storey buildings which, particularly if of light construction, are much less costly to construct than multistorey ones and generally easier to manage and provide internal transport (Chapter 11).

Consumers require services such as shopping, education, health and recreation, to be of high quality and conveniently located. Under current trading
conditions most goods have to be carried away by the purchaser. If private
transport is not available, purchasers generally prefer a good range of shops
close to home (shopping by bus usually involves carrying heavy and bulky bags
and parcels) especially if public services are not that frequent and do not stop
close to the place of purchase and home. On the other hand, consumers with
their own private transport probably prefer large shopping areas which offer
more choice and usually more competitive prices. Since many people have
freezers, shopping even for perishable food does not need to be frequent.
Again mothers generally favour schools close to their homes so that only the
youngest need be accompanied. If schools are at a distance from the homes of
their pupils busing is usually necessary, adding to public costs. Thus citizens
without private transport would generally favour local services, while those
with private transport might prefer consumer services to be centralized. The
costs-in-use of such services are probably more affected by size and density
than form and shape of settlement.

9.8 BUILDING FORMS AND TOWN FORMS

The form of a settlement depends on the form of the buildings and the way
these are disposed over the settlement. Land is required both to provide a
base for buildings and to provide a space for various outdoor activities. So far
discussion has concentrated on various forms of conventional settlement with
few buildings of more than a few storeys, and most capable of being lit and
ventilated naturally. With this type of development most of the land within
the curtilage of a settlement is used for open space, private gardens, roads,
parking and other space about buildings (Table 9.1). Only about one-eighth is
used as the base of buildings [7]. Piling one building on another does not in
itself appreciably reduce the amount of land required for a settlement.

Even in a densely populated country such as Great Britain less than
one-tenth of the land is used for urban purposes [8] and a substantial amount
is derelict or vacant. As explained earlier with rising agricultural productivity
and over-production there is little current pressure to retain land for that
purpose but there is pressure to retain land for amenity (Chapter 8). Again as
indicated earlier, saving land by building high multistorey buildings, decking,
tunnelling and so on, while it might sometimes reduce market costs, considerably increases real costs while saving little land. Nevertheless, situations do
arise where land for urban development is scarce at a particular location.
Such situations arise where a settlement to which activities and people are
migrating in large numbers is hemmed in by river, sea, mountains or some
other natural obstruction, or where part of a settlement, for example, the
central business district, is hemmed in by other development, and where the

convenience of maintaining close proximity to particular business centres such as the central bank, stock exchange and international commodity and insurance markets are considered of great value. The market value of space in such locations often rises sufficiently to justify the costs of developing to the highest possible densities.

In terms of the costs of development, land, construction, fees and interest, high density development raises real costs; real costs-in-use are raised even further because servicing high density development is more costly than low density. Whether or not the higher real costs are worth incurring depends on the economics of the operations housed in the buildings and the additional satisfaction and convenience to users and the community. Where face to face contacts for business deals, retail sales, the supply of goods and services are concerned, close proximity to customers tends to bring more trade and reduce travelling and transport costs. These advantages are reduced as communications become more convenient and efficient. Much of the crowding into central districts is a form of inertia. Many entrepreneurs have already found that only a small part of the organization needs face to face contacts, the rest being able to be sited wherever suitable workers can be attracted. Communication, within the firm or over long distances, becomes easier as electronic communications and transport systems improve.

While piling one building on another increases net densities, it has only a marginal effect on gross densities unless external space standards are reduced. In effect this happens when a developed area is redeveloped with higher levels of floor area. Generally, especially in central business districts, the new buildings cover the whole of the site, although some space under them at ground level may be left free. Frequently, however, floor space and the number of occupants are increased severalfold, while the volume of space for roads, footpaths and open space remain unchanged, increasing the density of users and often leading to congestion.

Using artificial internal environments does not in itself necessarily enable gross densities to be increased but it does enable a use of different building forms and possible radical changes in urban form. As long as spaces in buildings have to be lit and ventilated naturally, the buildings cannot be very deep and increasing their size involves more storeys and longer buildings. These then have to be further apart in order to allow sufficient light and sunshine to fall on their windows to maintain daylight and sunlight standards. If lighting and ventilation is provided artificially, even to some spaces, buildings can be much deeper and closer together; if to all spaces, there ceases to be a limit to the depth of buildings and there need be no spaces between them. Artificial environments are quite acceptable for many non-residential uses such as shops, restaurants, places of entertainment and in some cases for offices and industrial uses. Of course, artificial lighting and ventilation tends to raise both capital and running costs (Chapter 11). Artificial ventilation is generally necessary where the internal environment needs to be very clean, where plant generates excessive heat and where temperatures and humidity result in uncomfortable conditions within buildings, as in and near the tropics.

Technically it is possible to provide accommodation for a large group of people in a single large multistorey building as, for example, Le Corbusier's Unite d'Habitation at Marseille. The greater the complex of spaces under one roof, the greater the proportion of space needed for circulation and storage within the building. Such space is far more expensive to provide and service than space outside. Internal transport needs to be electrically powered in order to reduce noise, pollution and fire risks. If auxiliary functions such as parking, access and recreation are not accommodated around the building, so substantially reducing densities, spaces for these uses need to be provided within or on top of the building. The flexibility and safety of a settlement designed in this way tends to be far less than in a group of conventional buildings, and adaptation and extension is far more difficult. Accommodating a settlement in a single building creates economic and social as well as technical difficulties.

Some writers have suggested that roads should be run on the roofs of buildings and across bridges to adjoining ones, that settlements should be roofed over as a site for open space, or that they should be developed underground with open space on the ground above. Again the major problems would be economic and social rather than technical. If the roofs had to carry open space uses or roads with heavy live loads and support bridges, the frames of buildings and roofs would need to be stronger than otherwise necessary and hence would be more expensive. Ramps would need to be created at the terminal buildings. Roads and bridges at roof level would be more exposed to wind and frost; problems of noise and pollution would also need to be solved.

Even roofing over a settlement by roofing between buildings would require stronger frames for the buildings or columns and roof frames to be set up and clad. If the roof were glazed some light would be lost, especially if it was not kept clean or covered with snow. Solar gain, pollution and fire hazards would add to the problems of a roofed city. While more artificial ventilation would be necessary, the climate would be drier and warmer, reducing the need for heating in a cold climate but increasing the need for ventilation in a warm one. In a wet climate large quantities of storm water would need to be handled. With a roof between buildings the cladding of buildings could be lighter and many activities could be carried out between buildings without the need for additional covered space. The settlement would tend to be far less flexible and adaptable, and probably a great deal noisier than a conventional one.

An underground settlement would have environmental problems not dissimilar to those of a covered settlement and the costs which these are likely to create. In addition costs would arise from excavating and tanking the space in the ground for the settlement. Some idea of the scale of costs of construction and operating the type of settlements discussed above can be guaged from the cost relatives given earlier in the chapter.

9.9 PHASING AND ADAPTABILITY OF SETTLEMENTS

Most settlements take a considerable time to develop, during which large amounts of capital are tied up in partly completed buildings and works which do not yield any immediate return. At the same time the environment of a partly completed development is not usually very attractive. Finding purchasers and tenants for partly constructed areas is usually rather slow. Households are reluctant to take up housing until there are jobs and consumer services in the locality, while enterprises are reluctant to open until the locality has sufficient population to supply a work-force and customers sufficient to ensure viability. Clearly the smaller the settlement the sooner it is likely to be completed and occupied. If a settlement is planned in largely self-contained units, it is possible to develop one at a time and secure an earlier return on the capital employed. Moreover the experience is useful as a guide to the development of later units of development. As a result decentralized settlements are easier to phase than highly centralized ones.

Temporary services can be provided in temporary buildings, which if portable may be moved from area to area as development proceeds. This method may be economic by avoiding the need to create large buildings which are unlikely to be fully utilized for some years. Changes in demand may arise not only from changes in numbers as the population builds up but from changes in the age and lifestyles of the population as it develops and matures. For example, the early migrants are often young people building up families, so that each cohort of children tends to be of a different size. As families mature they tend to change their lifestyles. As a result the services required and the buildings for them tend to change over time. In addition changes in the national economy and tastes further change the demand for facilities and amenities, so that some facilities may be required in their initial form for only a few years. These problems tend to have greater consequences for a newly developed settlement than for a mature one because of the absence of obsolete buildings. As a result many of the buildings may need to be very flexible or adaptable (Chapter 11).

It is difficult to be certain how viable a new settlement will be. It may attract far more people and activities than were expected or far less. Settlements therefore need to be planned both to operate satisfactorily at each stage of development and to be able to be extended satisfactorily if their economy proves to be very successful and continues to attract people and activities after its planned completion. Again dispersed settlements tend to be more flexible than centralized ones. If the settlement is made up of more or less self-contained districts, or even self-contained subsettlements, it is fairly easy to add additional units or to leave some undeveloped. It is much more difficult to adapt a centralized settlement to a change of scale. A partially completed shopping and service area may not provide a satisfactory service. The expansion of a central service area may be difficult as it will tend to be hemmed in with other parts of the settlement. Additional neighbourhoods and residential areas will be at increasing distances from the central service area and perhaps from industrial areas.

9.10 MACHINERY FOR DEVELOPING AND REDEVELOPING SETTLEMENTS

The development of the New Towns has been carried out by Development Corporations set up and financed by the central government under the New Town Acts, 1946 and 1949. Town expansion has been undertaken by local authorities under Housing Acts and the Town Development Act, 1952.

New Town Development Corporations have enjoyed wide powers for acquiring land, planning and developing. They develop roads, sewers and other town facilities. Public facilities are handed over to the appropriate authority to maintain and service. Freeholds of houses, shops, offices, factories and so on are either retained for renting or sold, as are some plots for development. Appropriate housing is transferred to the district local authority, who obtains rates from the newly developed property to provide and support additional services.

Local authorities undertake a great deal of the development of housing, roads and other infrastructure and the redevelopment of obsolete areas in towns, but significant town expansion has often been undertaken under the Acts described above. Usually there has been a partnership between an authority which wishes to export population to reduce overcrowding and an authority wishing to expand.

Most of the town expansion schemes were in the home counties or in the midlands and were set up to absorb overspill, mainly from London and Birmingham. Such schemes were curtailed when the cities found themselves losing more population than they felt desirable. Generally the town expansion schemes were smaller and slower than the new town developments. Most of the local authorities who participated in these schemes were too small to afford the expertise acquired by the Development Corporations and did not have equivalent financial resources. Frequently they relied on expertise and finance from the exporting authority. They obtained 50% grants towards water and sewerage works (these had not been taken over by the Water Authorities at the time town expansion schemes were set up). In addition there were available government subsidies and contributions from exporting authorities towards housing. Most of the expenditure was met from rates and normal government grants (on a year to year basis). Borrowing was subject to government approval.

Although the development corporations are financed by central government and subject to departmental control, they operate much like private companies. They are able to take decisions far more rapidly and decisively than local authorities where professional officers are subject to the detailed sanction of the politicians and where many matters fall under the responsibility of more than one department, reporting to different council committees and often meeting at intervals of 3 or 4 weeks. Where more than one authority is involved, as often occurs in conurbations, and under town expansion schemes, problems can be greatly multiplied. Local authorities have no special finance for urban development. Much of their revenue and capital expenditure depends on current government financial policy, which varies from year to year. As a consequence local authorities are not as well placed as Development Corporations to carry out either the development of new settlements or the large scale redevelopment and rehabilitation of existing ones.

Private developers have not in the past operated on the scale of Development Corporations and would not generally be prepared to accept the risks of developing large new settlements or the development and rehabilitation of large areas of existing settlements for which demand was uncertain. Generally they have confined their attention to housing estates and small groups of industrial and commercial buildings, although they are now interested in building small residential settlements. However, private enterprise does create consortiums to carry out large, high-risk developments, now even one as large as the Channel Tunnel. It would appear, however, that public Development Corporations are the most likely instrument for large scale settlement development and redevelopment. (Chapters 7 and 10).

REFERENCES

1. Stone, P. A. (1963) *Housing, Town Development, Land and Costs*, Estates Gazette Ltd, London.
2. Stone, P. A. (1973) *The Structure Size and Costs of Urban Settlements*, National Institute for Economic and Social Research, Cambridge University Press, London.
3. Davis, Belfield, and Everest (1972; 1979; and 1987) *Spon's Architects' and Builders' Price Book*, 97th, 104th and 112th edns, E. & F. N. Spon, London.
4. Stone, P. A. (1962) *The Economics of Factory Buildings*, Building Research Station, HMSO, London.
5. Goldstein, A. (1966) Motorway Route Location Studies – Town and Country Planning Summer School, Town Planning Institute, London.
6. Townsend, C. B. (1960) *The Economics of Waste Water Treatment*, Institute of Civil Engineers 6424, London.
7. Stone, P. A. (1961) *The Impact of Urban Development on the Use of Land and Other Resources*. Journal of Town Planning Institute, **47**(5).
8. Best, A. H. (1976) The Changing Land-use Structure of Great Britain. *Town and Country Planning*, **43**(3).

10

Utilization, growth, decline and revival of settlements

10.1 EXISTING BUILT ENVIRONMENT

The national heritage of the built environment in its widest sense is very considerable; as indicated earlier it probably represents something of the order of fifty times the annual net additions (Chapter 5). It contains development of all ages, exceptionally going back to the building of the Romans. Clearly its continued existence depends on continuous maintenance and adaptation to meet current needs. While each year some of the built environment ceases to be useful because of physical, functional and financial obsolescence, most of it has a long potential life. There are many demands for change as population and human activities migrate from one place to another and change in scale, and as changes occur in technology, lifestyles and human preferences. Given the sheer scale of existing built environment and the limited resources available to extend, replace, adapt and maintain it, there is a need to make the best use of what is available.

10.2 UTILIZING EXISTING BUILT ENVIRONMENT

Often existing buildings can continue to provide satisfactory accommodation in their original use with only limited internal changes, leaving the external appearance and the street scene basically unchanged. While the internal facilities and aesthetics may be different from those of contemporary buildings for those purposes, they may be equally or even more acceptable.

There is a large range of small houses built in every age from the Tudors onwards which are still inhabited. While in some ways they fall short of current standards, they are widely accepted and some command a premium. Small houses have many other uses in addition to providing domestic accommodation. Many are suitable as small offices, surgeries and shops, and need not be changed externally in unacceptable ways in order to function satisfactorily.

The continued use of larger buildings often presents more problems. Large houses generally have more space than required by present day households but frequently their internal spaces can be reorganized for use as flats, hotels, offices, schools or galleries, depending on their location, on the local demand and on their flexibility and adaptability. Warehouses and multistorey factories can often be adapted to meet the current needs for such uses, or for offices and even flats, depending on their form and construction and local demand. Schools, prisons and cinemas can in suitable cases be converted to other uses. How far such changes of use are worthwhile depends on demand at their location, on their form and structure, and on their condition and expected future life.

In addition to the value of buildings to their owners and occupiers, many are prized for their aesthetics as individual buildings and for their contribution to the street scene. People may get pleasure from visiting them, from their presence in the built environment, or even from just knowing that they exist. Some of this pleasure may be lost through alteration and conversion, and inadequate maintenance, particularly when it affects the external appearance. The pleasure from streets of historical buildings can be considerably reduced, for example, by the addition of contemporary shop fronts. Old buildings often have little value in use unless they are adapted to meet new needs: without a current use they tend to be neglected and to deteriorate, their sites worth more for redevelopment than in their present form. While collections of historic buildings can, up to a point, enhance the urban scene, their value tends to rise less than proportionately as the scale of such a collection continues to increase.

Judgement about preserving historical buildings involves a consideration of costs and benefits, not just rarity, or even aesthetics. The amount of resources available to preserve them is not unlimited. The current and likely future public pleasure from a building and its value in use now and in the future can be set against the costs of maintaining and servicing it. Options include converting it to some other use or redeveloping the site. The costs and benefits of the options can be compared (Chapter 13). Clearly not every historic building can be retained and priority should be given to those providing the greatest net value to owner, occupier and the public. Not all the buildings which the public would like retained in their present form provide sufficient value for money to the owner or occupier to justify retention. If such buildings are to be adequately maintained in their current form to provide the values the public enjoys, the community may need to meet the excess of costs over values which otherwise would be left with the owner-occupiers, either through voluntary or tax supported contributions (Chapter 13).

While some buildings and developments have very long lives, some are soon physically, functionally or financially obsolete. Early physical obsolescence can arise from the design, construction or materials as a result of which the building becomes excessively expensive to run, uncomfortable to use or even unsafe. Early functional obsolescence can arise from inadequate attention to the needs of future users or from unexpected changes in technology or lifestyles. Financial obsolescence can arise from declines in value resulting from such changes and from new and higher valued potential uses for the site. Early obsolescence of flatted blocks has arisen from technical and social failures, for shops from falling demand for shop floor space, changes in sales technique and from changes in the relative pull of their location, while for commercial and industrial buildings obsolescence can arise from shifts in trade and technological change.

The faster lifestyles and technology change, and people and activities migrate, the more buildings and urban developments are likely to become obsolete in their current use and the earlier in their life this is likely to take place. Where such obsolescence gives rise to a need to change the use of the development, resources might have been saved had the development been designed to be flexible in use or easily adapted to a change in use. Whether or not this would be worthwhile depends on the additional costs of constructing, maintaining and servicing a development with built-in flexibility or adaptability as compared with the costs of adaptation or rebuilding when obsolescence occurs and the likely lapse of time before this becomes necessary (Chapters 11 and 12).

10.3 LOCATION AND DEMAND FOR SPACE

The demand for space for particular uses depends on the economy of the local area. If there is insufficient demand for the uses to which the development could be put, adaptation would be a waste of resources. In such cases the development, however physically sound and suitable to the intended uses, would be without value for that use. If there was a more economic use for the site, it could be redeveloped. Thus existing developments can be in one of four situations:

1. an adequate demand for them in their current use;
2. an adequate demand in a new use to which they could be economically adapted;
3. no demand for them in their current use but a demand for the site in a new use;
4. no demand for the site in any use.

No problem arises with the first situation since it may be assumed that the current use is the one acceptable within the location.

The second situation could raise planning problems since the new use may have unacceptable consequences for other occupants and users of the area. Adaptation might involve profound changes to the exterior of the building with unacceptable consequences for the street scene.

The third situation clearly is likely to have more radical consequences. The new use may not only result in pollution and the generation of more traffic but may greatly reduce the value of other property in the area for their current purposes and change the quality of the street scene. These consequences may flow not only from the new use of the site but from the scale, form and style of the new development. In considering the costs and benefits of the proposed development and its acceptability, it is necessary to consider not just the immediate locality but the expected development of the surrounding district and perhaps, the whole settlement. For example, the costs and benefits, and hence the acceptability of allowing the development of a massive office block in a street of small houses and shops would depend in part on whether this was likely to be a one-off development of this type, or the beginning of a redevelopment of the whole area in this way. The situation would also be affected by whether there were other acceptable sites for the block elsewhere in the settlement. Clearly the initial planning decision is important since it may result in that area coming under heavy pressure for developments of that type, which may or may not be the best way to use the land and other resources.

The fourth situation also raises problems of demand and location. There may be no demand for a site either because the site is physically uneconomic to redevelop, perhaps because of pollution, or because there is no demand for space on that site which would command a price sufficient to offset development costs. In the long run, of course, the level of demand may rise sufficiently to lift the price of a development high enough to cover development costs. Because redeveloping is more expensive than development on virgin land, redevelopment is generally only worthwhile if the new use of the site is of sufficiently higher value than the old use, or if new densities are sufficiently higher than previous densities to create enough additional value to offset the additional costs.

10.4 SETTLEMENTS AND THE DEMAND FOR LAND

There is likely to be a strong demand for better properties and additional properties in settlements with a buoyant economy, with an increase in economic activities and a rising number of households. This will encourage the development of new sites, the redevelopment of existing ones, rehabilitation and conversion. Demand is not usually uniform over the settlement. There may be areas of decline, even in a prosperous settlement, such areas are often in the inner city.

Historically settlements develop outwards from their original location.

Housing and workplaces tend to develop around the central commercial and service area, with successive waves of new dwellings, commercial and industrial premises developing at the periphery. Clearly it is generally the earlier properties which become obsolete first. If there is adequate demand for new higher value uses or development at greater density, and the values (market prices) of the obsolete properties are low enough, there may be redevelopment to meet current demands. In other cases demand is likely to be met on virgin sites at the periphery where development costs are usually lower than on previously used sites and operation costs may be less. Vacant property soon becomes derelict and casts a blight over the area in which it is located, reducing demand and values even further. Owners of both public and private property tend to hold out for prices which reflect the use value implied by planning zones and densities and which will compensate them for the resources they originally put into the development, further discouraging re-use or redevelopment.

In an expanding settlement new households and activities create a demand for additional premises; these might be attracted to areas of decline within the settlement if the environment of the sites is made acceptable and site prices fall to those justified by the costs of development and the prices likely to be offered for redeveloped or rehabilitated properties there. In a settlement with a declining number of households and activities there is unlikely to be sufficient demand for all the sites in the settlement to be used. In the less attractive parts of the settlement, especially where redevelopment costs are particularly high, site prices might need to fall nearly to zero or exceptionally, subsidies may be necessary to induce someone to redevelop them.

10.5 LOCATION OF SETTLEMENT GROWTH

While the populations of conurbations and cities are falling (Chapter 6), there is still pressure to build at their peripheries, especially in the south, and further out in the Green Belts, with the possibility that their outward spread might be resumed. The incentive to build at and beyond the periphery arises from the preference for these areas both by economic activities and people. The two reinforce each other, people moving out to take up jobs created by new economic activities and new areas of residence supplying labour for further economic activities.

The long-term trend is for households to move out of the inner parts of settlements to the periphery and beyond where housing standards and amenities are higher. Even in the relatively prosperous south-east there has been only limited demand for development in the inner city either for commerce, industry or residences. Even in London, the redevelopment of docklands was slow to start.

While life in an area being developed is difficult for those settling early, this has not been a serious problem in new and expanding towns, or for peripheral development. The major difference between new settlements and the inner parts of old ones is the future expectations. In the former case it is expected that in a few years a high standard settlement will emerge with contemporary buildings, infrastructure and amenities. In the latter case, in the absence of examples of the complete redevelopment and rehabilitation of extensive areas, the expectation is of piecemeal development within a crumbling area with only a few facilities and amenities improved to standards currently expected. In the past most inner area improvements have taken the form of large public housing estates. These are often less acceptable than the housing which was cleared (given that it could have been brought up to standard), and are not balanced by commerce and industry to provide the types of employment, nor the appropriate facilities and services, the occupants require.

As suggested earlier, comprehensive combined redevelopment and rehabilitation areas with a balance between residences, and commercial and industrial development, might be viable in the southern cities and conurbations, but it is doubtful whether they would be viable in the north without a radical change in the economic environment (Chapter 7).

In some parts of the country, especially in the south-east, the demand for new and expanded settlements is already strong. There is a strong demand for more commercial and industrial development and for more labour for many existing enterprises. The supply of labour is limited by the supply of housing. Where demand exceeds supply, house prices rise, making it difficult for available labour from other areas to obtain available housing without sacrificing the standards they currently enjoy. Many of the areas of high demand are either within Green Belts or in other protected areas, or are already heavily developed. The difficulties of diverting the demand for labour to areas with the largest surpluses have been considered earlier (Chapter 7); diverting demand for jobs to less congested areas in the south appear to be equally difficult.

10.6 ECONOMICS OF SETTLEMENT GROWTH

Settlements grow to house the natural increase of population and household formation, from attracting people and activities and as a result of planned migration and growth. The resource requirements depend on the scale of growth, its relation to the phasing and development of the settlement and its form (Chapter 9).

Many of the facilities which need to be provided in a settlement are 'lumpy'. There is a minimum practical size for many of them, (the unit size cannot be matched to the scale of demand) and as demand increases new units need to be added. For example, most roads have a lane in each direction and if traffic rises beyond their capacity two additional lanes are normally added. Often there are some economies of scale, one large unit may provide cheaper services per head than several small ones. Hence settlement facilities tend to be developed at their optimum scale for the projected demand. Costs per head tend to fall as demand rises to the level at which the facility operates at its optimum and to rise when this level is exceeded. Unanticipated growth may raise costs per head. Some facilities such as water supply and storage, and sewage treatment plant tend to be very lumpy and development costs can rise substantially when their threshold has been reached and a new plant becomes necessary. Sometimes it is economic to use temporary buildings or old makeshift ones until demand settles down to a level justifying new permanent units. For example, temporary classrooms may be worth using until either a wave of children born at a particular time has passed through or until numbers are great enough to justify an additional school or unit of school.

Because of this lumpiness, settlements will tend to have spare capacity in various facilities at various phases in their growth. Depending on whether such spare capacity is to be expected for natural or planned growth in the future, there may be economic advantages in attracting growth from one settlement to another. The savings might be considerable if growth in one settlement involved an additional sewerage works, a new main road system or town centre where as elsewhere the growth could be absorbed without such major development (Chapter 9). Such savings on development would not be worthwhile if the alternative settlement could not sustain the economic development of the additional enterprise and provide employment for the additional population.

Neither additions to settlements nor new settlements may yield sufficient revenue in the early years to cover interest on the capital costs of development and running costs. The situation is likely to change rapidly if the settlement is successful. The prices of property, both land and buildings, and rents will tend to rise with increases in population and purchasing power; revenues will tend to increase and more activities will tend to be attracted. Employment will rise as more firms are attracted and early ones expand; more population will be attracted and purchasing power will rise further. As growth feeds on growth, public revenues will rise to meet the costs of public services.

10.7 SETTLEMENT DECLINE

As indicated earlier there are a number of reasons why the economy of a settlement may decline (Chapter 7). These include a decline in the national industries upon which it has depended, the loss of local advantages for its industries such as supplies of raw materials and changes in technique which reduce its special advantages, reduction in the comparative advantages for access to its markets and a failure of management and labour to increase efficiency and to change designs and marketing in step with competitors.

Often a declining settlement is part of a declining region, which tends to increase the difficulties of revival. However, as indicated earlier, in this country deeper analysis suggests that problems are not so much from the decline of regions as the decline of cities and conurbations within certain regions, other areas of which may not be in decline (Chapter 6). There are, of course, towns and villages declining even in the more prosperous regions.

Settlement development is affected by changes in national population. A rise or decline in births first has an impact on the demand for maternity services, and services and facilities for young children but the consequences gradually spread throughout the age groups and affect their demands. If the change in birth-rate is sustained all settlements are likely to be affected. Rates of population growth tend to decline or increase in growth settlements and fall faster or more slowly in settlements already in decline. However, if there is a change in the levels of migration, it is mainly the settlements from or to which population moves which is affected. The changes tend to occur in all age groups but especially for younger adults and their children, those most likely to migrate.

The problems for unattractive settlements are both economic and social. It is not only that they offer fewer advantages than their rivals as centres for economic activities (lower property prices and labour costs might offset these) but that economic decline tends to destroy confidence both in entrepreneurs and in the inhabitants. The more active and able people tend to drift away during the early stages of decline. While the larger settlements do not usually suffer from poor communications as do some of the smaller ones, the decline and dereliction themselves discourage new enterprise. The longer the decline continues, the more dereliction occurs and the more run-down the economic structure tends to become.

In the past many settlements lost their vitality and ceased to exist, or continued to exist only as small dependent areas. Today there are many small towns and particularly villages which are unable to offer their citizens an acceptable livelihood or lifestyle. Unemployment is often high and in some cases there is no suitable public transport to other centres, and possibly no local school or shop. While they may continue to decline, it is unlikely that all the inhabitants would leave *en masse* of their own accord.

Closure of a settlement, even a village, is likely to be economically, socially, administratively and politically difficult. Some citizens are bound to be reluctant to move however poor local services and amenities become. Complete moves and closures have probably only occurred in recent times when an area has been cleared by a public body to make way for a public development such as a reservoir or for defence purposes. Inhabitants, however few, cannot be left without services; these become progressively more expensive per head the fewer to be serviced. Up to a point it is worthwhile to subsidize services rather than incur the expense of creating the urban facilities and services elsewhere and the resentment that would be created by a forced move of the inhabitants.

Sustaining a declining settlement, especially if reasonable services and amenities are provided, and closing a settlement, are both expensive. The first is a continuing expense; the second includes compensation for eviction, together with the cost of developing a new district to house the inhabitants of the closed settlement. This needs to provide not just homes and consumer services but viable enterprises to employ those moved. The cost depends on how the addition is created (Chapter 9). Against the costs of additional environment could be set savings from not needing to rebuild or rehabilitate the partly worn facilities in the closed settlement. Similarly, the costs of encouraging new enterprises could be partly offset by reducing social payments as additional employment was created. Thus the closure of a settlement creates considerable costs which can be avoided if the settlement remains viable. Such costs can be set against the alternative costs of rehabilitating the infrastructure and economy of the settlement.

10.8   ECONOMICS OF SETTLEMENT DECLINE

There is a danger that settlement decline will be cumulative and even accelerating and there can be no certainty that a declining settlement will reach a stable size. As a settlement declines the more skilled and enterprising labour and management tends to leave, particularly when the economy is expanding elsewhere. Unemployment tends to rise as firms contract and go out of business. The further decline proceeds the more difficult it is for households to leave. Owner-occupiers find the value of their homes declining relative to costs elsewhere, while the tenants of public authority housing find it difficult to transfer to similar housing in expanding settlements. Stagnant industry and unemployment result in declining income levels with less purchasing power. With a decline in trade, shops and other consumer services lose their viability and contract or shut, further depressing the local economy and adding to the vacant and run-down property. Rateable values and the level of local revenue decline. Local government expenses tend to decline less than revenue because vacant property tends to be spread widely, rather than be concentrated, so that servicing costs are not much reduced and some economies of scale tend to be lost. Public utilities are similarly affected. As a result it becomes difficult to find the finance to maintain standards let alone finance the revival of the economy, unless outside assistance is available.

10.9   LOCATION OF DECLINING AREAS

The major areas of dereliction, vacant and run-down buildings and worn out infrastructure are in the cities and conurbations. The problem is not confined to any one region but is concentrated in the midlands and north. The areas within the cities and conurbations are the most difficult and expensive to rehabilitate and the most difficult to which to attract enterprises on a sufficient scale. Rehabilitating depressed areas in the smaller settlements is a less difficult task because the scale is that much smaller and the task of making good dereliction and improving the infrastructure can be achieved more rapidly and generally at a lower cost per head of population.

The problems of upgrading the southern conurbations and cities is not as acute as for those in the north, partly because the rate of loss of population and activities is less and partly because they still attract new and expanded activities (Chapter 6). Since households are getting smaller the demand for dwellings falls more slowly than population and may increase while population falls. Generally there tends to be a shortage of land for development in the settlements preferred by firms and households but a reluctance to redevelop vacant inner city land, partly because of derelict and poor infrastructure and partly because of high development costs and insufficient demand for properties in those areas.

The problems of upgrading the midland and northern conurbations and cities are exacerbated by the lack of demand for properties and the sheer scale and depth of dereliction and run-down infrastructure. The cities and towns in these regions grew rapidly in the late eighteenth and nineteenth centuries on the basis of heavy engineering, mining, textiles and metal working; all industries which have suffered considerable declines with substantial losses of employment. The built environment grew up with the industries to serve them and their workers, and is of a form and standard not acceptable today. Further it is often found that workers experienced in heavy industry find it difficult to adapt to the requirements of contemporary production. Too few local entrepreneurs appear to have the expertise and capital to start new activities without assistance. The absence of local entrepreneurs is not made good by sufficient new ones from outside the regions. The problems of upgrading the smaller towns in the depressed regions are of the same form but on a smaller scale. Redevelopment has generally been less successful than in the south because, even with the attraction of new infrastructure, insufficient enterprises with long term viability have migrated to provide a viable economy.

10.10 POTENTIAL OF DECLINING SETTLEMENTS

Location is less important than it used to be. Industry and commerce is tending to become increasingly footloose as the economy is less concerned with winning and processing raw materials and more concerned with advanced processing and providing services, and as transport and communications become more extensive and less costly. As value added per unit of output increases and transport costs fall in real terms, production can take place further from its markets. Similarly the advance of electronic communications reduces the need for face to face contact and the transport of people, and facilitates the spread of work forces over long distances. As a result there should be more scope for settlements with declining traditional activities to find new ones.

Some small settlements developed to service agriculture and handle its products now flourish as centres for light industry and as office centres, particularly if they are in regions with a buoyant economy. For example, manufacturing clothes, printing and mail order business can be carried on almost anywhere as long as transport is adequate. Tourism is growing, particularly countryside tourism, and many towns and villages are developing substantial activities around potential tourist attractions. Even worked-out mineral workings and disused industrial buildings can be developed into tourist attractions. Again given adequate transport facilities small towns and villages can be developed as commuter dormitories to larger settlements in their vicinity. Others may serve a useful purpose by catering for the retired, leaving space in economically active settlements for economically active households. Clearly if settlements are to find new functions their services and communication links must be maintained and improved to current standards.

The possibility of reviving settlements tends to depend not only on their inherent attractions but also on the rate of national increase in population and household formation and on the strength of attraction of competitive settlements and regions. If population is increasing slowly, as is the case now in most of Europe, there are slower increases in the number of households and activities and it is easier to accommodate people and activities in the settlements of first choice. It is less necessary to expand other settlements and there is less natural growth to sustain activities in settlements which have declined. Demand tends to be greater for accommodation in the south-east and least for the north and west increasing the problems of reviving settlements in such areas of decline. Preference is for small settlements close to areas of high economic activity. Settlements with the lowest powers of attraction are generally those away from transport corridors, for example, at the upper end of mountain valleys and away from main rural roads, those despoiled by mineral workings and those with large areas of dereliction and a run-down local economy.

As indicated earlier despite the increase in footloose industry and the scale of government incentives for firms to develop in areas of decline, insufficient have moved to revive the economies of such areas and plants which have set up in such areas have not always proved viable (Chapter 7). While many economic activities could function effectively in many parts of the country, other things being equal, in practise areas which develop early as a home for particular activities acquire special advantages such as firms specializing in the services the activity requires and appropriate labour and management skills, attracting further businesses in that line of activity (Chapter 7). Again, unless firms need to site themselves close to local markets, they generally prefer to locate all their establishments in the same area. It may, therefore, be necessary, in order to attract footloose industry, to build up a local centre from firms who set up initially in the locality.

Clearly it is not possible for declining settlements to finance job creation on an adequate scale. The costs eventually work through into the rates and might reduce existing enterprise at the margin by as much as it was raised by the financial incentives to new enterprises. The problem for any agency of picking viable enterprises is considerable; there can be little certainty that those chosen will make good. Whether or not it would be worthwhile to use national resources to attempt to revive declining settlements depends on the likelihood of success and on the comparative costs and benefits of reviving declining settlements as compared with those of partial or complete closure with expansion elsewhere to house population and activities forced out.

10.11 REVIVING AREAS OF DECLINE

In order to revive a district in decline it is necessary to attract sufficient demand for vacant sites in it. If the settlement of which it is a part is not in decline it may be possible to attract demand from elsewhere in the settlement, that is from currently more attractive districts within or on the periphery of the settlement. One step might be to limit development and densities in such areas, for example, lowering densities in the business district might encourage those wanting space there to spread into adjacent areas of inner city and take up vacant sites there. However, unless the area in decline is given an attractive environment, planning restrictions may only drive potential occupants to properties in other settlements at home or abroad.

To make an area of decline attractive it will generally be necessary to provide it with a road layout suitable for its intended use, good access to the area for goods and people, adequate parking, sites of a suitable shape and size, appropriate public utilities and amenities, including a satisfying appearance, and to offer sites at competitive prices. The lower the value purchasers or tenants place on the improvements made to the area, the lower the site prices will need to be. It is usually advantageous to improve an area sufficiently large to remove the taint of decline and dereliction, and to bring it adjacent to an area of prosperity.

Often derelict areas are embedded in old housing areas, the improvement of which would increase the attractions of the area to be revived. Improving the two together would generally be to the gain of both. There are several government schemes to assist local authorities in improving the condition of run-down housing. These include grants for house renovation and area improvement under the Housing Acts of 1974 and 1980 and the exchequer grants to local authorities for 'enveloping' which provide for the renovation of the exterior fabric of badly deteriorated property at no cost to the owner [1]. Finance is also often available from urban development grants, the Urban Programme and other improvement schemes (Chapter 7).

In order to provide an acceptable layout for an improved area and sites of suitable size and shape, it may be necessary to reorganize the road layout and the arrangements of the sites. Much of the land may need to be acquired by the overall developer so that the road system can be rationalized and land reparcelled. Often the public utility services need to be reorganized. Where there are a multiplicity of owners, assembling sufficient land to redevelop the area may take a developer many years, during which the property already acquired and the finance for its acquisition will need to be serviced, resulting in high holding costs. Sometimes the participation of the local authority is sought to acquire key sites compulsorily, the private or public owners of which are holding out for prices higher than the worth of the sites themselves. Clearly the local authority must be closely involved with changes in the road layout and planning consents. In some cases local authorities themselves take the lead in acquiring and reparcelling the area. In fact a great deal of land in areas requiring redevelopment is owned by local authorities and nationalized industries, often without any specific purpose and the government is now ordering its release (Chapter 8).

Clearly acquiring land in a run-down area, while if successful in creating a substantial demand may lead to large profits, carries a high risk and local authorities often prefer to cooperate with a private developer, selling to him any land they compulsorily acquire. Costs borne by the local authority may eventually be covered by the excess of increased rate returns over the costs of servicing the additional property brought into occupation by the redevelopment. Government grants to local authorities have been available for the reclamation of land for more than a decade. Initially they were used for removing eyesores outside settlements but they are now increasingly used for reclaiming land within urban areas. The grants have now been extended in appropriate cases to private developers who are reclaiming land.

In the past local authorities have often accumulated inner city land for public housing. Large areas of inner city land have been used to develop estates of high rise flatted housing. Apart from the physical failures of some of these estates resulting from their design and construction, there have also been social failures, for a variety of reasons: from the frustrations from the physical conditions arising from the design and layout, and often inadequate maintenance, from vandalism and attacks on the occupiers and often because the estates were built in areas where there was a lack of suitable employment for the occupants. Inevitably areas of inner city with vacant land are those from which the traditional forms of employment have disappeared. Often the type of jobs the occupiers of inner city housing are equipped to undertake without retraining have either moved to the periphery of the settlement or have ceased to exist. If the land in these areas is to be used for housing, land needs to be available within commuting distance for industry and commerce likely to provide suitable employment for the occupants of the housing. Appropriate training may need to be provided. Housing developed on vacant inner city land may need to be designed to attract those who work in adjacent areas.

Consideration needs to be given to the best solution for the derelict and vacant land where there is little hope at that time of being able to attract more than a limited number of occupiers. As long as the area remains without improvement, it will be difficult to attract occupants and hence developers to the area. The attractions of the area are likely to be improved if derelict buildings and land are cleared and useful buildings refurbished for at least some temporary use. Land with no immediate foreseeable use could be grassed over and planted with suitable robust trees. Tree belts might be used to conceal any areas which cannot be cleared for the foreseeable future.

The revival of areas in a declining settlement may encourage demand in adjacent areas and stimulate an improvement in the economy of the settlement as a whole, creating more employment, private income and public revenue, and thus contributing to further demand and improvement. Generally, however, it will be much more difficult to stimulate the necessary demand in the first case, because this involves reversing the economic decline of the settlement itself.

Clearing derelict and unwanted buildings and sites, improving the infrastructure and utility services, rehabilitating housing and other useful buildings, and developing workshops, industrial and other buildings is the least difficult part in reviving a run-down settlement, but it makes a heavy use of resources; resources which a run-down settlement is not likely to have available. If nothing else, such improvements increase the quality of life for the local population, and help to stem migration from the settlement. However, clearly it would be unwise to use too many resources to provide facilities and amenities for potential new enterprises without some assurance that they would be used. Initially development for these purposes might be limited to a pilot scheme. Such development would need to be backed by a consistent set of measures to attract potential entrepreneurs and support existing ones.

Such measures might include the provision of advice and counselling on the lines of the small business scheme, managerial assistance in setting up enterprises, training, organizing local enterprises to subcontract and supply services needed by local traders and communal cooperative services such as secretarial, computing, legal and accounting. The costs of such services would be generally small compared with those of financial inducements often offered to firms to migrate to declining settlement, and would be partly borne by the enterprises themselves (Chapter 7).

Attempts to revive rundown areas need the cooperation and the close coordination of all public authorities both central and local. The revival of areas and their economy can be frustrated by bureaucratic delay and over fastidious implementation of planning, traffic, parking, licensing, fire, building and other regulations, and by delay in providing funds and such essential services as water, power and telephone.

The problem of selecting which areas to attempt to revive cannot be avoided, even if it only takes the form of priorities, since not all the less prosperous areas can be revived simultaneously. Priority could be by the scale of deprivation, however measured, or by the likelihood of its relief. The optimum solution might be to give priority to those centres likely to respond in the shortest time and on the largest scale, so not only to create the greatest number of new jobs, output and revenue but to create buoyant centres in each area which would assist in restoring confidence and attracting more enterprise. Selection would not be easy although perhaps less difficult than trying to determine which firms would be most likely to prosper and give the best returns for public subsidies.

Perhaps, rather than putting so much emphasis on attracting migrant firms to areas to be revived, more attention might be given to encouraging local firms and local people to expand and set up businesses, particularly in trades for which attractive centres have not already been created elsewhere on an adequate scale. This might be promoted through assistance to potential entrepreneurs as explained earlier.

National finance is likely to be needed not only for physical reconstruction but for retraining labour, creating and improving other services, and other confidence-creating measures. There are, as indicated earlier, a number of government schemes for financing the improvement of the built environment, particularly for housing and derelict land (Chapter 7). Government grants are available for training, work experience schemes, small business schemes and so on. The government has also introduced other schemes to assist the revival of the economies of settlements (Chapter 7). These include, in addition to the assisted area provisions, bringing additional employment to an area by transferring government departments to them and thus creating directly some additional employment; increasing spending to create other activities and employment through the multiplier effect; giving firms in the selected areas priority in placing government contracts. These devices have been used in the assisted areas. A more limited scheme is the enterprize zone. A number of small areas have been created under this scheme (Chapter 7).

The advantages of development corporations over local authorities in carrying out large scale redevelopment and expansion of settlements was discussed earlier (Chapter 9). Their advantages lie not only in the physical redevelopment process but in generating a balanced and prosperous social and industrial development. Some observers advocate setting up development corporations to carry out at least the major inner area redevelopments and point to the experience and expertise in the new town corporations, many of which, at the time of writing, are being run-down. The corporation would, of course, need to operate in close collaboration with the relevant public authorities. The government has in fact set up urban development corporations for London Docklands, Merseyside Docklands and now for four further areas (Chapter 7).

The limited success in reviving run-down areas and settlements does not appear to have been the result of indifference. Many schemes have been devised and considerable resources have been expended, not only by central government but by local authorities and private agencies. For the most part the resources have been spread thinly over the problem areas of the country; there appears to have been little coordination between physical, economic and social reconstruction or between the different agencies, even those within the same authority, so that the initiatives have often impeded rather than reinforced each other. There appears to have been insufficient realization that the problems of each area tend to be unique and that each needs a phased and coordinated development plan, based on a full understanding of the local situation, in which every step is related to create cumulative growth.

The resources likely to be available are unlikely to be sufficient to treat all the problem areas simultaneously. Priorities need to be worked out with an initial concentration on the revival of areas promising the highest and earliest returns, physical, economic and social, relative to the resources used and the generation of the greatest volume of additional resources for application to further areas.

REFERENCES

1. Department of the Environment (1982) *Improvement of Older Housing: Enveloping*. Circular 29/82, HMSO, London.

PART FOUR

Design and planning economics

11

Economics of designing and planning built facilities

11.1 ECONOMICS OF DESIGN

The costs and benefits of designs for built facilities follow similar lines to those discussed earlier for settlement structure (Chapter 9). Factors of internal layout, appearance and location affect the developer, occupiers and other direct users, while both location and appearance, and the facility's generation of traffic, pollution and the demand for public services affect the public authorities and the community.

The initial costs of built facilities depend on a large number of factors such as the properties of the site, the characteristics of the facility itself, such as size, shape, layout and the quality of the fittings and decoration, the efficiency of the designer and contractor, and on tendering conditions. Running and service costs depend on the design, on the quality of the erection process and on the way the facility is used. Inevitably there are many uncertainties as to how the facility will function and what demands will be made upon it.

It is helpful to combine initial and running costs into costs-in-use [1]. This is the sum of the two types of cost expressed in equivalent terms by discounting at a given rate of interest all the costs to a common time base, either at the beginning of the life of the building or as an equivalent annual cost, taking into account the life of the building or facility. If costs-in-use are minimized, real costs are minimized. Sometimes this may involve additional initial costs in order to save greater equivalent running costs. Developers sometimes argue that because capital is tight they cannot afford more than the minimum initial costs and that bearing higher running costs will be acceptable because they would expect rising incomes and revenues in the future. While owner-occupiers building for themselves are in a position to judge their best interests, developers building for sale or letting are more interested in initial costs unless customers take running costs into account in determining the price acceptable to them (Chapter 3).

The benefits of a facility consist of the services it provides to the occupiers and other direct users, either as satisfaction or in generated added value to the product or service in connection with which it is used and in the satisfaction it provides to the public at large. Consideration will be given in this chapter to some of the principal types of design and planning problems which involve both initial and running costs. Space is not sufficient for an adequate discussion of the application of the costs-in-use technique, this is given elsewhere [1]. However an example will illustrate its application and value as a guide to decision.

11.2 DEVELOPMENT NEEDS

The need for built facilities arises from the need for shelter whether for a household, an industrial, commercial, educational, social or health activity or for some other function. The stock of built facilities is large and a need for shelter does not necessarily create the demand for a new development. Sometimes it is more economical to adapt an existing building, either already owned or rented, or to be acquired. In some cases the building already occupied may be capable of fulfilling all the foreseen needs of the occupier. The current use may be inefficient; space may be used wastefully, for example on unnecessary storage or circulation; the arrangement of spaces may not fully utilize the potential. The most economic solution may be to reorganize the use of the building rather than the building itself. Where the building does not meet the new demands, the choice lies between altering and extending it, moving to another building better fitted for the purpose, or developing a new one. Alterations may be limited to the movement of partitions and creating new openings. More radical changes may be required such as lowering and strengthening floors, increasing clearance heights, removing columns and extensions. In other cases the changes required may relate to changes in styles and standards such as new windows, doors and floors, or a new system of heating. Where the location no longer fulfils needs, another existing building or a new development cannot be avoided.

Most decisions about buildings are relative; compromises are necessary between the best solutions over a wide range of demands. Few newly developed buildings, however well designed, are completely ideal or remain so for very long. The additional costs of getting one step nearer the ideal solution in one direction may soon reach a point at which they outweigh the value of the benefits. It is always necessary to weigh up the costs and benefits over the areas affected.

Past costs and benefits are of no account; economically bygones are forever bygones (Chapter 3); it is future costs and benefits on which decisions need to be made. The initial costs of a new development include those for land, construction, design and other fees, furnishings and interest until occupation.

For an existing building the corresponding costs include the purchase price, costs of alterations, fees, furnishings and interest. If the occupier already owns a building its sale price reduces initial costs but there will be costs for transferring from one site to another. These may include not only the costs of moving materials and equipment but losses until an efficient level of functioning is achieved at the new location and compensation to staff and others affected by the move. In the case of leased buildings initial costs will include the costs of acquiring and selling leases.

The initial costs can be amortized over the life, or remaining life, of the building to give an annual equivalent cost to which may be added any ground or other rents. The probable life of an existing building will generally be less

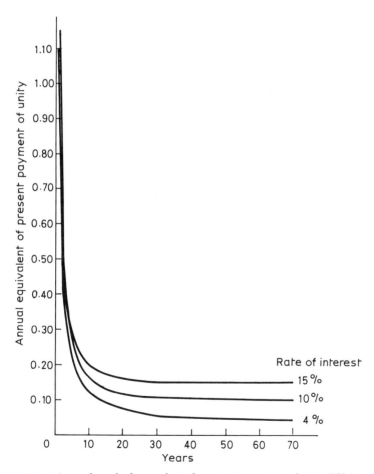

Figure 11.1   Annual equivalent value of present payment of 1 at 'i'% interest.

than that of a new one but it may be extended as a result of any alterations and rehabilitation. Most buildings have long physical lives if adequately maintained but technological or financial obsolescence may shorten effective lives. At the usual real rates of discount annual equivalent values change only marginally once probable lives reach 50 to 60 years (Fig. 11.1). As a result there is little economic significance between probable lives in excess of this length.

The running and service costs of existing buildings are generally higher than those of new buildings; the difference depending on the extent of rehabilitation work. Usually many old components will remain with failure rates higher than for new ones. Old buildings may have such defects as dry rot, woodworm, rust, defective electric wiring and corroded pipes, not all of which are easy to detect. On the other hand, new buildings may have design and building faults which result in early failures. The risks are usually greater where use is made of newly developed materials or new design and building techniques, although successful innovations may result in substantial benefits. Old buildings may cost more than new buildings to operate because they are less well insulated, have less efficient heating and lighting systems, are less easy to clean and have greater fire risks.

If a new building has been adequately designed for its future use, it should be better for its purpose than an old one and either give greater satisfaction to its occupiers and others, or assist in promoting greater efficiency in carrying out the purposes for which it was designed. Unless extensive rehabilitation was carried out on an old building, a new one should provide greater comfort. On the other hand, aesthetic values are subjective so that there can be no certainty that the appearance of a new building will promote greater satisfaction than an adequately maintained existing one.

While a new building may be developed on the same site as an existing one for which it provides an alternative option, it may be on a different site with a range of different attributes and different performances in the desired use.

11.3 LOCATION AND THE SITE

The location of a site will affect the costs of occupation through the costs of communication such as bringing in materials, energy and labour, taking out finished products, journeys to work, school, recreation and shopping, according to the type of occupier. Communication costs may also affect other users such as customers, visitors and patients, and the community through overloading public transport and roads. Public authority costs and hence charges to the public may be affected through the need to provide additional road and public utility services.

A good location might mean greater convenience, greater flows of customers past the door or a higher quality environment. The latter may include both physical facilities and amenities, aesthetic values, freedom from congestion and pollution. The location of an activity at one site rather than another may bring benefits to the community through enhancing aesthetics and convenience of the district or settlement affected. Again an activity may itself create differential external costs through the way it generates traffic and pollution.

The site itself will affect development costs through its shape and size, gradient, weight-bearing capacity of its soil, chemical composition, moisture content and exposure. The surrounding environment will affect costs and benefits through the quality of light, noise, air pollution and congestion.

11.4   SIZE, SHAPE AND FORM

Usually there are some economies of scale in constructing and servicing buildings. The nature of these economies vary with the type of building. A dwelling for eight persons tends to cost only about twice as much as one for one person [2]. The economies arise partly because there is a minimum to the floor space and facilities (kitchen and bathroom etc) necessary even for one person, and because perimeters increase less than proportionately to floor space [2]. Other things being equal, costs per unit area of floor space of factory buildings tend to decline by about one-fifth as the area increases by a factor of ten [3].

A significant proportion of the costs of developing a building and of servicing it arise from the shell which encloses the space. The shell has a minimum surface area in relation to the space enclosed when spherical but this is not a convenient shape for human occupation, although it has attractions for vessels containing liquids and gases. Cubic space is more convenient and is comparatively efficient in the sense discussed. Other things being equal efficiency declines as the shape moves away from the cube, the surface area of the shell increases relative to the space enclosed increasing the costs of construction, maintenance, cleaning and heating. For example, the costs-in-use for a large single storey factory building were found to rise by about one-fifteenth as plan ratios increase from a ratio of 1:1 to 1:8 [3]. Of course, other things are often not equal; cost relationships are generally more complex than the geometry suggests. Different parts of the shell, floors, walls and roofs have different costs-in-use per unit area. Cost relationships are further complicated by the structure and the provision of internal environment.

If natural lighting is to be provided, the depth of a space is limited by the strength of the light at the rear of the space. In order to increase the depth at a given level of natural light, the height of windows need to be raised, eventually to storey height, thus increasing costs of fabric and frame, maintenance, cleaning and heating. Alternatively the inner part of the space can be provided with permanent artificial lighting. These problems do not arise in top storeys or single storey buildings where top lighting can be provided. Deep spaces are generally more difficult to ventilate naturally than narrow ones; artificial ventilation or even air-conditioning is usually necessary; particularly the latter raises costs considerably. Where external noise is unacceptably high or a controlled and clean environment is required, air-conditioning may have to be provided in any case and savings from the construction, maintenance and heating a deeper space may offset the additional costs of lighting (Chapter 9).

Costs-in-use tend to rise with the number of storeys, the cost relationships varying with the type of building (Chapter 9). In some cases ground floors are much cheaper to construct and maintain than upper ones. For example, where large loads have to be carried, as in many industrial buildings, a light shed over a ground floor is often quite adequate and much cheaper to construct and service than a multistorey operating space. A ground floor car park does not need a roof, whereas a heavy frame is necessary to support upper floors. As the number of storeys of a building is increased the frame needs strengthening, more circulation space is needed with an increasing provision of vertical access (lifts and staircases) and cleaning and maintaining the exterior becomes more difficult, raising both initial and service costs per unit area.

11.5 BUILT-IN FLEXIBILITY

It is difficult to foresee future needs. Households can grow or decline, both over the life of a household and nationally as demographic habits change. More and more personal possessions and more household equipment tend to be acquired, and members of households tend to become more diverse in their activities, requiring more space. Work spaces tend to increase in size as more equipment and services are provided for each person; a feature common not only in industry but in offices, hospitals and other buildings. Replacement plant is often a different size, shape and weight to that it replaces. Buildings often have to be adapted to meet the needs not only of changing techniques but changes in use and hence often need to be very flexible.

Up to a point, additional space provides greater convenience and comfort, and greater flexibility for meeting changing needs. For example, a three-bedroom dwelling can accommodate households of up to six, with space available for smaller households to have diverse acitivities. A one-bedroom dwelling can only meet the needs of one or two person households and provides little space for guests or a range of activities. Additional space in commercial and industrial buildings allows for possible increases in plant and workers, and additional storage space, while in hospitals it allows for more beds and treatment rooms and in schools for more pupils and teaching space. Additional height allows space for taller plant and for additional services to be fitted between floors. Stronger structures provide a margin for accommodating greater floor loads.

However, while a loose fit increases the flexibility of a building and increases the chances that it will meet future needs without alteration, it entails greater initial and running costs. The larger the floor area and the greater the clearance heights and strength of the structure, the greater the costs of construction and the greater the costs of cleaning, maintenance, heating and other service costs. Whether such costs are worth incurring depends in part on the type of alterations likely to be needed and in part on when such alterations are likely to be necessary.

The most common requirement is perhaps changes in the distribution of spaces. Internal walls of masonry, especially if load-bearing, can be expensive to remove, create dirt and involve a loss of space while the building work is being carried out. New masonry walls usually need plastering and decorating; even temporary partitioning tends to create dust when removed and needs to be redecorated. The latter tends to be more expensive than permanent partitioning and to have poorer sound insulation properties. Raising clearance heights and strengthening floors may involve substantial reconstruction and loss of useful space for long periods, involving considerable construction costs and inconvenience costs to the occupiers. Re-equipment and new finishes, while less difficult to provide can still involve considerable costs and temporary loss of space.

In order to decide whether it is worthwhile to build-in flexibility, it is necessary to compare the additional costs of constructing and servicing a flexible building over one which just meets current requirements, against the costs of conversion when the need arises. However, whereas building-in flexibility creates an immediate and certain cost, the costs of conversion may not arise for a considerable period and may never arise at all, at least in the form expected. The costs-in-use of built-in flexibility compared with those of later conversion can be compared in the following way.

The costs-in-use of built-in flexibility 'A' would be:

Additional initial costs of construction plus additional running costs.

These different types of costs have to be expressed in equivalent terms before they can be summed [1]. It is convenient to express them in present equivalent values, that is the face value of the initial cost and the discounted values of future costs for t years, where t is the number of years to elapse before conversion is expected to be necessary. The discounted value is the sum which if invested now at a given rate of interest would accrue to the sum required at the end of the period.

The costs-in-use of conversion 'B' would be:

The costs of conversion discounted over t years.

The breakeven point between built-in flexibility and conversion occurs when the equivalent values of the two expressions A and B are equal. Usually it is not difficult to estimate the three cost items; the major uncertainty lies in estimating the elapsed period before conversion is expected to be necessary. Rather than trying to estimate t, it is easier to find the value of t necessary for equivalent values of the two cost groups A and B to breakeven, then to ask whether the elapsed period is likely to be as great.

Clearly the greater the number of years before conversion would be necessary, the more the equivalent cost of built-in flexibility would be relative to conversion. Built-in flexibility would be worthwhile if the expected elapsed period is less than the value of t at which the costs-in-use of built-in flexibility and conversion breakeven.

It is convenient to calculate R_s and R_c in relation to values of t such that:

$$R_s = \frac{\text{additional annual running costs}}{\text{additional costs of building}}$$

$$\text{and } R_c = \frac{\text{costs of conversion}}{\text{additional costs of building}}$$

These two expressions can be equated at an appropriate rate of discount and plotted on a decision diagram such as that shown below (Fig. 11.2). This was calculated at a discount rate of 5%. The value of t at which the costs of built-in flexibility and conversion breakeven can then be read off Fig. 11.2 in terms of R_s and R_c.

Suppose, for example, that the costs of built-in flexibility were £1 million, the additional running costs were £80 000 a year and the costs of conversion were £2.5 million. Reading from the diagram (Fig. 11.2) it will be seen that the two methods would have comparable present values at an elapsed period of something over 8 years. Hence it would not pay to build-in flexibility if it was thought that the building would satisfy needs without changes to the building for something over this period. It is also necessary to take account of the possibility that when changes are required, they might be different to those anticipated at the time of briefing for the building, so that further work might be necessary or that the occupier might decide to move or other contingencies might arise.

The need to change a building might arise from changes of occupier as well as from the changing needs of a single occupier. Such an event would be difficult to project. Given the rate of possible changes of demand for buildings, consideration might be given to the desirability of creating a building sufficiently flexible to meet a number of totally different types of need. Recently there have been examples of factory buildings and large shops being converted to offices, cinemas to shops and shops to small industrial units (Chapter 10). Changes in technology and in the function of areas might result in large numbers of buildings no longer required in their designed used.

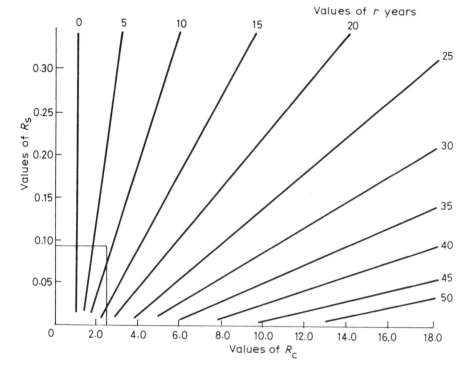

Figure 11.2 Break-even points for built-in flexibility against subsequent conversion.

Whether constructing them to satisfy multiple purposes would be worthwhile requires careful investigation.

11.6 STRUCTURE AND CLADDINGS

For small low buildings such as houses, shops and schools it is not generally necessary to provide a frame. The walls on their foundations are generally strong enough to carry the floors and roof provided that spans are not very great. A frame may be introduced to facilitate the use of curtain walls and other features or to facilitate the erection process. For example, dwellings may be built with a timber frame so that a roof can be erected at an early stage to provide protection and allow several operations to proceed simultaneously. It is claimed that such procedures reduce erection costs, in part by allowing capital to be turned over more rapidly.

As spaces in buildings become larger, and spans and floor loads increase, frames tend to become necessary. As column spacings are increased, beams tend to become deeper, increasing storey heights, and the area of walling to be constructed and maintained and through which heat can be lost. The additional costs-in-use arising from such changes may be offset at least in part by utilizing the space within the beams for service connections or for accommodating tall pieces of plant. The form of roof frame may affect the type and costs-in-use of roof covers and roof lighting. The type of frame also affects the percentage of space which can be profitably used. Costs are also affected by the type of frame, including the form of material used, relative costs varying with the state of supply and demand in the market [1].

Wall claddings vary considerably in appearance and cost. While some have much better thermal efficiency than others, deficiencies can easily be made good by adding additional insulation. Brick cavity external walls tend to be comparatively cheap both to erect and maintain, especially in flettons but walls of corrugated sheets on timber frames are even cheaper [4]. Appearance can be an important consideration. Using facing bricks, rendering and painting add to the costs. Decorated surfaces generally need frequent maintenance. Reinforced concrete is generally more expensive than brickwork, especially if its surface is provided with some type of decorative finish, stone facing being particularly expensive [4]. Metal and glass curtain walling is also generally very expensive, especially if frequent cleaning is required.

Roof shapes affect the types of construction and covering, maintenance, heat losses, appearance and possibilities of top lighting. Flat roofs are generally difficult to construct satisfactorily and frequently have high maintenance costs.

11.7 GLAZING

The use of glazing has considerable consequences for the convenience, comfort, appearance and costs of buildings. Most occupiers prefer natural to artificial lighting and like to have a view out; for some processes natural lighting is more valuable than artificial lighting.

Glazing near the floor does little to improve the level of lighting. Light penetrates further into the room the higher in the wall it is placed. The value of natural light can be measured in terms of the cost savings from a lower use of artificial lighting. Such cost savings depend on the design and placing of the glazing, the strength of natural light and the periods during which the building is used. The shorter the periods of daylight during which the building is used, the lower the value of the light penetrating the glazing. Additional glazing, beyond a certain point may contribute little additional light of value. While glazing admits useful light, it also admits solar gain and lets out heat. Solar gain can be useful in winter but a nuisance in summer: it complicates temperature control. The position of the glass has less effect on heat losses and gains per unit area than on light gain but generally temperatures are greater nearer the ceiling, increasing the rate of heat losses there.

Clearly the net costs-in-use of glazing are the consequence of a number of factors. Allowance needs to be made for the costs of erecting, maintaining and cleaning glazing in relation to those of the solid walling omitted, for the costs of double- or treble-glazing to reduce heat losses and tinting to reduce solar gain and glare, for the value of the useful light gained and the heat lost, and for the value of a view out and the effect on the appearance of the building. Generally conventional windows are the most cost-efficient but the longer the periods during which the building is used during daylight hours and the nearer outside temperatures to internal comfort levels the greater the justification of larger windows [1]. While double-glazing in walls may improve comfort standards, it is not generally very cost-effective [5].

Roof lighting generally allows more useful light per unit area of glass than wall glazing, its value and quality depending on the design of the roof and the roof glazing it allows. Because temperatures are generally higher at the ceiling, the rate of heat losses will generally be higher than on average through wall glazing. Where the building is used more or less continuously, double glazing may be worthwhile [1]. Because roof glazing is generally away from the view of the passer-by, its affect on appearance may be small.

11.8 HEATING AND VENTILATION

Heating and ventilation are important factors in determining the comfort of the internal environment. The levels of heating and ventilation required depend to a large extent on the way the building is used. Active occupants do not require internal temperatures as high as the sedentary. Heat in a building is gained from the occupants, machinery, processes, artificial lighting, solar gain and heated objects brought into the building. Heat losses arise from ventilation, heat escaping through the fabric and from heated objects leaving the building. There is usually a critical heating period for human occupants, the period of occupation; temperatures at other times may not be important from comfort consideration but it may not be economical to allow temperatures to get too far out of line from those required during the critical period.

In some cases heat gains may exceed losses during critical periods when the main requirement may be ventilation. More often, however, losses exceed gains and thermal insulation must be improved, ventilation reduced and space heating provided. As indicated earlier, it is usually easy and cost-effective to increase thermal insulation to a reasonable level. The degree to which it is cost-effective varies with the building element, walls, roof and floor, with the form of structure of the component, with the type of insulation, with the required internal temperature in relation to external temperature and with the length of the critical period [5].

Ventilation losses can be reduced by improving the fit of doors and windows, fitting double doors, double-glazing and blocking gaps in floors, walls and roof. Some ventilation is necessary for the health of the occupants and for the durability of the fabric and the goods stored in the building. Excessive moisture, fumes and other pollution needs to be removed. Inadequate ventilation can result in condensation and the growth of fungi with damage to the fabric and contents, and to the comfort and health of the occupants.

Ventilation is provided naturally through doors, window frames, flues and other vents and can be increased by additional controlled openings, mechanically through extractors or by air-conditioning. Natural ventilation is generally satisfactory in small rooms but it can create draughts and may emit noise, fumes and dust. Compared with other forms of ventilation it has low costs-in-use. Opening windows and other vents becomes less satisfactory as rooms become deeper and in upper parts of tall buildings, especially where there are several crowded together. Forced ventilation or air-conditioning is then generally used. The latter enables the internal environment to be controlled to eliminate dirt and fumes, and provide regulated temperatures and humidity levels. For some types of buildings such as cinemas, theatres and large departmental stores the spaces are so deep that some form of artificial ventilation is unavoidable. Again artificial ventilation enables higher standards of comfort to be provided in countries where temperatures and humidity create unpleasant conditions. In other cases the need for artificial ventilation arises from the design of the building.

The use of artificial ventilation frees the design from limitations of depth and height, shape, fenestration and opening lights (Chapter 9). Generally the volume of auxiliary space will need to be greater to accommodate the ventilating plant, particularly where air-conditioning is used, and the loads on the building will be increased. In addition to higher structure costs, there will be additional costs for the ventilation plant itself. Heating and ventilating plant is perhaps two to three times as expensive as heating plant alone, and air-conditioning plant is four or five times as expensive [1]. Maintenance costs tend to be broadly proportional to capital costs, while energy costs for mechanical ventilation tend to be one-third to half as much again as for heating only, and about three times as great for air-conditioning [1]. These costs may to some extent be offset by lower cleaning costs.

There are many forms of heating from the traditional open fire or stove burning solid fuel: radiant types such as electric and gas fires; hot water systems circulating heat through radiators or under-the-floor pipes; circulation of warmed air. The choice available depends on the type of building, on the standard of heating required and on the accepted cost. The choice for space heating to an acceptable standard narrows as the spaces get larger. In large buildings, where it is only required to warm the occupants, such as large storage and assembly buildings, and churches, heating may be by unit heaters for each group of occupants, for example, at each workplace or in each pew.

Where cost is an important consideration heating may only be provided in a single communal space such as the sitting room or kitchen of a small house.

The choice of form of heating also depends on the critical period. Where this is very short, for example, in a doctor's waiting room, flexibility may be more important economically than efficiency. The longer the critical period the more importance is likely to be attached to an efficient heating system. The critical period for most commercial and industrial buildings is about eight hours for five days a week during the heating season; for schools the hours and the number of weeks is lower; for hospitals it is continuous.

Fuel costs form a large proportion of the running costs. Unit fuel costs tend to be volatile in the short to medium period. Competition between secondary and the primary fuels on which they are based tends to reduce large cost differences in the long run. Coal, oil and gas can be used directly as a fuel or to generate electricity; gas may be generated from coal or oil and may be a byproduct of the latter. While the winning and generation of fuels are often state monopolies, the fuels may still be in competition. Some power sources, for example, electric generators, can often easily switch from coal to oil and in the long run may be able to make a greater use of nuclear, hydroelectric or tidal power. The volatile nature of fuel prices makes the projection of long term prices difficult and creates uncertainty in costs-in-use comparisons. Nevertheless, some forms of heating are more cost-effective than others. If unit fuel prices rise in real terms the higher initial costs of some forms of heating installation may be offset [5]. How far it is worthwhile to fit heating systems which currently have relatively high costs-in-use in the expectation that relative fuel price changes will result in lower costs-in-use in the long term can be tested through costs-in-use comparisons [1].

In comparing the costs-in-use of different heating systems allowance is necessary for the space requirements of the heating plant and for fuel storage, and their consequences for initial and maintenance costs. Allowance also must be made for the affect of the system on the creation of dust, and damage and staining of the fabric, and its decoration. Some systems require more servicing than others; servicing can sometimes be reduced by the installation of automatic controls. Service labour can add significantly to running costs or to the load on volunteers.

The form of the building, its size and type of cladding affect the fabric heat losses, the size of heating plant and the consumption of fuel. For example, the heat inputs necessary to compensate for fabric losses from dwellings increase substantially with the degree of exposure, being over three times as great for a detached house as for an intermediate flat otherwise similar [5]. As indicated earlier, fabric heat losses increase broadly in proportion to exposed shell area; they are also affected by the degree of exposure and, of course, the standard of thermal insulation. Heating plant tends to be lumpy. Reductions in heat losses may be highly cost effective if as a result the plant size can be reduced.

Alternatively it may be worthwhile to provide a supplementary source of heating to top-up at critical times.

11.9 FINISHES AND FITTINGS

Finishings affect not only appearance but maintenance and cleaning, and possibly heating and lighting. Many finishes have a short life and need frequent replacement, maintenance and cleaning, the incidence of each varying with the type of material, environment and use. Often, of course, finishes are changed to meet a change of taste. Some finishes absorb less light than others; the lighter the finish the more light it reflects, reducing the amount of artificial light required. Some finishes have poorer thermal insulation properties than others and if greater fabric heat losses are to be avoided, need to be backed with more insulation material. The costs-in-use of finishes also depend on the effect of building work and cleaning on the use of space. Depending on the type of occupant, space may need to be vacated while building work or even cleaning is carried out. This would be particularly important in buildings used continuously such as hospitals. For example, if maintenance operations necessitated clearing floor space for 2 weeks every 4 years, about 1% of the accommodation would effectively be lost.

The costs-in-use of fittings and equipment include not only the costs of purchase and installation, maintenance and servicing but also the costs of providing and servicing the space they occupy. It is often pointed out that in offices in the City of London it costs £20 to £30 a year to provide space for the waste paper basket.

The building may not only have to be larger to accommodate the equipment; in exceptional cases it may be planned to make the best use of it. Even in domestic kitchens so much equipment is now installed that the size and shape of the kitchen may need to be modified to accommodate the equipment conveniently. In industrial buildings the size of plant may determine the space between the columns and the clearance height. Storage buildings now tend to have greater clearance heights to allow the capacity of fork-lift trucks to be fully utilized. The space between floors and ceilings is tending to increase to accommodate the increasing volume of services. It is often cost-effective to provide a generous amount of space to facilitate maintenance and replacement. Vertical access can be expensive and it is sometimes cost-effective to group spaces around the vertical access core to utilize the full capacity of the equipment, even although this may change the shape of the building and perhaps increase the cost of the shell.

Manpower tends to be costly relative to manufactured goods and the cost relatives tend to be getting wider. Automation of lifts and other equipment may be cost-effective relative to manual operation. Where operators also carry out other functions, automation may save time but not useful time and may not result in reducing manpower. However, equipment (for example) for the vertical and horizontal movement of people and goods, may significantly reduce unproductive time, reduce the need for staff to assist customer movement or increase the number of customers visiting upper floor sales and service areas, and therefore be cost-effective despite increasing costs.

11.10 STANDARDS OF COMFORT AND CONVENIENCE

Decisions on standards of comfort and convenience depend on resources and valuations of the occupiers and on what developers and owners think these might be. The costs-in-use indicate the resources likely to be necessary to obtain and service a building to particular standards. How much can be afforded depends on the availability of capital to meet first costs and of income or revenue to meet annual costs. Occupiers have many needs and aspirations, and in a general way will try to obtain equal marginal returns from each item of expenditure (Chapter 2). Because their evaluations of satisfaction from different goods and services vary, so do expenditure patterns. For example, some households are prepared to spend much larger proportions of income and capital on their dwellings than others, who may have higher levels of preferences for other goods and services. Commercial and industrial undertakings may value the worth of high class buildings very differently. The less value occupiers place on comfort and convenience, the less resources they will spend on the building.

Site costs are often a major part of the costs of development and of rents (Chapter 3). Location can provide a substantial part of the comfort and convenience obtained from a property. These arise both from ease of communication with other buildings and people, and from the many qualities of the local environment.

There are a large range of options for building standards. A household, for example, can choose between standards for space, heating, lighting, decoration and equipment. One household may obtain relatively high satisfaction from a well equipped kitchen or a second bathroom, while another may prefer larger rooms. A keen gardener is likely to have a preference for a comparatively large private outdoor space at some cost to the standards within the dwelling. However large a households' resources, it must generally choose between different attributes. It must weigh up the values it attributes to each against their costs-in-use and trade off one against another. Appearance, an important consideration, will be considered later.

As indicated earlier (Chapter 3) the private person sets his personal valuation against the costs of each option; the businessman can to a large degree relate the values of the standards of the building to a return on capital, through additional business expected to arise in one location rather than another, or through higher standards in the building itself, or through better staff relations. A high-standard building is thought to give customers confidence in the stability and efficiency of a firm, characteristics important for finance houses and high-class shops. Lavish decorations are thought to raise the prestige of hotels. A convenient location and comfortable conditions may aid the recruitment and retention of staff. On the other hand, building standards and location are less important in low prestige trades and are often given low importance by industrialists, transport and storage organizations, the premises of which are not frequented by the general public. In part the standards reflect the ability to meet their costs. Broadly, the lower the added value generated by the firm the less they can afford high-standard premises.

In the public sector the decision-taker is not backing his preferences with his own resources; often the capital cost is limited by a cost target set by others. Nor is there a concern with returns on capital; generally there is no specific charge for public services, costs being met through taxation and rate revenues (Chapter 14).

The range of standards is very wide, with wide cost consequences. Sites are very variable, some costing many times more per unit area than others. Buildings for the same purpose can vary in cost by a factor of two or three [4]. The range of prices for individual building components is naturally wider still. For example, demountable partitions cost two or three times as much as plaster board on studding; suspended concrete floors have a similar price range compared with timber floors; internal doors can have price variations three- or fourfold, while the prices of floor finishes per unit area can vary by a factor of ten [4].

11.11　APPEARANCE, VALUE AND COST

Appearance is another attribute for which costs and values need to be related. Whereas comfort and convenience generally only affect the satisfaction of the users of the building, appearance also affects those of the public at large.

The appearance of a building depends mainly on the form, shape and style, on the materials used for cladding, fenestration, external fittings and on decorative features, whether of form or colour. The aesthetic impact depends not only on the building itself but on its relation to its environment. Many buildings take a form and shape dictated by the uses to which they are to be put; for others form and appearance are considered of such importance that the form is not closely related to its function. For example, the height (and often size) of churches have generally been quite unrelated to functional needs and some post-modern buildings take a shape dictated more by aesthetic ideas than functional needs. While costs generally rise less than proportionately as space increases, providing space not required for functional purposes clearly adds to the cost. Again, costs tend to rise per unit of useful space as the height of a building increases and as the area of walls and roofs containing the useful space are increased. Some forms and shapes are much more expensive to construct than others.

The structure and style of buildings have changed over time reflecting the availability of materials and technology, and changes in fashion. Before the development of railways transporting materials was difficult and expensive; each locality tended to develop its own style and form of structure based on the materials available in the area [6]. Most buildings were erected by local craftsmen following the local traditions. Today building materials can be moved more easily and cheaply and there is a wide choice of both materials and techniques in developed countries. Whereas once building materials were obtained from the land (e.g. stone, slate, clay and timber) now such materials are supplemented by a large range of man-made materials such as a range of steels, asbestos and plaster sheets, boards and plastics. While the range of forms and styles is greatly increased, choice is much more difficult requiring a knowledge of the performance and costs of using many materials and forms of structure and the techniques of their use.

The appearance of buildings is much affected by the materials used for claddings, particularly wall claddings; often roofs are not visible, especially on tall buildings or ones with flat roofs. Claddings vary considerably both in their qualities and in their costs. Some claddings have a self-finish which is generally acceptable; others need some further treatment such as paint or an additional material to cover them. Some are robust, others easily damaged; some keep their appearance for long periods without cleaning or resurfacing, while others rapidly become dirty and stained, depending on the cleanliness of the environment, the weather and the design details. For example, concrete, especially when not protected by overhanging roofs or other devices to keep the walls dry, tends to show dirt and to stain much more rapidly than brick. Some coverings such as glass, metal and plastic sheets tend to need frequent cleaning and renewal to preserve their appearance. Little use is now made of such finishes as decorative plasterwork and carved stone because of the high costs of the large amounts of skilled labour such finishes require.

The range of prices for different options is very wide. For example, cavity, fair-faced brickwork can be twice as expensive as sheeting on a timber frame, while solid reinforced concrete with a hammered finish can cost three times as much and a stone face ten times as much; glazed curtain walling is equally expensive [4]. Roofs vary in price in relation to shape, structure and finish, prices varying by a factor of four to five [4].

The treatment of space about buildings is also important for the appearance of the building. If the area is untreated it soon becomes unsightly. Prices vary by a factor of ten to twenty as between the cheapest surfaces such as gravel and the more ornamental paving slabs and bricks [4]. While grassing over is not that costly initially, regular attention is quite costly and is required frequently throughout the growing season. Planting with shrubs, trees and other plants also creates the need for regular maintenance.

Occupiers normally trade off appearance, comfort and convenience within their cost limits. Most families are content with a dwelling of traditional form and style. Forms and styles change over time. Few choose either the cheapest finishes or the most expensive. Today most accept a machine-made facing brick and concrete tiles. At one extreme some accept common fletton bricks as a cladding, at the other there is a demand for hand-made facing bricks and hand-made clay tiles, or even stone facings. Claddings of galvanized iron are unusual in Great Britain for dwellings but not unusual in some other countries. For example, in Australia many good class dwellings have galvanized iron sheets as a roof covering. Claddings, particularly wall claddings, cannot readily be changed once erected, except at considerable expense as compared with changing internal finishes. As a consequence savings on external finishes may be less economic than savings on internal finishes.

Industrialists tend to be more concerned with the convenience of the building for their production operations than with its appearance. Industrial and warehouse buildings are generally single storey sheds, the shape and height tailored to suit the nature of their opponents. Industrialists tend to choose the most economic claddings, except for the street elevation, often an office block, and the only part seen by the public.

In the commercial field more attention is usually given to the appearance of a building, although considerable weight is given to its convenience in use. Most attention is given to the street frontage, especially in the case of terraced buildings and especially to the ground floor. Unless a building is surrounded with extensive open space only the lower floors are generally noticed. The higher a building the less noticeable are upper floors and roofs, and the less impact they have on appearance. Attention is therefore usually concentrated on the first few floors. Shop frontages are mostly of glass, appearance being determined as much by the total impact of the display inside as by the facade. Rear and flank walls are usually given little attention. Hotels must also attract trade and may be designed in a spectacular form and style; most attention is usually given to the facade, particularly that of the lower floors. Offices vary from modest, almost domestic architecture, to soaring, eye-catching forms and styles, with claddings of brick, faced concrete or stone or curtain walling of metal and glass. Generally small traders and professional firms choose modest, low-cost forms and finishes, while the wealthy financial firms such as banks and insurance companies, and international traders such as oil companies choose expensive prestige buildings to demonstrate their wealth and solidity. High quality and opulent building even by the wealthiest firms is frequently confined to head office buildings in city centres. The quality and appearance of commercial buildings tends to be related to the prestige of the location; the greater this is the more likely that the sites will be occupied by firms achieving high added values per unit of floor space and able and willing to pay for high quality and appearance. Usually the most prestigious buildings are erected for owner-occupiers. Developers of rented property try to cater for a wide market – price is usually more important than high standards.

Public buildings also range widely in quality and appearance. Most attention is given to the appearance of buildings thought to confer prestige on the politicians who order and use them, such as legislative chambers and town halls. Less attention is given to the appearance of buildings providing supporting services. Value for money considerations are generally less compelling than for buildings in the private sector where personal responsibility for raising the finance is more acute. Often existing buildings are maintained at standards of quality and appearance far lower than those demanded for new buildings (Chapter 14).

It would appear that expenditure on the external appearance of buildings depends on considerations of costs as against satisfactions. The latter are probably measured by the commercial occupiers as the value of enhancing their reputation and of influencing potential customer opinion in favour of the product or service. Potential customers may be only a small part of the public at large and may not embrace many of the public most likely to be affected by the appearance of the building. Clearly the building's appearance is another aspect of external costs considered in earlier chapters.

While many members of the public lack the training to appreciate the finer points of form and finish, they are still affected by them and obtain some degree of satisfaction or dissatisfaction from the appearance of buildings. Most people probably react not just to the building but more to the building in its environment. Individual buildings may barely be noticed by many people if they fit unobtrusively into the street scene. If they stand out levels of satisfaction may be determined by the extent to which they enhance or spoil the street scene. The relationship between form, style and materials within and between buildings is important. Not only may a new building be found unattractive relative to surrounding buildings but existing buildings may be found unsatisfactory in relation to the new one. This is an inevitable problem of piece by piece redevelopment. As pointed out earlier, the public may only be conscious of the lower part of a building, especially where the building is in a terrace on a narrow street. It is difficult to determine what value the public is likely to place on the appearace of a building, but it can be thought of in terms of how much individuals would be prepared to sacrifice to obtain a level of satisfaction from the appearance of a building on each sighting, how often they would sight it and how many would be affected. Without some measure of the way the public values the appearance of buildings there is no basis for deciding to what extent developers should take public interest into consideration. In its absence official planners can only make a judgement on the basis of their own aesthetic values (Chapter 15).

11.12 DESIGN AND ERECTION

While the capital cost of a building depends largely on the design, which determines both the quality and quantity of materials and the labours involved in erection, it also depends on the erector and the relationship between the designer and erector, and on the client.

The client does not always adequately specify the nature and quality of building required and may not obtain an efficient solution to meet his needs. Some clients offer little guidance in the brief and rely on the designer offering successive options until an acceptable one is found. Since there is a practical limit to the number of options that there is time to design, this may not produce a satisfactory solution. Changing the design as erection proceeds tends to raise costs.

Designers need to be aware of the erection process. Very similar designs can make very different demands on the erection. Some design details are more time consuming to carry out than others. Erection time can be minimized by such factors as the repetition of design features, long continuous operations, simple fixings, the use of standard components and providing adequate operating space. For example, if the detailing of concrete work is repeated for each floor and for each building unit, the formwork can be reused; long continuous operations reduce preparation, cleaning up and idle time; using a limited number of standard units involves smaller stocks and less learning time, and the provision of suitable space for manoeuvering and fixing components reduces labour time [7].

It is far easier to estimate the quantity of materials from drawings and specifications than the quantity of labour. The drawings generally provide a better indication of the form of the building than how it is to be erected. The more the design departs from the familiar, the less certain the erector will tend to be about the erection process and the labour involved. The more uncertainty, the larger the contingency allowance the estimator will tend to add. If the uncertainties are very great, the erector may not be prepared to tender for a fixed sum but only on the basis of costs plus profits. Such terms provide no incentive to efficient construction and tight pricing.

The most accurate method of estimating the labours involved in erecting a building is usually considered to be that based on an erection plan and programme. This involves working out the erection process operation by operation, with the sequence and manning levels, and timetable [7]. While the plan may have to be modified on the job, it provides a basis of management, to which can be added rules for dealing with departures from the programme.

An effective plan can only be prepared if the erector has an adequate understanding of the design, for which complete design documents are needed.

While good communication between the designer and erector is necessary if full weight is to be given by the erector to the design economies, good communication is not itself sufficient to secure a satisfactory contract. Prices will also depend on such factors as market conditions, the keenness of erectors to obtain the contract, their efficiency, the quality of their work and the way they present the tender price. Erectors who are short of contracts, who regard the job as prestigious or who wish to establish goodwill will tend to reduce their allowance for overheads and profits to a minimum and to give a detailed consideration to the technical nature of the job and reflect this in tight costing. The less keen an erector is for the job, the less attention will generally be given to possible construction economies and to minimizing overheads, profits and contingency allowances. Choosing between tender offers is difficult because low prices may not reflect keenness and efficiency but low standards of work and juggling with the items in the tender price. This, for example, may involve pricing work likely to be underestimated in the bill at high unit rates and items likely to be reduced at low rates, so as to produce a final settlement price substantially higher than the tender price.

The quality of erection and the quality of the materials used are clearly important; poor materials and workmanship will tend to be reflected in building performance and in the costs of servicing and maintaining the building.

11.13   RISK AND UNCERTAINTY

However carefully a building is designed and erected some building and component failures are inevitable; no component will last for ever. Durability, however, depends not only on the quality of the building and its components but also on the quality of maintenance and servicing. Over time a knowledge has been built up of the behaviour of building components and of their likely durabilities. Estimates of maintenance costs can be based on programmes of preventive maintenance which aim to rationalize operations in an economic way, while just avoiding the need for emergency treatment (Chapter 12). Such programmes are based on past experience. Of course, in practice there is a wide range of durabilities even for similar components. The risk of a failure generally increases with time. While durabilities cannot be known with any great accuracy, the accuracy is usually sufficient, at least for traditional components, to provide a fair guide to maintenance and replacement costs, and hence to the ultimate costs of a design. Thus the risks associated with most traditional designs can be estimated with reasonable accuracy and if it is required funds can be set up to cover the costs of meeting the risks as and when they occur. In the case of risks such as fire, past experience can be used to estimate the probabilities of an incident occurring in a particular building. By coming together on a mutual basis, through a fire office, uncertain but possibly heavy costs can be converted into a small certain cost.

The performance of new materials, components and design features can only be assessed accurately over their period of use. In some cases the ageing process can be simulated but this is not generally a satisfactory substitute for the natural ageing process, which reflects many factors of exposure and use. Some guide to possible rates of failure can in some cases be obtained by analogy with existing components. However, even prolonged and thorough technical analysis does not necessarily provide an adequate measure of possible failures. For example, in the case of system house-building in Great Britain the Interdepartmental Committee set up to examine alternative methods approved no less than 101 systems as suitable for development and use by local authorities [8]. Many of these systems have failed in various ways, with costs of maintenance substantially greater than for traditional houses. Similarly despite expert technical appraisal many systems for high multistorey flatted blocks have failed. There does not appear to be any satisfactory substitute for the experience of performance in use; for this to be available some building users must be prepared to accept the uncertainties inseparable from innovations.

Many failures have been experienced with new materials, with new uses of existing materials and with new systems of construction. Failures have not been confined to dwellings: roofs on libraries and cathedrals and wall claddings on office buildings have all been casualties. Dr Allen (Beckerdike, Allen Partners) has been quoted as expecting a high level of failures in the materials used for filling cavity walls, for curtain walls, mastic seals, roofs and floor screeds [9]. Failures have also been reported in civil engineering works such as motorways, box-girder and concrete road bridges.

Risks are more acceptable than uncertainty because risks can be estimated and often covered by insurance; the cost is knowable at least in broad terms. While often innovations may be fully satisfactory and result in large savings, they may also result in considerable additional costs. Advance, however, depends on the uncertainties of innovation being accepted so that their performance can be ascertained.

REFERENCES

1. Stone, P. A. (1980) *Building Design Evaluation – Costs-in-use*, 3rd edn, E. & F. N. Spon, London.
2. Stone, P. A. (1970) *Urban Development in Britain*, National Institute for Economic and Social Research, Cambridge University Press, London.
3. Stone, P. A. (1962) Economics of Factory Buildings. Factory Building Studies No. 12, HMSO, London.

4. Davis, Belfield, & Everest, (1987) *Architects' and Builders' Price Book*, 112th edn, E. & F. N. Spon, London.
5. BRE Working Party Report (1975) *Energy Conservation*, Building Research Establishment CP 56/75, Watford.
6. Clifton Taylor, A. (1972) *The Pattern of English Building*, Faber & Faber, London.
7. Stone, P. A. (1983) *Building Economy*, 3rd edn, Pergamon Press, Oxford.
8. House Construction Post-war Building Studies (1944; 1946; 1948) *Nos 1, 23 and 24*, HMSO, London.
9. The Times, 17 August 1984.

12

Maintenance, rehabilitation and replacement

12.1 MAINTENANCE AND DURABILITY

The durability of building components varies considerably with their nature: paint lasts only a few years, while brick and stone units often last a century or longer. Durability also depends on use and on the quality of maintenance. Some materials such as glass and asbestos cement goods are brittle and easily damaged on impact, others such as reinforced concrete and stone are very strong. How long materials and components last depends on where they are and what forces they have to endure. Dampness, chemicals in the air, rain and ground, impact and rough usage, all tend to shorten the lives of materials. Durability can be extended through an adequate programme of maintenance, including cleaning.

Buildings, engineering works and even recognized building components consist of many subunits. Durability depends on the maintenance of the whole complex. For example, the functioning of a plumbing system depends not only on the fairly durable pipes, taps and valves but on such short life components as washers, while the durability of joinery, especially external joinery, depends on an adequate protective coat of paint or other protective coating without which water would soak into the wood and cause rot. If water penetrates a roof covering, it is likely to lead to the deterioration of the roof structure, services within it and to the contents and floors below. The cost of making good the damage to components as a result of inadequate maintenance can be many times the potential cost of the neglected maintenance. Consideration will be given in this chapter to some of the problems and options in maintaining properties.

Maintenance is necessary if a building is to retain its initial functional efficiency and appearance. It is not only plumbing, mechanical and electrical equipment which needs regular attention if it is to function efficiently. Windows and doors may cease to open smoothly and may allow required heat to escape; broken floors, loose handrails and even peeling paint may create hazards, causing injuries, contamination and loss of production. Similarly, inadequate maintenance, especially decoration spoils the appearance of a building and reduces the level of comfort.

Initially maintenance needs may arise from unsatisfactory design, the use of incompatible material and poor detailing, from inadequate workmanship during erection or from the use of inadequate materials. In the long run they will arise from wear and tear on the building and from the natural soiling and deterioration of the building components. The rate at which components deteriorate and get dirty depends on the nature of the component, its use and the environment. The costs of maintaining a building to the standards for which it was designed are considerable and need to be taken into consideration at the design stage (Chapter 11). For example, in a dirty atmosphere a painted wall requires much more attention to retain an acceptable appearance than an untreated brick one. Plastic floor tiles may have adequate durability where the traffic is light but may break up rapidly under heavy traffic or where chemicals and fats are dropped. The costs of maintenance are not just the costs of the building and cleaning work but also the costs of disturbance arising from the maintenance process which often involves vacating the area or room in which the work is to be carried out.

Disturbance costs can be an important element of the costs of maintenance. For example, where sterile conditions are necessary as in hospitals, kitchens and some production spaces, all surfaces will need to be cleaned frequently. Frequent cleaning can lead to shortening the life of the surface and more frequent replacement. While some cleaning can be carried out outside working hours, this is not always possible. It is usually necessary to vacate space for resurfacing walls and floors and repainting. Where space has to be vacated costs arise for moving furniture, equipment, materials and people; often there is a temporary loss of output and a cost for temporary space (Chapter 11).

There are often several options at the design stage, each of which has different construction, cleaning and maintenance and other running costs. The costs-in-use of the options can be compared to determine which provides the best value for money. For example, a painted surface might cost less for a complete redecoration than for a replacement by a more durable surface. The painted surface might need annual cleaning, touching up every 2 or 3 years and redecoration every 5 or 6 years. The alternative more durable surface might last 10 years with only annual cleaning. There might be no disturbance costs for cleaning but for other treatment disturbance costs would tend to arise. Since the durability of the options differs the costs-in-use comparisons would be made in terms of annual equivalents [1]. Of course the more expensive solution might be preferred on other grounds, such as appearance.

12.2   REMEDIAL AND PLANNED MAINTENANCE

While it is not possible to know when a particular building component will fail, it is possible to estimate the average life and probability of failure in relation to age. The inconveniences, hazards and costs of failure vary with the type of component. If one electric bulb amongst a group fails the level of light will only be slightly reduced but if a lift motor fails, at the very least vertical communications will be held up and at the worst there might be an accident. In some cases the labour costs of maintenance are considerable in relation to material costs and it may be more economic to economise on labour than on materials. For example, it may be cheaper to replace all the bulbs or tubes in a lighting system just before failures are expected to start, than to replace units as they fail.

Planned maintenance may not only be more economic than remedial maintenance in itself but it may result in lower disturbance costs. Often it can be carried out at times when disturbance will be at a minimum, possibly when the users of the building are not working. Moreover, the costs which might arise from the failure of a component such as interrupted production, injury, spoilt work and damage to other building components and equipment, may be avoided. The comparative costs of planned and remedial maintenance can readily be estimated by costs-in-use analysis.

12.3   REPAIR AND RENEWAL

Often there is a choice between repairing and renewing a component. A roof cover or a road surface may be patched or renewed, or a heating unit may be repaired or replaced. In most cases the costs of repair will be lower than that of replacement but a new component may last longer than a repaired one. Again the comparative costs can be analysed. Often, of course, the replacement component will be an improved model with perhaps lower operating costs. An allowance needs to be made in such cases for operating costs as well as maintenance costs.

In some cases the improvement in the design of the component may be so great that replacing the existing one may be economical even if it still functions satisfactorily. This situation would arise only if the annual running costs of the existing component exceed those of the replacement one by more than the annual equivalent of the initial costs of the replacement, minus any resale value of the existing component. Clearly the improvement has to be large for replacement to be worthwhile [1].

12.4   ALTERATIONS AND ADAPTATIONS

The need to consider alterations or adaptations to plant or building generally arises where new techniques have been developed or where the plant or building must be put to some other use. It is necessary to consider the costs of the change itself, the consequences for running and operating costs and the life of the building in its new form. For example, suppose an old school could be used by a printer. A choice has to be made between altering or adapting the building to the new circumstances or accepting the inconveniences of the building in its current form. An estimate is needed of all comparable costs-in-use. There might be many inconveniences unless extensive changes were made. The costs of alterations and the costs of running and operating in the building with or without alterations can generally be estimated fairly easily. Estimating how long the building would be operated in its new use is generally much more difficult, depending not only on the probable durability of the building but on the length of leases, on the rates of technological change, on the demand for the output from the building, competitive forces and so on.

Consider the following approach to the analysis as an example of the use of the costs-in-use technique to maintenance and renewal problems [1]. Suppose the costs of alterations or conversion were estimated to cost £C, the annual costs of running and operation after alterations £B as against £A if no changes were made and that the building was expected to be useful in its altered form for n years. The alteration would be cheaper if the annual savings were greater than the annual equivalent cost of the alterations.

As indicated above the greatest uncertainty usually lies in the future useful life of the altered building. The shorter this period needs to be to satisfy the criterion of cost reduction, the firmer the proposition. In order to avoid calculating for a range of lives, it is convenient to prepare a decision diagram, expressed in terms of the length of life at which savings and costs, in terms of annual equivalents, breakeven.

It is convenient to express both the annual savings from carrying out the alteration ($£A - £B$) and the annual equivalent costs of the alteration ($£C$) as ratios of the current annual running costs ($£A$). Thus

$$R_s = \frac{£A - £B}{£A} \text{ and } R_c = \frac{\text{the annual equivalent of } £C}{£A}$$

At the breakeven point $R_s = R_c$

The values of R_s and R_c lie between 0 and 1 and can be plotted against n. The values of n at which R_s and R_c are equal can be read off a decision diagram such as Fig. 12.1. For example, if A is 100 000, B is 80 000 and C is 200 000:

$$R_s = \frac{100\,000 - 80\,000}{100\,000} = 0.2$$

$$R_c = \frac{(a_n)^{-1} 200\,000}{100\,000} = 2\,(a_n)^{-1}$$

where $(a_n)^{-1}$ is the factor by which £C is converted to its annual equivalent; a_n is the present value of equal annual payments for n years.

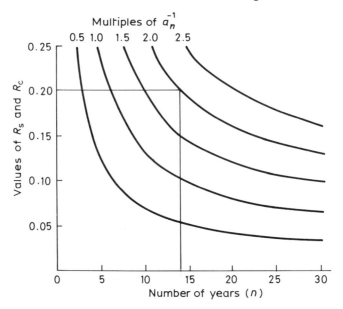

Figure 12.1 Break-even point between alterations and no action

Since R_s equals R_c at the breakeven point, the value of n is that which corresponds to $R_s = R_c = 0.2$ and the curve $2(a_n)^{-1}$. It will be seen from Fig. 12.1 that n would be about 14 years if the rate of discount was 5%. It might be thought that such a period is too long to be very certain. In some cases the alterations would create additional satisfaction from appearance and comfort. These would increase the value of $(A - B)$ and hence reduce n.

12.5 CONVERSION, REHABILITATION AND REBUILDING

In social buildings like houses, changes in the levels of satisfaction may be far more important than changes in running and operating costs. In commercial buildings also, such as shops and hotels, satisfaction from appearance and comfort may enhance trading prospects. The owner-occupier sets costs against satisfaction or the expected increase in profits. In some cases further lets or sales might depend on rehabilitations. Landlords could look at the difference in net revenue obtained by rehabilitation and compare it with the costs. Using a decision diagram similar to the one above they could work out how many years they would need to let the rehabilitated building to secure a reasonable return on their investment. Again, they would need to judge the likelihood of letting for such a period against market, planning and other factors.

An additional test needs to be applied to conversion, rehabilitation and

Table 12.1 Equivalent levels of expenditure on rehabilitation and new building (discount 5%)

Life expected for rehabilitated building (years)	Equivalent level of rebuilding cost (%)
10	41
20	66
30	81
40	91
50	97
60	100

alteration options, that is whether rebuilding would be more economical. While a new building will generally cost more to erect than the alteration or rehabilitation of an existing one, its running costs tend to be lower and operations cheaper to carry out because it is better fitted for its purpose than the original building, however much work is done on it. Further, its life will generally be longer and it may give more satisfaction.

Some idea of the scale of expenditure worth incurring instead of rebuilding is given above (Table 12.1). This table indicates the percentage of demolition and rebuilding costs which give the same equivalent annual costs if spent on rehabilitation, for various lifespans of a rehabilitated building with similar running and operating costs, assuming a rate of discount of 5%. If the rehabilitated building has an expected life of 10 years, the percentage would be 41, rising to 100% for an expected life of 60 years. Taking the life of a new building as infinite would make little difference to the percentages. The higher the rate of discount the greater the proportion of rebuildings costs it is worth spending on rehabilitation. Allowance must also be made for the difference in annual costs and in the value of satisfaction. The greater the net annual savings in favour of the rebuilding option, the less it is worthwhile spending on rehabilitation. In some cases conversion or rehabilitation may be preferred to rebuilding because the resources to finance the more costly option are not available.

12.6 CONSERVATION

Rehabilitation may be preferred to rebuilding in order to preserve the building in its present form. Exceptionally a building can be re-erected in its original form and style, at least externally, or a new building can be erected behind the original facade or a reproduction of it. Often it is difficult to obtain materials similar to those used in the old building, especially ones which have weathered to the preferred texture and colour. Such materials may only be available from old buildings which have been carefully demolished. Moreover, much more craftsmanship is usually required to re-erect buildings in their original form than in contemporary ones. The appropriate craftsmanship is generally in short supply. Clearly re-erecting buildings in their original form can add considerably to costs and it is generally cheaper to rehabilitate a building. Even so, it will usually be more expensive to preserve the building in its original form than simply make good neglected maintenance.

Often the preservation of old buildings and conservation of old areas is carried out for aesthetic and civic purposes, to create or preserve appearance and atmosphere which would not be obtained by repairing or rebuilding. It is, of course, still necessary to weigh up the costs in relation to the benefits, especially if total resources are limited. Resources used for conservation in one place cannot be used for conservation elsewhere, nor for increasing the built stock to meet additional needs. The volume of buildings and areas of aesthetic and historical interest is considerable and tends to grow as new styles and ages of development become accepted as worthy of preservation. Some conservation offers better value for money than others. Comparative tables could be drawn up of the comparable returns from alternative options of conservation and other development (Chapter 13).

The values to be considered include not only appearance and comfort to the occupier but the satisfaction obtained by the public from appearance, environmental impact and historical associations. The costs include not only the costs of building operations, the running costs of the buildings and the costs of carrying out operations within them, but also the costs of not using the land for some other purpose. Since resources are not without limit, priorities need to be established if resources are to be used to the best advantage.

Conflicts of interest and limitations of resources equally arise in the conservation of non-urban assets such as trees, historical earthworks and sanctuaries for flora and fauna. While a persuasive case can be made for their preservation, preservation has costs as well as benefits; some conservations provide better value for money than others. As more people become aware of assets in danger of being destroyed if conservation is not undertaken and their interests widen, the number and scale of conservation options increases. Inevitably the resources available are limited and resources used for conservation of natural phenomena and their sites are not also available for improving the environment in other ways.

Trees within development sites are often in conflict with buildings; their roots damage the foundations and leaves block gutters and cause rot where they pile up. Changing the layout of a building in order to be able to preserve a tree can be very expensive, often more expensive than moving the tree to a new site or replacing it with another mature tree.

Preserving natural sites has a cost in terms of what use might otherwise be made of them. There are often strong grounds for opposing the siting of reservoirs, airfields, damming rivers for power plant and other development, and in the past much damage has been done to the natural heritage. However, a balance needs to be struck between the costs and benefits of each preservation option, setting out the gains and losses from preservation and development.

As indicated earlier (Chapter 8) agricultural output in the EEC greatly exceeds demand. Output at the current level costs the consumer in taxation to cover price supports, grants, and in shop prices nearly double its costs on world markets. As a result while the costs of preserving natural habitats on farmland may be costly to the farmer, the real costs to the community, after allowances for taxation, are often only half the total financial cost. Similarly the real costs of preservation through not improving husbandry by drainage, ploughing up grasslands and so on are often far less than the subsidized prices the farmer might have obtained as a result of the improvement.

REFERENCES

1. Stone, P. A. (1980) *Building Design Evaluation – Costs-in-use* 3rd edn, E. & F. N. Spon, London.

13

Evaluating development and planning projects

Generally there is a large range of options for every development whether a simple building, a district or settlement; one of which may be 'no action'. As explained earlier (Chapter 2) resources are almost always limited if only because they have alternative uses. It is, therefore, rational to select the alternative which makes the best use of the resources, that is which gives the best value for money (Chapters 11 and 12).

13.1 COSTS AND BENEFITS

Resources imply materials and labour, the use of which creates costs as well as creating benefits. Benefits can take many different forms such as factors of appearance, convenience and function. Benefits for some will be disadvantages to others. Many of the benefits can be evaluated in money terms for example, usable daylight and solar gains, the usefulness of internal and external space, and the convenience of communications. Other benefits are intangible and difficult to evaluate in money terms; for example, it is difficult to put a valuation on benefits such as appearance and lack of noise. Evaluation is sometimes possible by using a measure of what those people affected would be prepared to pay in order to gain a satisfaction or avoid a dissatisfaction. Considerable ingenuity has been used in developing these 'shadow prices'. Another approach is to list the intangible satisfactions and dissatisfactions against the measurable costs of the different options so that the decision-taker can decide whether he is prepared to meet the additional costs in order to secure the additional benefits. For example, a person having a house built for personal use might have to decide whether a tree was worth preserving despite additional costs in constructing the house.

Benefits and costs arise in different ways and at different levels to different groups of people. There may be a net gain to the occupiers of a proposed development and net costs to various groups outside the development. The occupiers may value the satisfaction they obtain from the form and shape of the development, from its convenience in use and from its access and communications at more than the costs of land, design, construction, maintenance and servicing. Occupants of surrounding sites may feel that the dissatisfaction from the intrusion of the development, from the noise, dust and traffic it generates outweighs any advantages. Local service undertakings may find that the additional demand the development creates is too great for the capacity of their installations and that the costs of carrying out additional development outweighs the revenue likely to be derived from the new development. The sum of the external costs may be greater than the gains to the developer and its occupants.

Several techniques have been developed to assist in evaluating plans and designs. They have in common the analysis and evaluation of costs and benefits, and the equating of streams of costs and benefits arising over time. Differences in technique arise from differences in purpose, and the treatment of errors of estimating.

13.2 DECISION TECHNIQUES FOR COMPARING DEVELOPMENT AND PLANNING OPTIONS

There are two groups of decision techniques applicable to the economic analysis of planning and design projects [1]. The first group is concerned with the best means to a given end; that is the best plan or design from the point of view of value for money to solve a particular planning or design problem. The techniques are variously known as costs-in-use, life-cycle costing, total costs, ultimate costs analysis and terotechnology. They were developed independently as analytical solutions to slightly different problems. The second group, which includes cost–benefit analysis, cost-effectiveness and threshold analysis, are concerned with ends as well as means. They are really investment tools concerned not only with the plan or design which gives the best value for money but also with which of the projects would make the best use of the available resources and give the highest return.

The techniques are concerned with setting the costs of construction, maintenance, renewals and other servicing costs over the life of a development against the benefits of function, convenience and appearance. As far as possible each cost and benefit is evaluated in money terms. In some techniques, for example, costs-in-use, each item is evaluated separately and expressed in a balance sheet together with its possible errors of estimate [1]. This facilitates both the comparison of cost differences between plans and designs with allowance for the effect of possible errors in the estimates and taking into account items for which no money value is possible. Generally it is found that the plans and designs to be compared contain large common elements, even if the quantities are different: common structural elements and engineering services, for example. This has the effect of reducing the comparative errors, so that they are small in relation to the cost–benefit differences. Differences which cannot be valued in money terms can be set against the differences which can be valued in that way, the decision can then be made on whether the differences in qualitative factors, for example, appearance, are worth the additional costs of construction and operation (Chapters 11 and 12).

Where the developer is concerned with the development that yields the best return on the available capital, for example the most cost-effective road or town expansion scheme under consideration, a measure in money value is needed for each item and a wide range of assumptions are generally necessary. The criterion becomes the internal rate of interest on the investment. Errors of estimate are taken into account by variation analysis, that is by calculating the internal rate of interest over a range of assumptions.

Evaluating the consequences of planning alternatives is worthwhile even if no common measure is applied to the items. Evaluation matrices are often prepared for the environmental consequences of developments such as major roads, for which evaluation in money terms is difficult or impossible. The valuation exposes the items which need to be considered and sets them against costs and other benefits.

Cost–benefit analysis is more powerful than costs-in-use but more difficult to use. It is not just concerned with which alternative gives the best value for money but with which gives the best return on capital. Thus it can be used to determine which of the possible projects to finance in order to maximize the return from a given amount of capital or public resources. It is thus similar to discounted cash flow, a technique widely used in the business sector, where all costs and returns can readily be measured in monetary terms. In the public and community sectors it is used to find which group of developments is likely to make the best use of available public resources. Problems arise in obtaining a cash value for the intangibles.

With cost–benefit analysis the rate of discount is determined by the analysis, but for costs-in-use it has to be chosen. In either case the rate of discount affects the weight given to the items. The higher the rate, the less weight is given to costs and benefits arising well into the future. This tends to lead to the choice between alternatives being based on short-term considerations. The lower the rate of discount the more weight is given to items in the future. At a zero rate of discount equal weight is given to initial costs and benefits and to those in the future.

In costs-in-use analysis the costs and benefits are usually expressed either as equivalent first costs or equivalent annual costs. The relative worths are naturally not affected by the type of equivalent used. The choice depends more on whether the decision-taker is more interested in capital costs or annual costs. In choosing the rate of discount an allowance is necessary for inflation and taxation. As explained earlier inflation reduces the value of capital, lenders add an allowance for inflation to the rate of interest, so that a nominal rate of interest of 15% when inflation is running at 10% implies a real rate of interest of about 5% (Chapter 3). In the business sector interest is charged against tax, so that a rate of interest of 12% implies at current rates of taxation a net rate of about 8%. A rate of discount is generally composed of a pure rate of discount together with a risk premium, the amount of which depends on the expected likely risk of failure. A highly speculative business venture would generally be discounted at a rate of interest which allowed for a high risk factor, while a community venture would be discounted at little more than the pure rate of interest.

13.3 SECTORS OF SOCIETY AFFECTED BY DEVELOPMENT

It was explained earlier that a development affects different sectors of society in different ways (Chapter 3). In addition to initial and running costs over the life of a development met by the developer and occupier, external costs arise for other sectors. Generally the main benefits are enjoyed by the occupier but other sectors may also obtain benefits, some of which will be negative and contribute to external costs. The major sectors concerned with a development include the developer, the occupier, the local authority, central government and its agencies, members of the public and the community as a whole.

13.4 DEVELOPERS AND OCCUPIERS

It was explained earlier that the costs which developers can bear depend on the prices which occupiers are prepared to pay for the resulting property (Chapter 3). The prices depend both on the qualities of the properties and their location. In evaluating the worth of a property, potential occupiers will try to take into consideration the costs they will have to bear, including rents or amortized purchase costs, rates, heating, lighting, ventilation, maintenance, cleaning, insurance and other service costs arising from occupying the building and access to it. They will attempt to set against the costs the benefits they expect to enjoy such as savings on their operations, additional business, prestige and goodwill, comfort, convenience and aesthetic pleasure (Chapter 3). In some cases, of course, the occupier will also be the developer.

Location tends to be an important factor in determining value, a value which relates to the site rather than the building (Chapter 3). The site value depends not only on geographical position but on the types and qualities of development in the vicinity of the site. Where the site is large enough to develop an estate, district or settlement, the developer determines a large part of site values by the way he lays out the development, the infrastructure and buildings he provides or licences and even the types of occupiers to whom he sells or leases the properties. Good access and parking facilities, attractive buildings, open space and other amenities are attractive in varying degrees to different types of occupier. For example, commercial occupiers tend to place a value on their neighbours; being next to a successful chain store justifies a higher rent than having a boot repairer or a food take-away shop as a neighbour.

While developers are concerned with financial costs and returns, as are occupiers in the business sector, those in the private sector are concerned partly with financial costs and partly with non-monetary satisfactions and dissatisfactions. For example, the householder meets the costs of a property as a rent, or as interest and repayments on a mortgage or loss of capital and interest on it, and the costs of maintenance and other services. All these costs have monetary values. The benefits to set against these costs include some, such as costs of travelling to work, school, shopping and so on, which can be expressed in monetary terms, and others such as satisfactions from the environment, and the comforts and convenience from the dwelling, which are intangible. The householder can only ask whether the monetary differences between alternative options are worth more or less than the differences in intangible satisfactions and trade them off against costs and each other.

The public developer of buildings does not necessarily have to balance financial returns exactly against costs as the private developer does, since losses can be covered by subsidies paid from general taxation and the rates. Some account can therefore be taken of the desirability of providing amenities which do not produce a monetary return.

13.5 PUBLIC AUTHORITIES AND LOCAL PUBLIC SERVICES

While the private developer usually provides access roads to the estate and estate utility services, it generally falls to county and district councils to provide for the inhabitants and users of the estate the main infrastructure, including open space and public services such as schools, local health and social services. The central government provides hospitals and other services. The costs of these public services are borne partly by the rates and partly by general taxation, that is by the community. The public utility organizations are also affected by developments through the need to provide further infrastructure such as water, sewage and power networks and terminal facilities. The costs of these and their operation will affect the charges such bodies level against users and possible government financial policy.

13.6 THE COMMUNITY

In the long run developments have consequences for the community as rate and tax payers and as customers of the public utility organizations. In addition, of course, the community enjoys any wider advantages developments may bring such as a more attractive built environment and better services but suffers disadvantages such as congestion and pollution.

13.7 NATIONAL ECONOMY

From the point of view of the national economy it is real costs and benefits which need to be considered together with the total impact of development on the economy. The costs of land, grants, subsidies and taxes represent payments from one part of the community to another, that is they are transfer payments and do not measure the consumption of real resources. Similarly some of the benefits enjoyed by one group are costs to others. It is the balance between the real costs, the value of resources used, and the additional national welfare, real output and net satisfactions which needs to be considered in deciding which option is best for the country. It is not possible to detect all the consequences from an analysis of individual developments. A substantial rise in public development in aggregate might result in such consequences as additional imports, additional public borrowing, a rise in interest rates and higher prices (Chapter 2).

13.8 OFFICIAL PLANNING DECISIONS

Each sector of the community has to decide between development options in relation to the costs and benefits to itself; indeed it will generally not be able to assess the external costs and benefits to others. Here lie the seeds of conflict and the need for official planning machinery to make an overall assessment of the costs and benefits, and to trace their consequences through the various sectors, in order to find out which options give the best value for money and minimize the penalties that some sectors may need to bear, and to seek more generally acceptable planning solutions.

13.9 PLANNING BALANCE SHEETS – COSTS AND BENEFITS

In order to find which development option offers the best value for money and is fair as between those affected by it, it is necessary to prepare comparative balance sheets in terms of equivalent costs-in-use; discounted present costs or annual equivalent costs [1]. The form such comparative balance sheets might take is indicated below in generic terms (Table 13.1). The most suitable form and detail depends on the nature of the development being considered. In some cases the consequences might be so limited that it would be clear from a preliminary assessment that some cost and value sectors and items could be eliminated, while in other cases the item headings would need to be detailed out into subheadings. Clearly items common to the

Table 13.1 Annual equivalent costs and benefits of development options

Sector	Items of costs and benefits	Development options 1, 2, 3, 4, 5 ... n
Developers	1. Construction 2. Fees, interest, profits 3. Land	
	4. Total development costs 5. Equivalent sale value or rent	
Occupiers	5. As above 6. Rates 7. Building maintenance, servicing and management 8. Consequences for costs of operating within building 9. Taxes less grants	
	10. Total occupiers costs 11. Gain or loss of net output/satisfactions	
Local government	12. Construction of buildings, works and other infrastructure 13. Land for 12 14. Maintenance, servicing and management for 12 15. Additional costs of other services	
	16. Total additional costs to L.A.s 17. Total additional revenue from rates, sales and grants 18. Value of net addition to infrastructure	
Central government	19. Construction of buildings, works and other infrastructure 20. Land for 19 21. Maintenance, servicing and management of 19 22. Additional costs of other services 23. Grants to other public authorities	
	24. Total additional cost to central government 25. Additional tax revenue and sales revenue 26. Value of net additions to infrastructure	
Public utilities	27. Construction of buildings, works and other infrastructure 28. Land for 27 29. Maintenance, servicing and management of 27	
	30. Total additional costs to public utilities 31. Total additional revenue 32. Value of net additions to infrastructure	
Community external to development option	33. Additional costs for transport, and other goods and services 34. Additional rates, taxes and public utility charges 35. Gain from land sales 36. Balance in value of satisfactions/losses from option 37. Value of total consequences of option to community	

Table 13.1 *Cont.*

Sector	Items of costs and benefits	Development options 1, 2, 3, 4, 5 . . . n
National economy	38. Development 1 + 12 + 19 + 27	
	39. Maintenance, servicing and management 7 + 14 + 21 + 29	
	40. Other real costs 2 + 8 + 15 + 22 + 33	
	41. Intangibles 11 + 36	
	42. Total real costs	
	43. Value of net additions to built environment 5 + 18 + 26 + 32	

options being considered or little different could be eliminated to keep the comparisons as simple as possible. In making comparisons, possible errors of estimate need to be considered.

Such balance sheets assist in indicating which options are likely to provide the best returns from the resources used. For example, development on one side of a settlement might be uneconomic because it required utility services beyond the threshold current facilities could meet, while on the opposite side of the settlement there might be spare capacity. It would be necessary to take into account whether the development was likely to be a one-off project or the first of a series. Planning balance sheets cannot be as precise as costs-in-use comparisons made for a developer or occupier because of the need to evaluate costs and benefits to the community as a whole.

REFERENCES

1. Stone, P. A. (1980) *Building Design Evaluation – Costs-in-use*, 3rd edn, E. & F. N. Spon, London.

PART FIVE

Financial and planning machinery

14

Demand and resource allocation

14.1 NEED AND SUPPLY OF RESOURCES FOR THE BUILT ENVIRONMENT

The volume of resources needed to provide and maintain the built environment is greater than is generally available (Chapter 5). As a result potential demand for the built environment exceeds supply and standards are lower than is generally thought desirable. The evidence available points to a considerable backlog of desirable construction work, particularly maintenance and rehabilitation (Chapter 5). At the same time the construction industry is under-employed. Because of inadequate maintenance some built assets eventually cost much more to maintain than necessary, give a poorer service or cease to be useful at a prematurely early age. This chapter considers why the allocation of resources is inadequate and why some resources are used in an uneconomic way.

14.2 SECTORS OF THE BUILT ENVIRONMENT

Most sectors of the economy have a responsibility for the development and servicing of some of the built environment (Chapter 3). There is a wide variety of economic objectives, of sources of finance and of criteria for acquiring and servicing property. It is convenient to divide the economy into sectors according to their approach to the built environment: owner-occupied housing; private rented housing; public rented housing; other public authorities such as those for the public estate, hospital services, highways and education; public corporations for the supply of such services as water, energy, and transport and the business sector, mainly industry and commerce.

14.3 OWNER-OCCUPIED HOUSING

The owner-occupier of a dwelling obtains satisfaction both from living in it and from its investment potential. Up to a point the greater the resources put into a dwelling the greater the comfort, convenience and satisfactory appearance and the larger the investment potential. Thus there is an incentive to plough in as large a proportion of wealth into house purchase as can be afforded and will yield adequate additional satisfactions.

Few households can find the capital from their own resources to purchase their first dwelling. Borrowing capital for this purpose is facilitated by the financial institutes, (Chapter 3). They all compete to lend on mortgages to potential house purchasers. Generally they will lend 80–90% of the value of the property, exceptionally more, subject to the borrower's potential ability to service the loan.

The cost of borrowing for house purchase is reduced by tax relief on interest paid in respect of (currently) the first £30 000 borrowed on the principal dwelling; similar relief is allowed on loans for house improvement. The consequence of the tax relief is to increase the financial return to owners who borrow to facilitate purchase and who do not have offsetting income from investments. The tax concession is of particular value to first time buyers and in the early years of a mortgage when interest is high and earnings generally low. Furthermore, capital gains on the principal dwelling are not taxed, so that the owners of such dwellings retain the full real value. Particularly in recent years house prices have tended to rise faster than the rate of inflation, being broadly related to rises in the level of earnings.

Many households raise their housing standards broadly in step with their incomes, either by selling and purchasing a dwelling of a higher standard or by improving and extending the dwelling they currently occupy. Such house owners tend to maintain their property to a high standard and most expect the price of their property to continue to rise in real terms. However, prices of dwellings, as of other buildings, can move in both directions. Market prices depend on supply and demand in a locality and on the condition of the dwelling. The popularity of housing areas can change rapidly in a short time as the quality of its internal and external environment changes. Migration can change the level of demand relative to the stock. Considerable shifts in house prices can take place.

While the price of dwellings tends to rise with improvements, it tends to fall if maintenance is neglected and if no effort is made to up-date fixtures and fittings in line with changing fashions and expectations.

While the current tax regime in this country assists the purchase of a dwelling, it discourages maintenance and improvement work, both of which are subject to VAT at 15%. Such work, even without VAT tends to be considerably more expensive than the equivalent amount of new work undertaken at the time of constructing a dwelling.

Much maintenance and improvement work is within the scope of house-holds especially now that preprocessed materials, easily fitted components, together with improved tools and techniques have considerably reduced the skill content of much of the work. Given the incentive of rising costs and an increased capacity to tackle DIY work, it is not surprising that a great deal of maintenance and improvement work is now carried out by householders with considerable savings in costs. It is estimated by the National Home Improve-ment Council that about two-fifths of such work is now carried out by the householder but this estimate appears high in relation to other estimates (Chapter 5).

The incentive to maintain dwellings up to contemporary standards probably declines with the age of the householder. As householders become older they are probably less inclined to make changes, to face the disturbance of building work and to put perhaps decreasing financial resources into a dwelling they have no intention of selling. They also become less able to carry out the work themselves. Householders purchasing a dwelling do not always appreciate the scale of the costs of maintaining standards and find it difficult to finance such work. When finance is tight it is generally easier to postpone maintenance and upgrading work than expenditure on other aspects of living. For these reasons the owner-occupied dwellings of older and poorer households tend to be those most likely to fall into decay or to lack improvements now necessary to maintain the value of dwellings.

14.4 PRIVATE RENTED HOUSING

Most dwellings rented privately are expected by their owners to cover their management and maintenance costs and provide a market return on the capital invested in them. Most rents have been controlled by government regulations since the first world war (1915), and rents are now generally considerably below economic costs. As a consequence little capital is put into constructing dwellings for rent, except in the public sector; both the number and proportion of dwellings in the private rented sector have fallen consider-ably, from about 90% before rent controls were introduced to about one-tenth of that proportion now [1].

Leases for dwellings do not usually require tenants to accept responsibility for maintenance and improvements, although some may require the tenant to carry out internal decoration and minor repairs. Tenants are not generally compensated, when they vacate their dwelling, for improvements they have made and are generally reluctant to pay for repairs and improvements, particularly short-term tenants. Landlords are also reluctant to spend money on repairs and improvements when rents do not cover economic costs. Many landlords are themselves not well off and depend on rents to supplement their incomes. As a result rented dwellings in the private sector tend not to be improved to current standards and often are not adequately maintained; the greater the delay in maintenance, the greater the costs and the use of resources. Many eventually become unfit for occupation and are condemned as slums.

The government has an incentive to encourage maintenance and to arrest the deterioration of the housing stock because in the long run it is advantageous to maintain a stock of dwellings for renting; grants and subsidies are sometimes offered to rehabilitate and replace deteriorating stock (Chapter 10). However, the government has never accepted that taxing maintenance and improvement work discourages the maintenance of a good quality stock or considered tax relief for such work. While grants encourage the improvement of dwellings, they may also encourage owners to put off such work in the hope of future grant payments.

14.5 CONTROL OF LOCAL GOVERNMENT EXPENDITURE

Before considering public rented housing it is necessary to consider how the central government controls the expenditure of local authorities. Some of the services will be considered in more detail later. Capital and revenue expenditure are dealt with separately.

The present controls on capital expenditure in England (there are variations in relation to Wales) were introduced in 1981–82 under the *Local Government, Planning and Land Act, 1980*, but there have been some modifications since they were first introduced. The government's objectives include the control of aggregate local authority capital expenditure in line with its annual public expenditure plans, the encouragement of the disposal of assets, expenditure in line with government priorities for the services concerned and the promotion of cost-effective capital programmes [2]. There are now six blocks of capital expenditure covering most local expenditure other than law and order, but the allocations for each block can generally be moved from block to block. While allocations are on an annual basis in relation to agreed programmes, local authorities can carry forward or anticipate 10% of the allocations from adjacent years and can use prescribed proportions of capital receipts and other moneys. Additional allocations may be made if national expenditure is below the level required by central government.

Revenue expenditure is supported by the central government through the Rate Support Grant. This is allocated to local authorities on a basis which attempts to take account of local need but no reliable or equitable basis of allocation has ever been devised. The Rate Support Grant is not earmarked for particular services or projects within them. Total local authority expenditure is limited by central government by cash limits on expenditure and rate-capping.

It is perhaps not surprising to find that the Audit Commission does not think that the systems give the government the control it seeks.

The Commission considers that it encourages resources available for capital expenditure to be wasted in various directions [2]. The consequences of the short time horizon (1 year) and abrupt changes in annual capital programmes are thought to lead to rushed work, inadequately evaluated projects and wasted resources [2]. The system appears to do little to encourage cost-effectiveness or the adequate maintenance of the stock.

Local authority revenue expenditure is financed from the rate support grant, the rates and to a small extent fees. Maintenance can always be postponed when other claims for expenditure are pressing. In the long run if maintenance is neglected more expensive renovation becomes necessary. This can be treated as a capital project but inevitably when capital expenditure is limited, it reduces the amount available for new capital development [3].

14.6   PUBLIC RENTED HOUSING

Public rented housing is provided mainly by local authorities but there is also public support for housing associations. Within a context set by central government, local housing authorities are responsible for deciding the quantity, quality and location of their housing estates. The rents charged for such housing do not generally cover the economic costs and are subsidized both through central government housing grants and from the rates. Total revenues are not always sufficient to cover amortization and management costs, let alone contribute to maintenance costs. Rent levels and most decisions about public housing are decided on political rather than economic grounds.

Central government issues advice on the size and quality of individual dwellings and prices; these used to be mandatory but now only indicative costs are provided [4]. Price criteria are generally limited to initial costs with little or no consideration of maintenance and running costs. It is difficult to control quality and cost by regulation. Quality and cost depend on the design criteria (Chapter 11).

Local authority capital expenditure on housing is vetted by central government in this country through the Housing Investment Programme (HIP) [5]. Central government is concerned not only with the quantity and quality of the stock of local authority housing but also with the contribution local authority expenditure makes to the total public expenditure and to public borrowing. The housing investment programmes of local authorities have to be agreed with central government for a period of 2 or 3 years ahead but sanction is on an annual basis. In recent years restraining public expenditure and borrowing has been considered more important than increasing the stock of local authority housing. The smaller Housing Association Programme is also subject to central government financial control.

Rehabilitation and improvement expenditure is included in capital expenditure, while maintenance expenditure is treated as revenue expenditure. This is not subject to detailed control by central government but is influenced as part of revenue expenditure through government action to limit rate support grant, cash limits on local government expenditure and rate-capping.

With less money to spend, local authorities look for expenditure which can be postponed. Generally they are reluctant to lay-off staff and prefer to postpone purchases and outside contracts. In the case of housing maintenance this tends to result in the postponement of cyclical work, such as external painting, resurfacing flat roofs and paved areas and rewiring.

The financial controls imposed by central government do not preclude the application of economic criteria to decisions on the planning, location, design and maintenance of public authority housing but they provide little incentive to their use and tend to make their application more difficult. Local authorities are particularly critical of the short timespan of sanctioned expenditure – 1 year. Capital investment programmes are generally long-term, lasting several years and have long lead times. Cutting back or hastening the pace of committed projects can be both difficult and expensive [5]. The short-term nature of HIP allocation also tends to encourage short term projects at the expense of possibly more desirable longer term ones. In times of financial stringency HIP allocations tend to be considerably less than planned programmes of development and improvement. Essential work may be held up, increasing subsequent costs and delaying urgent housing provision. Dwellings emptied for rehabilitation may have to be left unused. Because of long lead times and the long-term nature of housing projects, additional funds, especially if short-term, tend to be spent uneconomically. Whatever the scale of expenditure on housing national expenditure policies can support, housing authorities need firm budgetting over several years, if they are to plan expenditure effectively. Firm forward budgets are difficult for central government to provide if housing expenditure is used for marginal adjustments to national capital expenditure.

Difficulties also arise from the treatment of repairs and maintenance expenditure in part as capital and in part as revenue expenditure. As argued earlier, if economical designs are to be produced, life-cycle costs (costs-in-use) need to be considered (Chapter 11). Equally if the most economic use of housing funds is to be made, it is necessary to consider new building, improvements and repairs together (Chapter 12). Indeed, there are often interactions between management services and building work. The division of housing resources often impeded the economic use of the developments.

Local authorities are critical of the cost yardsticks which are blamed for false economies [5]. On the other hand, there appears to be little evidence that life-cycle costs are considered in any formal way either in the design of new buildings or in rehabilitation and improvement work [5]. A better understanding is needed of what can be achieved and how. Such an understanding has to go well beyond the designers and housing managers, to include those responsible for allocating finance.

14.7 OTHER PUBLIC AUTHORITY ORGANIZATIONS

Public authorities, both central and local, are concerned with many aspects of the built environment. Central government, for example, is concerned with the management of its own estate of properties and the health service, as well as with services in which local authorities play a part such as highways and education. Many of the points made about the organization of public housing apply equally to these other services. There are, however, a number of differences in organization which affect the way resources are used. A few examples of services will indicate the problems.

14.8 CENTRAL GOVERNMENT ESTATE

This includes offices, workshops, stores and so on owned by the central government and used in administration and in the provision of services such as defence. The estate is now managed by a quango, the Property Services Agency (PSA). It operates through a territorial organization with regional and area offices. Government departments are responsible for expenditure on specialized new works. For the rest they pay rent for their accommodation, an allowance for which is made in their annual allocation of expenditure. Funds for the PSA are allocated annually in the course of the Public Expenditure Survey as with other government agencies and departments. The levels of funding are related to levels of expenditure in earlier years. The allocation of funds to the regions is based on bids. Thus the criteria for allocating funds is based more on government expediency for the control of its overall expenditure and borrowing than for the efficient management of the PSA resources. It is claimed, for example, that funds for maintaining the stock are quite inadequate [5]. Little attempt appears to be made to secure cost effective design and management of property. As it is currently organized there is little incentive towards economic efficiency and no test of the cost-effectiveness of its operations [5].

It is generally accepted that economic efficiency in large organizations can usually be improved by dividing the organization into separate cost centres, each of which charges market prices for its services. Each can measure its effectiveness in terms of the return it obtains on the capital it employs. Economic discipline is reinforced by providing that customers within the organization can purchase goods and services in the market if this is in their interest [6].

If, for example, this discipline were applied to the PSA, the Treasury would deem that it owned the total shares in the PSA, which would in turn be deemed to own the Central Government Estate, together with an appropriate amount of working capital. The Treasury would look for a market rate of return on its share holding. The PSA would manage the estate, letting to government departments at market rents and conditions, with the power to let surplus property to other tenants. The departments would be able to rent from other landlords if this were more economical. Employment and rewards to the staff might be related to economic performance.

14.9   HOSPITAL SERVICE BUILDING

This service is again operated through a quango but for this quango, unlike the PSA, property management is only a small and subsidiary part of the total operation. The service operates through regional and district organizations. Again funds are allocated on an annual basis, largely in relation to previous levels of expenditure, through the Public Expenditure Survey [5]. The regional distribution takes account of regional demand on the hospital service, its quality and expenditure levels. The greater part of expenditure is on hospital staff and supplies. When funds are short it is likely to be the maintenance of the building stock which is postponed, particularly preventive and cyclical maintenance which is generally carried out on a contract basis.

Annual funding encourages putting aside funds to meet contingencies later in the year; unused balances being released for use at the end of the year when there is little time to plan their most effective use. The amount of resources dispersed in this way can be quite large since such contingency funds are set up at central, regional and district levels.

Central government gives some attention to the economic use of resources spent on building development. Cost limits are set for the many types of hospital buildings and building notes are issued describing cost-effective methods of maintaining and operating buildings and appropriate methods of costs-in-use analysis. Their application is left to the hospital service.

It would be possible to set up cost centres for the management of the property on lines not dissimilar to those described for the PSA but it would be more difficult to introduce market discipline in the absence of a large private sector hospital service to provide a yardstick.

14.10   HIGHWAYS

Responsibility for highways, roads and bridges, is divided between central government and the two tiers of local government. Trunk roads, including motorways, are the responsibility of central government, which decides what roads are necessary and the appropriate standards. They are responsible for design, construction and servicing but use private consultants for much of the design work and county councils as agents for maintenance. Other roads are the responsibility, in the main, of shire counties, and in the past, metropolitan counties. Counties may delegate some responsibility to district councils.

The budget for highways is also fixed annually in the course of the Public Expenditure Survey in relation to previous years expenditure and current financial policy, the division of the funds is left to the discretion of the administrating department [5]. Cost–benefit analysis is used to determine the acceptability and priority of schemes for new trunk roads but questions have been raised as to whether the methods of evaluating road benefits as trade offs are satisfactory, and whether adequate allowance is made for the maintenance consequences of different designs. It is suggested that a higher specification would be more cost-effective [5]. Of course, higher and more expensive standards would reduce the length of road which could be financed without increasing the budget. Most of the maintenance costs are charged to capital, the costs charged to revenue are mainly for servicing.

The length of local roads greatly exceeds that of trunk roads. Additions to the stock are mainly estate roads built by estate developers and subsequently accepted by the local authorities. While roads once built generally remain in existence, they are reconstructed, realigned and widened as the need arises.

The funds for the care of local roads are derived from the rate support grant, the transport supplementary grant and local rates. The central government considers the capital programmes put forward by the counties who decide broad priorities and road design on the basis of cost–benefit analysis. Over half the local expenditure on roads is on minor maintenance and particularly servicing, with declining expenditure on major repairs [5]. It is suggested that while the methods of assessment and decision making are adequate, a lack of funds is resulting in the erosion of road surfaces and even foundations, and creating a backlog of expensive work, so that maintenance is no longer cost effective [5]. The revenue expenditure on local roads is allocated by local authorities from their general revenue funds.

14.11 EDUCATION BUILDINGS

Overall responsibility for education lies with the central government but control lies with the University Grants Committee (another quango) and, for non-university education, the local education authorities, mainly the counties but also some London and Metropolitan boroughs and districts. Non-university education is funded from the rates, rate support grant and to a small extent fees.

Capital expenditure is broadly controlled by central government who approve new projects on a value for money basis [5]. Schemes which comply with cost guidelines issued by the central government receive automatic approval. The University Grants Committee also issues 'Notes on control and guidance' setting out planning and cost norms.

Maintenance expenditure for local authority education buildings are derived from the authorities' revenue allocated to education. Again the main revenue costs of local education are the costs of staff and equipment, against which building maintenance must compete for funds. As in the case of other public sector buildings, when funds are tight it tends to be cyclical and other planned maintenance which is postponed. Again a large backlog of maintenance work is reported to be building up. Local authorities could hive-off property management on lines similar to those described for the PSA.

14.12   FINANCIAL CONTROL OF PROPERTY FOR PUBLIC SERVICES

Clearly neither public nor private organizations have unlimited funds and there are occasions when funds are insufficient to finance all the new work and the maintenance work which is desirable. The total allocation is generally related to anticipated revenue and borrowing in relation to the total demand for funds. Where the supply of funds is inadequate to meet demand the best value for money is obtained by giving priority to projects giving the highest returns. Clearly, capital and revenue projects should be considered together Central government has already gone a long way to create the machinery for deciding priorities. Systems for allocating capital funds such as Housing Investment Programmes and Transport Policy Programmes could be extended to cover maintenance as well as capital expenditure and to other policy areas, and applied to central government departments and quangos as well as to local authorities. Firm allocations need to be extended from 1 to 3 to 5 years. The expenditure on the public built environment is small enough to leave ample scope for adjusting total public expenditure in other areas where the consequences of a poor allocation of funds on the economic use of resources are less.

As long as there is common funding for a whole service, the maintenance of building and infrastructure are at risk of being squeezed, since maintenance is so easy to postpone. Local authorities and other public organizations could set up property units with separate funding. These could be operated on the lines of property companies as indicated for the PSA, with the closest possible links with the property market to provide incentive to efficiency.

14.13   PUBLIC CORPORATIONS

Public corporations such as those for water, transport and energy differ from the quangos discussed earlier in that they sell goods and services they produce in the market. They are not, however, subject to full market forces since most enjoy at least a partial monopoly of supply, they do not compete in the market for finance, this is provided by central government, and they are subject to government control over investment and pricing.

The funds available for capital development generally depend on government policy on public expenditure and borrowing. Usually the corporations are set target rates of return on the capital they use. In some cases the government sets price levels high enough to create surpluses to enable past government debt to be repaid and in in some cases the government provides subsidies.

The external financing limits are set annually creating problems not dissimilar to those already discussed in relation to central and local government departments. For example, a water authority may, towards the end of the financial year, be offered additional spending as a result of underspending by other water authorities [5]. With such a short time-scale it is difficult to find worthwhile projects which can be planned efficiently. Annual financing does not sit comfortably with the long lead times necessary for planning capital works.

The conditions under which the corporations operate offer only a limited incentive to efficient operation and frequently a shortage of funds prevents essential work which would be cost-effective, being carried out. As indicated earlier (Chapter 5) there are considerable backlogs of both capital and maintenance work in some of the areas covered by the corporations concerned. Again separate profit centres for property management would be likely to enhance the effective use of funds but much of the property is too specialized to have a market price.

14.14 BUSINESS SECTOR

The business sector, broadly commerce and industry, is generally exposed to competition (although in some cases this may be rather muted), is not affected by government financial controls but is subject to the effects of monetary and fiscal policy. However, even in a highly competitive market the use of resources for buildings and other property may not be very cost-effective.

As indicated earlier, the range and quality of buildings is very wide (Chapter 11). In some cases the process carried on in the building demands particularly expensive buildings. Financial organizations generally have very high added values in relation to costs, especially at their head offices and it is usually only these which are of exceptionally high standard. At the other extreme, where added value is relatively low, entrepreneurs are likely to try to minimize the costs of their properties. If they build they tend to opt for minimum standards. Often they purchase or rent existing property for which there is little demand and which is sometimes semi-derelict (Chapters 3 and 11).

While ultimate costs can often be reduced by better quality building to reduce maintenance and running costs (Chapter 11), usually higher quality buildings only continue to provide the comfort, convenience and aesthetic satisfactions they were designed to give if they are maintained to a high standard. This tends to be relatively costly because the fixtures, fittings and finishes are expensive to replace. Clearly where a good standard of building is required for commercial, technical or prestige reasons, there is likely to be an adequate level of maintenance. Inadequate maintenance is likely to occur in businesses with relative low added value or in businesses which are failing. Where funds are tight, expenditure on maintenance may be the easiest to delay. However, property may be rented on a fully repairing lease and the tenant may be forced to maintain an adequate standard whatever the state of his business. Landlords may also neglect the maintenance of property they cannot let or sell but, on the other hand, they may spend heavily on improvements and updating in order that they can continue to command satisfactory rents or sale values.

Tax regulations affect building maintenance. VAT, currently at 15%, is charged on maintenance and improvements but not on new buildings. Maintenance is an expense for business taxation purposes. Some types of business can write-off capital costs against profits over the tax life of the building. As a result of the incidence of taxation in some situations it may be relatively more economic to rebuild rather than rehabilitate.

Business buildings, for which there is a profitable current use are likely to be adequately maintained but those not used or under-used may be allowed to deteriorate. Such buildings tend to be in the inner areas of cities and on declining industrial estates, and will be more likely in towns which are declining in population and employment than in prosperous and growing ones.

Property costs may be a relatively small part of total costs and less attention to cost-effectiveness may be given in managing the property than to other parts of the business. Problems of allocating resources for property management do not arise in the same way in the business sector as in the public sector, since ultimately both inputs and outputs are purchased or sold through the market. It does not follow, however, that costs-in-use will be adequately analysed to provide a well-based discipline for property management and the effective use of funds.

REFERENCES

1. Department of the Environment *Housing and Construction Statistics 1974–84*, HMSO, London.
2. Audit Commission (1986) *Control of Local Authority Expenditure*, HMSO, London.
3. Audit Commission (1985) *Capital Expenditure Controls in Local Government in England*, HMSO, London.
4. Department of the Environment (1981; 1985) *Circulars 7/81 and 11/85*, HMSO, London.
5. National Economic Development Council (1985) *Investment in the Public Sector Built Infrastructure*, NEDC, London.
6. Stone, P. A. (1983) *Building Economy*, 3rd edn, Pergamon Press, Oxford.

15

Economics of the official planning process

15.1 THE MARKET AND THE OFFICIAL PLANNING PROCESS

In a perfect market developers would make the best use of national resources by operating to maximize returns on their own expenditure. In fact, the market for the development and care of the built environment is far from perfect. Developers have only a limited knowledge of national, regional and local trends in the future needs for the built environment and are affected by only a limited part of the costs and benefits which arise from their operations.

At the national level market forces may concentrate economic growth, and new and improved development in a limited number of favoured settlements and regions, where demand is the strongest and the risks of development the least. Success in such places may stimulate further growth at the expense of other areas. Growth may continue to the point at which advantages arising from a supply of suitable labour, easily accessible raw materials and markets, attractive environment, good communications, public utility and other services are lost. At the same time growth in the favoured areas may cream off potential growth in other areas. Settlements tend to decline when the volume of new activities is too small to stimulate the redevelopment or rehabilitation of facilities which have become obsolete (Chapters 7 and 10).

The best balance of growth can only be worked out if all the factors are taken into consideration. The facilities and their potential, at both places from which migration comes and to where it might go, need to be considered, together with the cost and benefits of alternative patterns of change.

In a similar way market forces may result in the redevelopment of sound and useful property in one district of a settlement, or develop at the periphery of a settlement, while other areas are left to run-down and become derelict. As a result, additional services may need to be created in some districts, while existing ones are under-used in others (Chapters 7 and 10).

Developers do not set out to damage the environment or to create costs for other land users and the community. Their function, interest and knowledge is limited to the interests they represent. An electricity board, a hospital authority and an education authority are concerned, respectively, with supplying required power as cheaply as possible, using resources as well as possible to relieve and cure the sick, and providing the best possible education the resources will allow.

15.2 PURPOSE OF OFFICIAL PLANNING

The purpose of setting up an official organization can be defined as 'to guide developers collectively to make the best use of national resources in the interests of the community as a whole'. While the purpose is positive, planning powers can only have a negative effect. That is, official planners can prevent a development taking place, and they can plan positive improvements to the built environment but they cannot force a developer to carry out development against his interests. They can secure modifications in developers' plans as the price of granting planning consent, providing that the modifications do not reduce the value of the development in relation to costs to the point at which expected profits in relation to risk are much below normal market levels. Public authorities can provide incentives to developers to carry out development considered to be in the public interest by land transactions, public development and redevelopment of infrastructure, and grants and subsidies (Chapters 7 and 10). The objectives of planning control can only be achieved in the long run if basic market demand can be modified. This is the demand by individuals, firms and organizations for goods and services in particular places.

If planning control is to achieve a more effective use of land and other resources than the market, it is necessary to base decisions on an analysis of expected future demand and to take into account all the costs and benefits of development, including all the external costs. Such analysis is difficult, time consuming and can never be absolutely complete or accurate. As indicated earlier it is difficult to project future demand, especially in the detail necessary to provide a context to guide planning control. It is comparatively easy to estimate the developers' costs but difficult to estimate all the external costs and benefits (Chapter 13). In particular it is difficult to evaluate benefits which have no market price such as aesthetics and other environmental values. In the final analysis, judgements (usually political) have to be made. Their value depends on the quality of the analysis on which they rest.

15.3 PLANNING CONTEXT

The built environment is all embracing. As soon as a country is settled man starts to develop a built environment. In long developed, easily inhabitable countries this tends to cover all the land and waterways; only a few remote and inaccessible areas are not modified in some way by man. It is only in vast continents with inaccessible and inhospitable forests and deserts such as South America, North Africa and Australia, where there are large tracts devoid of built environment.

If official planning is to guide development and make a more effective use of resources than developers, it needs to have a knowledge of the built development which already exists, some understanding of future likely demands on it and some concept of how these demands can be met most effectively. Given a context and a strategy for the future development of the built environment, it is possible to examine the compatability of developers' plans with the desired overall development of the built environment.

The official planning process can conveniently be divided into strategic and tactical planning. Strategic planning is concerned with analyzing existing built environment and its potential, projected future needs and developing a plan of the most effective way of meeting them. Tactical planning is concerned with guiding developers to fulfil the strategic plans. The official planning process is supported by a large range of government initiatives such as regional grants, grants and subsidies to encourage development and rehabilitation of land and buildings, development of public infrastructure and so on. These aspects of official planning have been discussed earlier (Chapters 7, 8, 9, 10 and 14).

Strategic plans can be developed for the whole country or for a neighbourhood, and for the whole spectrum in between. Clearly the scale and detail at which plans are prepared varies with the area covered and the level of development anticipated. While a plan for a neighbourhood to be developed or comprehensively redeveloped might indicate the road layout and even plots for development, plans for large areas would be much less detailed. At the regional and national levels, strategic plans might indicate little more than the location and proposed size of settlements, together with strategic transport and communication links. Not only is strategic planning labour intensive but plans rapidly date as demands and achieved development change from those anticipated. To be feasible plans are limited to the detail actually needed during the period of the plan. It would be a waste of planning resources to draw up plans for areas unlikely to experience development or redevelopment over the period of the plan.

In order to make the most effective use of the available resources in meeting future needs, accurate predictions are required of both future demands and the resources available to meet them, including the future potential of the existing infrastructure. Because built facilities are so expensive and have such long lives, supply and demand need to be predicted over long periods. However, the future cannot be predicted, only projections can be made and the margins of error increase the further ahead projections are pushed (Chapter 4). Hence plans need to be revised regularly as new information becomes available. Numerous factors: population size and structure; geographical distribution; industrial and other activities; economic growth and government financial policy; need to be taken into account (Chapter 4). There are usually numerous possible options for development at every level. While not all can be fully explored, rational choice is not possible without some examination of them. When to terminate studies of particularly options and to choose between them is largely a matter of judgement, usually political. However, unless options are worked out in some detail they cannot be rigorously tested and neither developers nor the community can appreciate the nature of the solutions being offered.

Planning at this level is a highly technical process and the methods and forms of presentation are difficult for the layman to appreciate. Both the politicians responsible for the final decisions and members of the community find it difficult to visualize the consequences of implementing the plans.

Tactical planning is concerned with actual development projects. These are expected to conform with the strategic plans. At the local planning level the plans may specify use class and density criteria together with criteria relating to the form of development and other matters.

15.4   PLANNING AND THE COMMUNITY

In a democracy the official planning process is a public exercise. While planning research and plan preparation are clearly tasks for trained professionals and final decisions are taken by politicians, there is usually provision for public consultation before final decisions are taken. Usually strategic plan proposals are publicized and consultations with the community, usually informal, are carried out. When the public have serious disagreements with the plans proposed by the official planners, formal inquiries are usually set up to examine and try to resolve the differences.

The lay public often have considerable difficulty in appreciating the consequences of planning proposals, particularly where the plans cover large areas at a broad level, for example, in terms of projected population and employment growth, broad land uses and indicative road routes. It is less difficult in the case of local plans where proposed changes can be indicated on existing, large-scale town maps and it is possible to visualize how the street layout would be modified by the proposed developments. Even so the public cannot usually work out the consequences in terms of traffic, noise and other nuisances, or visualize the impact on the area. This is the job of the official planner but he may not share the community's values, or trade off benefits in the way in which they would. As a consequence the proposals finally incorporated into the plans may not make the most effective use of the resources from the point of view of the community.

The applications of developers for planning consents are related to the adapted official plans. If developers' proposals are not compatible, they are either rejected or where possible modifications which would achieve compatibility are suggested. There is usually an appeal procedure which might invoke a formal planning inquiry.

15.5 PLANNING MACHINERY IN BRITAIN

Plan-making in Britain has gradually but considerably been revised since the *1947 Town and Country Planning Act*, particularly by the *Town and Country Planning Act, 1971*. Central to plan-forming are the county structure plans. These are prepared by the shire counties and (until their abolition in 1986) by the metropolitan counties. They are vetted by the central government. They and groups of counties prepare regional strategic plans as a basis for the coordination of county plans within the region. District authorities prepare statutory and non-statutory local plans.

Inevitably there is a great deal of difference between plans for new areas and those for existing areas of development. Plans for the development of new towns and estates are prepared as a guide to actual physical development, while most town and country plans only set out guidelines for any development which may take place. Implementation depends on actual demand by people and firms, on the acceptance of the implication of demand for public infrastructure and on the availability of private and public finance to cover the costs of development. Development is likely to take place where either the demand for replacement or additional development is strong. There is little likelihood of more than a few areas being developed in the course of a decade and hence little to be gained by preparing detailed development plans over the whole country.

Structure plans are concerned with identifying the broad needs of an area and objectives for it in relation to all the agencies concerned with development. In order to maximize human welfare they need to take into account economic and social factors as well as environmental ones. The value of each type of gain and loss needs to be set out against the development costs to determine which plan offers the best value for money. It is necessary to consider benefits and costs from the point of view of each type of development agency as well as the community (Chapter 13). It is then possible to consider whether the development is likely to be sufficiently attractive to the various types of developer to be implemented.

The nature of structure plans as broad guides to the scale and direction of desired development results in difficulties in relating proposed changes to development on the ground. As a result it is difficult to determine exactly what the plans mean in relation to the interests of those affected, particularly in the case of members of the community, and people wishing to carry out minor developments. Unnecessary anxieties may result, with objections at planning enquiries, and the submission of development proposals not conforming with the plans. It may also inhibit acceptable proposals.

The district planning authorities prepare their plans within the context provided by the county structure plans and use their plans as the context for determining planning applications, most of which they now handle [1]. The county authorities now are mainly concerned with planning applications for mineral and related developments, cement works, waste disposal and development which straddles National Parks [1]. The division of planning powers is not always clear-cut and situations occur in which there are differences of interpretation. In the end these have to be resolved by the central government, either directly or through a planning inquiry.

Town planning is concerned not only with the types of development and their location but also with their form and scale. Land uses tend to generate various types of traffic and affect the environment through noise, fumes and other nuisances. Appearances are also of importance: they affect the quality and amenity of the townscape. Buildings are not necessarily compatible: this depends on their style and form, and on the materials used for their structure and cladding. Inevitably aesthetic judgement is involved, which can only be subjective. If it is not to be biased, it requires the planner to develop a catholic taste. In the past new development has not always been compatible with the existing townscape of the area and alterations and changes in the use of buildings have sometimes sacrificed the qualities for which the buildings were valued.

In making regulations to control development the ideal solution must often be modified in the light of what is achievable. If densities are set too low, use-zoning set too rigid, and form and design too restricted, there might be no or an inadequate scale of development and conversion. An absence of new users for land and buildings would result in vacant and undisposable properties with inevitable physical deterioration and eventually dereliction. Sufficient flexibility is needed in the regulations to encourage enough users to maintain the viability of each area.

Plans are published in draft and explained at public meetings but because of the difficulty for the lay public in interpreting them, there is considerable doubt as to whether such procedures provide an adequate test of public acceptance. The setting up of a formal inquiry under an inspector appointed by the central government throws the matter open to detailed discussion and the presentation of evidence. However, the inquiry is concerned not with the best planning option but only with the acceptability of the plan submitted. Formal planning inquiries may be set up where developers dispute local planning decisions, where the government considers area plans or development projects raise issues of national importance, or where there is considerable public disquiet.

Usually the government appoints an inspector to hear arguments for and against the proposals. Promotors of plans and development projects and objectors give evidence before the appointed inspector who either makes a decision himself or advises the Minister on his decision. Where costs and benefits are large, the principal protagonists may hire expert witnesses and learned counsel to put their cases. Often much of the opposition is from pressure groups who may not represent local interests. Generally it is organizations and members of the public who object to a proposed plan or development who give evidence, rather than those who support the proposals, or are prepared to accept them, so that the weight of opinion tends to be negative. Planning inquiries for large controversial plans or projects can take many years to set up, hold and report. Objectors can hold up projects for long periods.

Public authorities and public developers tend to be in a more dominant position than private developers. Government departments can authorize planning permission for development by local authorities and statutory undertakers. Crown land, which includes Duchy land and land belonging to government departments is largely exempt from planning regulations. Moreover government departments and other public developers are not subject to market forces and can spend far more on development and on planning appeals than would be worthwhile for private developers. Government departments also have opportunities to influence planning decisions on behalf of those they sponsor, e.g. quangos, through pressure on the department taking the final planning decision.

While official plans generally define areas of restraint such as Green Belts, National Parks, area of outstanding national beauty, conservation areas, and areas of architectural, natural, historical and scientific interest, such areas are dealt with flexibly. This has the effect of inviting developers to test the resolve of national and local planning authorities to safeguard such areas. As a result public and private developers put forward plans for towns in Green Belts, nuclear power stations in heritage coastal areas and roads through national parks. The possibility of challenges by developers should encourage official planners to take considerable care in determining the best way to use land.

15.6   CRITICISM AND CHANGE IN THE PLANNING PROCESS

The planning process has been subject to considerable criticism. Developers and building users argue that planners impose conditions, unjustified by the public interest, which stifle worthwhile developments by increasing the likely costs of development and servicing, and reducing the use value of the resulting property. This reduces opportunities for industry, employment and the economy.

It is claimed that while planning controls are applied rigidly to private urban developers, application of regulations is very limited in the case of agriculture and that public bodies are often largely outside planning regulations. It is often questioned whether the presentation of plans and applications, and plan inquiries provides the public with an adequate opportunity to make a positive input to the planning process. The adversarial nature of planning inquiries, in particular, tends not to provide a forum for working out acceptable alternatives. For objections to carry weight it is generally necessary to employ expensive expert witnesses and learned counsel to analyse and put forward well-argued objections. Only well financed interests can afford the expenses involved; local communities likely to be affected by the plans have considerable difficulties in financing equally strong teams of witnesses and legal support. It is argued that too long is taken over processing planning applications (3 years is said not to be uncommon for large commercial and industrial applications) and that too much information and plan revision is required. This adds to development costs and leads to development opportunities being lost. When an application goes to inquiry, several years may be added to the process and costs considerably increased.

The government has recently shown considerable sympathy with many of these views. In 1980 the Department of the Environment and Welsh Office issued a circular aimed at speeding up planning decisions and limiting the imposition of restrictions without good reason and without taking account of the economic effects [2]. It argued that planning control should facilitate development, especially for the 'economic regeneration' of the country. Planning authorities were asked to take into account the loss of production, employment, income, rates and taxes and lower profitability from planning delays and refusals. They were told to be aware of the costs of asking applicants for unnecessary information and expensive redesign work.

The circular said that zoning should not be applied rigidly and that a 'non-conforming use' was not a sufficient reason to refuse planning permission. Permission it said, should only be refused where there are convincing objections such as intrusion into open countryside, noise, smell, safety, health or excessive traffic generation. Zoning could be replaced by criteria directly related to the objections such as those listed above.

Both the appearance and the impact of buildings on the urban scene are affected through controls on density, plot ratio, daylighting regulations, building lines and so on. Such controls can affect the form of the building. It is difficult to define rules for controlling aesthetics which it said, were extremely subjective. Planners were told not to impose their own tastes in processing planning applications [2]. While designs out of scale or character with their surroundings should be rejected, control should not be over-fastidious and planners should not insist on designs conforming to the fashion of the moment or unpopular with customers or clients [2]. The circular also discouraged the issue of enforcement notices unless there had been a really objectional wilful breach of planning law.

The central government has taken several additional steps in the last five years to reduce the possibilities of planning control delaying or inhibiting development which might lead to the creation of more employment or of reducing the employment potential of existing developments. More power has been transferred from the Minister to the government-appointed planning inspectors to decide planning appeals, subject only to a final appeal to the High Court but the right to a planning inquiry is preserved [3]. The Secretary of State proposes only to decide appeals of national significance or where there is interdepartmental conflict. Greater use is also being made of special development orders under the *Town and Country Planning Act, 1971*, to speed-up development of industrial estates and in other special situations. This device can be double-edged: while it can speed up obtaining planning consent, it may result in inadequate examination of the planning proposal and leave the public without adequate means of appeal.

In 1984, the Department of the Environment and Welsh Office was again calling for more consideration for industrial development [4]. It said that industry was not to be confined to traditional areas earmarked for such development and that priority was to be given to processing planning applications related to job creation. Barns and other disused buildings in the countryside were not to be excluded from industrial use. There was a call for blanket permission for science parks. Even so there is a considerable contrast between the width and detail of planning control for urban uses and its lack for agricultural uses. Clearly care is necessary in streamlining the planning system to avoid weakening controls to the point where undesirable development can be carried out.

Structure plans have now been prepared and approved for most of England and Wales. These will need to be reviewed and kept up-to-date and further local plans will need to be prepared. The procedures were streamlined under the *Local Authority Planning and Land Act, 1980*, reducing some of the central government statutory controls and reducing the information which needs to be published and the necessity of the examination of the plans in public. More emphasis is put on early discussion to avoid appeals and on appeals based on written documents; there is still the right to be heard before a planning inspector in public.

Generally whether it is a public authority presenting a statutory plan or a public or private developer presenting a plan for developing infrastructure or developing a site, only one plan is presented. In most cases there would be a number of feasible alternatives, some or all of which may have been considered before the chosen plan is published. Which plan is best depends in part on the set of values used to judge them. For example, there might be a number of possible locations for a proposed settlement, a range of shapes and forms for a building and several routes for a road. Unless either the planning authority or an objector works out and presents possible alternatives, and analyses the balance of advantages to concerned groups of people, they may never be considered. The problems and methods of analysis and evaluating plans was considered earlier (Chapter 13).

By the time the proposer has developed his chosen plan a great deal of work has been carried out and his views have hardened in favour of it. A better stage for the public consideration of the proposed plan might be after the proposer has completed the research and analysed the options but before the favoured solution has firmed up, when suggestions by interested parties would be generally more acceptable. If the application went public at this stage the planning authority could invite reactions and suggestions informally or in writing which would indicate the level of acceptability of the range of options offered. Both the developer and the planning authority could subsequently proceed with a better knowledge of the implications and public acceptability of the options available. In the event of disagreement at that stage the dispute could be referred to a planning inspector as at present.

If the community is to be adequately consulted so that their system of values can be taken into consideration, some method needs to be devised of reaching them. The usual methods of press announcements and local meetings often fail to inform more than a small proportion of the community and planning documents are usually far too expensive except for developers and their consultants. Perhaps more attention should be given to reaching those living in areas directly affected by proposed changes. One method might be direct mailing of a concise, easily understood statement of proposals affecting them with an invitation to ask for more information and to comment. Another would be by means of sample surveys but unless those questioned fully understood the nature of the proposals and the questions were completely neutral, their comments would be of little value.

Further changes in the planning system are now proposed to meet observed inefficiencies in the system[5]. Following the introduction of the single-tier development plan in the metropolitan areas of England and Wales, the Unitary Development Plan, under the *Local Government Act, 1985*, it is now proposed to set up a single-tier system outside the metropolitan areas. Each district would prepare a District Development Plan (DDP) and there would no longer be county structure plans, or local plans whether statutory or non-statutory. The DDPs would contain all the land use policies for the district, except possibly for mineral working. The plans would be made in conformity with national policies, regional strategies (drawn up by groups of counties in association with central government) and statements of county policies. The latter would be published for consultation and could be subject to Examination in Public but the county would generally not need the approval of the central government. It is suggested that the district should consult the public before it has formulated a draft plan but no suggestions appear to have been made on the form this should take. There would be provision for Examination in Public and for the Inspector to consider the plan as a whole, not just parts subject to objection. Again the plan would not need central government approval. Since approved structure plans and adopted local plans would remain in force until replaced by plans proposed under the new system, it would be some time before a complete change could be achieved.

The new system suggested would appear to be faster and less expensive to operate than the current system. Central government would lose a large proportion of its statutory checking function and the counties would no longer formulate detailed county plans. On the other hand, all districts would be required to formulate the DDPs, but unless an early date was set for their completion, the current confusion of plans might continue for many years. The machinery would be simpler but there would be fewer checks that the District Plans were consistent with higher plans and each other and met reasonable objections. It is not clear to what extent public consultation would be improved and no change appears to be suggested in the adversarial method of planning inquiry with its inordinate length and high costs, which make it difficult for individuals or communities to make their case adequately against large developers, particularly public ones. It has been suggested that much time and money might be saved, without reducing safeguards, if all evidence was written and verbal exchanges at public inquiries were confined to the examination of witnesses who had submitted written evidence, by the inspector. Such a step might reduce the costs of objectors and the handicaps experienced by local communities in putting their case.

15.7 PLANNING COSTS

Official planning has various costs which need to be set against the benefits. The costs include for the planning organization itself, additional resources used by developers and net losses to the community from the implementation of the developments.

Costs and benefits of official planning depend on its scope and on the way it is administered. In some countries official planning is very limited. It may cover only large settlements or settled regions and may be concerned only with broad use classes and large zones. Planning consent may not be concerned with the form, density and style of development or with such use classes as agriculture and forestry. In other countries planning may regulate every aspect of a development and apply to alterations as well as to new development, at least in urban areas. This is broadly the situation in Great Britain. Clearly the more detailed the planning regulations and the more comprehensive, the greater the costs but also the greater the potential benefits. Planning administered through tiers of authorities, especially if their powers overlap, is likely to add to delays and costs.

Public inquiries can be long and expensive. For example, the consideration of the 5-mile Okehampton Bypass took over 20 years and the Public Inquiry sat for 96 days; the more controversial Sizewell Nuclear Power Station Inquiry sat for 340 days and the third of the three inquiries into the expansion of Stansted Airport sat for 258 days and cost taxpayers and ratepayers about £5 million. In addition to the direct costs to the public purse and to those presenting or objecting to developments, the costs in delay to developers and potential users can be considerable.

Local planning authorities in Great Britain employ about 23 000 equivalent full-time staff on planning research and administration [6]. In addition, large numbers of staff are employed by central government and by planning consultants in the preparation and defence of planning applications. Allowing for overheads, the direct costs of the official planning machine are likely to be of the order of two-thirds of a billion pounds per year, perhaps more. To these costs can be added the costs of presenting applications, modifying plans, possible additional construction work and delay in developing projects. Relating the costs to the value of new work would suggest that official planning costs something of the order of 5–10% of the cost of work. Development values may be reduced by reductions in the extent and attractions of development. As a result of development control some developments may be frustrated, all will be more costly and fewer will be worthwhile. Occupiers may incur costs through planning delays and through reductions in operational efficiency. The costs of the official planning machine will marginally raise taxes and tend to raise the costs and reduce the economic activity of marginal enterprises. The community may incur higher costs in the absence of potentially advantageous developments. Against such costs must be set the gains to owners and occupiers from the frustration of developments which would have raised their costs, reduced their amenities and lowered the values of their properties. The community also gains from a better balance of development than would have been provided by the market in the absence of planning control.

REFERENCES

1. Department of the Environment and Welsh Office (1981) *Local Government Planning and Land Act. Circular 2/81*, HMSO, London.
2. Department of the Environment and Welsh Office (1980) *Development Control and Practise. Circular 22/80*, HMSO, London.
3. Department of the Environment and Welsh Office (1981) *Planning Enforcement Appeals. Circular 33/81*, HMSO, London.
4. Department of the Environment and Welsh Office (1984) *Industrial Development. Circular 16/84*, HMSO, London.
5. Department of the Environment and Welsh Office (1986) *The Future of Development Plans – A Consultation Paper*, HMSO, London.
6. Department of Employment (July 1986) *Employment Gazette*, HMSO, London.

16

Conclusions

16.1 THE CONTEXT OF DEVELOPMENT AND PLANNING

Development and planning, together with maintenance, conversion and rehabilitation are the activities which create and sustain the built environment. This forms a large part of the physical environment in which we live. The form, distribution and condition of the built environment are important factors in determining the nature and functioning of the national economy, social conditions and lifestyles. The built environment constitutes a large part of national capital. Annual development generates about half of national fixed capital formation and consumes about one-twelfth of national income, the proportions currently being much lower than in the past.

Development and the way it is planned determines the availability, quality and distribution of housing, the built assets of industry, commerce, education, health and social services, the linkages between them and the public utilities which service them. The demand for development arises from the activities of the community, both as individuals and collectively. Both development and planning are subject to the forces of demand whether from a market economy or from a state monopoly. While a totalitarian state can ensure that development conforms with its plans, it cannot escape the consequences for production and distribution. If the form and distribution of the built environment does not conform with the economic and social needs of the community and its activities, economic efficiency will be impaired and the standard of life of the community will be depressed. In a market economy consequences are more direct: built assets with forms and locations less than optimum will not secure the highest values and may not be used at all.

Planning as a state activity usually involves public authorities at all levels; national, regional and local. The distribution of planning powers between authorities and the extent of such powers varies over time and from country to country. On the other hand, development is partly a private and partly a public function. In market economies private developers are responsible for much of the housing, factory, commercial and recreational building, while the public authorities develop buildings for education, health, social and other services, for some housing and other purposes, and develop communications and public utilities. Public and private development depend on each other and need to be coordinated, one of the functions of official planning.

16.2 SITES AND DEVELOPMENT

The efficient use of land and sites, and the way they are developed with buildings and services, depends on their physical environment as well as on the condition of the sites themselves. The demand for a site and its desired use generally depends as much or more on the surrounding environment, including infrastructure, as on its own attributes. A site in a town surrounded by sites in intensive use for human activities is usually much more in demand and valuable than one in the country. Site values can vary substantially for sites within a short distance of each other, and change with changes in local development. They also depend on the nature of any available planning consent. Planning control can both destroy and create site value.

The better sites are situated for particular uses, particularly high value uses, the more valuable they tend to be. Often the most desirable sites for a particular use have already been taken. If the new use is of a higher value or more intensive than the existing use, it is likely that the use of the site will change. Where this occurs buildings are often converted or cleared to allow the site to be redeveloped.

The value of both developed and undeveloped sites also varies with the economic, monetary and fiscal climate. Demand, hence purchase prices and rents, tend to rise as the economy becomes more buoyant and as incomes and revenues increase. Both owners and tenants tend to regard property costs in terms of an annual rent; hence capital values tend to rise as interest rates fall. Values are also affected by property taxes and subsidies; the first tending to reduce values and the second to enhance them.

Demands for sites and desired patterns of use change with changes in population and its activities. Changes in the volume of population, its demographic structure and spatial distribution, in household formation, and in work and leisure activities, result in changes in the type, quality, quantity and location of demand. Demand patterns also change with changes in taste, technology, wealth and lifestyles. Changes in the levels and quality of demand result in changes in price levels, creating incentives to change site uses, to adapt and convert buildings, and to redevelop sites. Changes in the development of a site and its buildings, and in its use can affect the potential values of other sites in the locality. While the consequences of collective changes to sites may only affect the immediate locality, a chain reaction may be started.

Development is dependent for its success on bringing together a range of factors in the most appropriate time sequence. Such factors include market demand, land, planning consent, local services, finance at a suitable price for both developers, and building users and owners, an acceptable tax base and building resources at an acceptable price. The planning and development of a site often takes many years, during which an unacceptable change in some of the factors may stultify the project.

The developer's objective is to maximize returns over the project with which he is dealing. Returns may be measured in terms of the surplus of sale price over costs or as streams of rent in relation to capital employed or returns from a business process in relation to costs, or in terms of satisfactions in relation to expenditure. The exact nature of the measure will depend on the criteria of the developer and on whether the development is for sale or for an investment, or for business or private use.

16.3 ECONOMIC, TECHNOLOGICAL, SOCIAL AND REGIONAL CHANGE

At the national level the built environment consists of cities, towns and villages, together with isolated developments in the countryside, communications and public utility services, energy plants and other man-made changes to the natural environment. The existing pattern has evolved partly through the requirements of the developing economy and partly through the developing pattern of lifestyles and consumer preferences.

As the national economy develops within the context of the world economy, the nature of home production tends to change. At first advanced countries tend to increase their reliance on other countries for food and raw materials, and later for simple manufacturing. They tend to concentrate more and more on the manufacture of advanced technological products and on the supply of services. Developing countries tend to change from subsistence economies to market economies producing raw materials and simple manufactured goods for export. Changes in home production result in changes in patterns of activities and in the relative importance of different settlements and regions. The location of raw materials, access to ports, climatic conditions and traditional manual skills tend to become less important in developed countries and more important in developing ones. Changing industrial structures tend to be accompanied by changing industrial location patterns. Improved communications widen the choice of location for both industry and people; favourable living conditions become of greater importance relative to sources of raw materials, markets and ports. As a consequence both people and industry migrate around the country changing the relative importance of both settlements and communications, and leading to the growth of some settlements and the decline of others.

Growing affluence and better communications, especially in developed economies, provide a wider choice of location for both households and firms. Workers can commute long distances to their place of employment, and they and entrepreneurs can choose to locate between central, peripheral and out-of-town locations. Population migrates from the inner areas of cities and towns to peripheral residential districts, and small towns and villages in their hinterland. Footloose industries and particularly office services tend to migrate from central business districts to outer suburbs and towns in the hinterland to take advantage of lower costs and new sources of labour created by the migration of population. Shops move from central districts to out-of-town locations. At the same time there tends to be migration from villages and the countryside as the mechanization, scale and forms of agriculture and related industries reduces employment opportunities, and transport and other services decline relative to those in towns. The relative scales of these migrations depends on the rates and timing of development in different parts of the economy.

As a result in developed countries there tends to be both regional and intraregional migration. This coupled with current declining or static populations tends to result in population decline in the settlements from which migration originates and increasing population in the new settlement areas. Developing countries tend to have exploding populations which migrate to the cities to find employment opportunities not available in the countryside, creating congestion in the cities without necessarily much reducing populations elsewhere.

The development of communications assists the spatial distribution of population, industry and commerce. For passengers and goods the development of road transport in place of fixed rail routes provides greater flexibility and access to most parts of the country, while the development of air transport reduces the importance of distances. The development of containers and roll-on/roll-off shipping facilities reduces the time and cost of overseas movement of goods and tends to reduce the relative importance of ports not able to cater for the new demands. The growth of telecommunications, together with electronic office equipment, reduces the time and costs for exchanging information, reduces the need for face to face contacts and hence close linkages and further assists dispersion, and may eventually reduce the need to bring office workers together in order to be able to function and open the way to home working.

16.4 SETTLEMENT STRUCTURE

The development of communications also increases the options for settlement structure. Large cities become less essential and need not be high density or form a single unit. Settlement size, density, shape, form and modes of internal transport affect the costs of development and operation and need to be taken into account when planning a settlement or the further development of one.

Complete freedom of choice of settlement structure is only ever possible where a completely new settlement is to be developed. Even in such cases the natural features of a site and its hinterland may impose severe physical and cost constraints on the structure of a settlement. Most areas suitable for a settlement have some urban facilities already on the site, often a village or even a small town. Since urban structure and services are very durable, they usually have considerable future potential and value. Given also their flexibility and adaptability, it may be more economic to integrate them into an expanded settlement, even though its structure may be distorted from the ideal, than to demolish them and redevelop.

16.5 SETTLEMENT DECLINE

While additional population and activities in a settlement create additional incomes and revenues, which are reflected in local property values and in their earnings, a decline in population and activities generally results in a decline in local incomes and revenues and hence narrows the financial base available in the settlement for meeting the costs of redevelopment. Redevelopment in declining areas tends not to be very attractive to private developers, because demand is often not great enough to create sufficient value to meet the costs. Settlement contraction tends to be accompanied by declining tax revenues, which are not fully offset by declining public costs. Since overheads of public services are fixed in the medium-term, costs per head for public services tend to rise. Public authorities tend to be left with insufficient resources to redevelop and improve the built environment and services.

Where demand is falling much of the property tends to become redundant, ceases to be adequately maintained and eventually becomes derelict. Such property is usually dispersed rather than concentrated in one area and sows the seeds of decay and a decline in property values widely over the settlement. This results in greater difficulties for rehabilitating the settlement and in servicing it. Such conditions create social, administrative and political problems. Comparable problems arise where decline occurs in districts within settlements.

16.6 DESIGN ECONOMY

In the past too little attention has often been placed on the costs, and economic and social consequences of developments, particularly on running costs, external costs and social consequences. This is reflected in the volume of abortive development and development which has given rise to unexpected economic and social problems.

Changing and new activities do not necessarily require new buildings. It may be possible to reorganize an activity or to modify a building, to match one to another. Specification of requirements, and the planning and design of a built facility largely determine both initial and running costs. The two types of cost need to be considered together, particularly in the case of service costs such as lighting, heating and ventilation. Most built facilities have a long potential life. They usually become financially or functionally obsolescent before they become physically obsolescent. Even physical obsolescence can be postponed by rehabilitation, while functional obsolescence can be postponed by adaptation, or conversion to new uses. Whether or not extending the life of built facilities is worthwhile, depends on the costs to be met now and in the future, compared with the value of the additional benefits which treatment would generate. Maintenance tends to become more expensive with age and a point may be eventually reached when redevelopment is less expensive than continuing to maintain the existing facility. The shorter the expected period of demand for a built facility, the more economic it is likely to be to build in flexibility and adaptability, to use short life forms of construction and to provide for easy demolition. The more rapid changes in technology, and economic and social climate are expected, the more important it is to take account of possible changes on future life.

16.7 FINANCE AND BUILT ENVIRONMENT

Poor returns from the use of building resources arise not only from inadequate specification, design and planning but also from inadequate financial resources and inadequacies of financial administration.

In the private sector limitation on capital expenditure may result in insufficient expenditure on the initial construction of a built facility. Similarly shortages of income or revenue may result in inadequate maintenance. Monetary and fiscal policies may distort real costs and result in a poor use of resources.

In the public sector governments tend to give but little priority to the economic use of funds for built resources. It is generally easier to reduce expenditure on capital projects, and on capital and maintenance contracts, than to cut staff or reduce the costs of ongoing policies. As a result resources for the built environment tend to be limited relative to need. The policies pursued to control expenditure often lead to their wasteful use. Expenditure on buildings by local authorities, quangos and other public bodies is also often easier to postpone than expenditure on staff and supplies. Often in the long run built facilities have to be rehabilitated or redeveloped at costs far greater than would have been the equivalent costs of adequate maintenance. As a result the backlog of construction work may become very great at the national level and, in the meantime, the inconvenience arising from inadequate built environment reduces amenity and creates additional costs to the community.

Building users are more likely to finance new and improved building when economic conditions are buoyant than when the economy is slack. Similarly public authorities usually spend more on developing and maintaining the urban fabric when the economy and tax revenue are buoyant. Thus private and public development tends to move together, fluctuating more in relation to the state of the economy than to potential need. Such fluctuations tend to be larger than the construction industry can accommodate without a loss of efficiency.

At times, development demand is greater than the construction industry can meet resulting in delay and rising costs and prices, and eventually the creation of additional capacity. Often periods of high demand are followed by substantial falls in demand, falling prices, increasing unused capacity and a reduction in the potential of the industry. As a result the industry may have insufficient capacity to meet demand when it rises again, causing a tendency of prices to rise and capacity to be increased again. This uneven flow of demand tends to waste resources. The first step in eliminating such fluctuations is to project needs over longer periods so that there is a better knowledge of likely future needs and a greater opportunity to plan a steady flow of work. This needs to be coupled with more attention to value for money and a greater priority for expenditure to improve and sustain the built environment.

16.8 RESOURCE CONFLICTS

Resources for development are not unlimited. Mistakes in planning and development not only waste construction resources but reduce the usefulness of the physical capital available to generate national income and well-being. The total available land is generally fixed; more land for one use can only be obtained at the expense of less land for other uses. Urban land users are in competition with each other and with rural land users. Up to a point market forces shift land from low value uses to higher value uses but market values do not always reflect social values and may be based on short-term consider-ations. Such market inadequacies help to justify official planning. The availabil-ity of finance for development depends on the demand for finance for other purposes, on rates of interest, inflation, incomes and revenues, propensity to save, and government monetary and fiscal policy. Development cannot be isolated from the economy but is a reflection of it.

When local activities decline, employment tends to fall in local services as well as in local industry and commerce. A decline in activities results in redundant built facilities and services. At the same time a shift in populations and activities elsewhere creates the need for considerable new investment in the built environment and associated services in other localities; some of which duplicate those in existing settlements. Thus there are grounds for attempting to sustain the existing pattern of population and activities. How-ever, changes in economic and technological conditions, and social needs change demand patterns with declines in demand in some areas and rises elsewhere. For example, mines become worked out, new forms of energy and communications widen possible locations; they, and changes in materials and skills, change relative locational advantages.

Official planning can be justified, not only to prevent a waste of public resources and to encourage the most economic use of national resources, but also to protect other site owners and users. Developers consider costs and benefits to themselves but every development has consequences for its neighbours and users of the area. It creates external costs and benefits. The consequences may be aesthetic or change physical or economic conditions; they may create nuisances such as noise or pollution, induce or take away trade, or destroy treasured natural or man-made features which cannot be replaced. Official planners need to consider not only market demand but also the balance of external costs and benefits both for the individuals affected and for the community as a whole. The planners' difficulty lies in recognizing the full consequences of a development and of measuring the incidence of the costs and benefits which arise as a consequence of change.

Planning control can prevent undesirable developments by rejecting plans or attaching conditions to its permission which result in the development being uneconomic; it cannot compel developers to undertake development however well conceived which they do not consider worthwhile. Public authorities can seek to influence development through grants, subsidies and taxation. They can carry out developments they consider desirable themselves but, if they do not meet market demands, prices will be generally less than costs and rents will need to be subsidized.

16.9   OFFICIAL PLANNING PROCESS

At the highest level the official planner is the government itself with maximizing the welfare of the community as its overall objective. The range of policy issues it needs to consider is substantial. At the national level the issues include the use of land for urban and rural purposes, the distribution of population and activities, the location, size, form, density and shape of settlements, their growth and decline, communications within and between them, the national resources and finance which can be made available for building and preserving the built environment, the balance of private and public development, its programming, and the extent and form of official planning and development control. Many of these issues also arise at the regional level. At the local level the official planner is concerned with the scale, form, density and location of development, with land use and quality of development, with the provision of public facilities and with maintaining built environment acceptable to the local community now and in the future.

The primary planning options arise from the way in which the official planners react to the market. The easiest option is to plan with the market.

This involves anticipating developers' needs by zoning and servicing the land the developers plan to develop. Such a policy does nothing to eliminate the possible wastage of national resources arising from market operations or to balance external costs and benefits.

An alternative is to try to rationalize the way developers meet market demand. This involves zoning land uses, setting densities and priorities so that land and uses are developed in the best sequence. A large range of options are then available according to how far such attempts to rationalize development are taken and to the criteria for such rationalization. This might imply, for example, disallowing development in peripheral areas as long as there are unused sites within existing settlements and restricting development in growth areas such as the south-east while there is unused land and facilities in northern towns. Restricting developers' freedom implies planning against the market. Whether this results in a more economic use of national resources depends on whether planners can evaluate planning options with sufficient accuracy, whether they can convince developers that their proposals are financially as sound as those of the developers and on whether restrictions in some places result in matching development where planners desire it.

Interference with the operation of the market is likely to create costs for the developer or reduce the value of his product and so reduce returns and the incentive to undertake the development. Planning cannot in itself force private development to take place. If there is no demand for property, it would be a waste of resources either to offer subsidies or to undertake public development. Where there would be a demand if prices were below market price, subsidies could be offered to developers or to potential occupiers. Subsidies could take the form of subsidized land prices to developers or grants and tax allowances to occupiers as in the case of assisted areas and enterprise zones.

Withholding development consents in areas to which population is migrating would not necessarily prevent migration either within or between settlements, and might encourage emigration to other countries. Since built facilities are flexible and adaptable, they can be converted to other uses and used more or less intensively. While up to a point changes of use can be controlled, such controls can never be complete and market forces cannot usually be completely frustrated. Nevertheless, it is generally accepted that there are firm grounds for attempting to rationalize built development.

The more buoyant an area and the more migrants it attracts, the greater the pressure from developers and the easier it is to direct development as long as the preferred development plan is coherent and rational. Some public participation in development is necessary in order to ensure an adequate supply of fully serviced sites. The lower the demand for built facilities, the less easy to persuade developers to accept what they consider second best and the greater the need to provide incentives to encourage development.

Public planning can assist but cannot on its own achieve policy aims for the national and regional distribution of economic activities. It is the economic and social activities which create the demand for built facilities, without them development and rehabilitation do not occur. Important issues arise in relation to policies for encouraging enterprise. Such policies include those for the provision of financial and tax incentives, for the training of labour and for conditions of employment, for creating additional local market demand and providing business services as well as for the provision of premises and attractive built environment. Issues arise relative to the weight to be given to each type of policy and their timing, and for the type of public machinery best suited for developing and redeveloping districts and settlements so as to stimulate balanced physical, economic and social development.

16.10 PLANNING ISSUES

An important issue for government is how to develop and implement coherent national plans. Planning can start at the centre or at the local level, regional, county or district, or the two can be developed simultaneously and be reconciled at each stage. While national planners are likely to be more open-minded about the most economic locations, local planners will have a better understanding of the needs and problems at the local level. If the best results are to be obtained planning is needed at all levels with continuous integration between local and central plans.

At the same time planning issues are generally indivisible. For example, at the national level policies for roads, ports, airports, the Channel Tunnel and so on interact with policies for land use and economic enterprise. The current policies for communication increase the attraction of the south-east for entrepreneurs and people, increasing the difficulties of implementing policies for controlling urban spread and safeguarding the Green Belt in the south-east and for implementing policies for attracting new enterprise in the north and improving its built environment.

Issues therefore arise as to the form best suited to national, regional, county and local plans, and with what issues each should deal. If official planning is to make the best use of resources, the policies for the various levels need to be compatible with each other and with economic and social forces. The plans do not need to cover the whole country equally comprehensively but need to demonstrate that policies as a whole are coherent.

Plan detail is another issue which exercises government. The greater the detail the better the understanding of both planners and members of the community of the consequences of what is proposed. This makes it easier to appreciate the implications of a plan and to estimate costs and benefits, but the greater the detail the more likely it is to be out of date on completion and the less likely that revision will be sufficiently frequent. The difficulty is to produce plans detailed enough to indicate their implications, well enough evaluated to carry conviction that they represent the best compromise and prepared rapidly enough to be relevant for a sufficient period on their completion.

The problem of ascertaining the wishes of the community are no less for planning than for any other public service. Many members of the public have no views about development outside the immediate areas in which they live, work and take their leisure and for routes between them. They have little appreciation of the possibilities until alternatives are put before them. Members of the community cannot generally judge between plans unless they are very clear, and the costs and benefits are worked out. Generally the possibilities are too numerous for a plan to be prepared for each option in full detail and the planner is forced to make some selection. While the planner can evaluate the costs and benefits, it is difficult to obtain any measure of the way the community would trade off different costs and benefits. This can only be discovered, as can plan preferences, by consultation. It is difficult to reach all those likely to be affected by a plan, to explain the issues simply and effectively, and to encourage them to express their views, positively as well as negatively. Open consultation meetings may only attract an unbalanced sample, mainly objectors. Unless issues are understood valid preferences cannot be given. Timing of consultation is also an issue for government; the firmer the plans at the time of consultation, the less the public can participate effectively in planning and the more negative they may be. Issues arise in relation to methods of public consultation both at the strategic and tactical level, and as to the best form of planning appeal and inquiry.

Because of the scale and cost of research needed to evaluate plans adequately, individuals are at a serious disadvantage in questioning the proposals of planners and developers. Often it is only special interest groups and large private and public organizations who are able to mount an effective challenge to planning proposals. The difficulties arising for individuals and small communities in taking advantage of public planning inquiries are further increased by the form and procedures normally followed. Many planning appeals are decided by planning inspectors entirely on the basis of written papers, saving much time and costs over full public inquiries. Much time and cost might be saved at public inquiries if all evidence was written and examination of witnesses was confined to the planning inspector.

Issues also arise in relation to the details of planning control. They often cover not only land use, densities and building form but design detail and apply to developments of all sizes and to minor changes of use. Planning and planning control have two types of cost for the community. Central and local government incur costs for administration, data collection and planning, handling planning applications, holding inquiries and so on. These costs are borne by the community in the form of higher rates and taxes. In addition developers, owners and building users incur the costs of supporting planning applications and additional costs imposed by planning delays and planning refusals, and any plan and design changes which may be imposed. Such costs are passed on to the community as a whole through higher prices. Clearly both types of costs need to be minimized in relation to the benefits of the planning system to both the local and national communities.

16.11   ECONOMIC ISSUES

Perhaps the most important current development issues for Great Britain include the drift of population and activities north to south, and outwards from cities and conurbations, the future use of inner cities and other areas no longer in demand and the protection of the countryside from excesses of both urban and rural development. These issues interact and combine with a range of further issues.

North–south migration is following market demand. As explained earlier the advantages for industry and commerce now tend to lie in the south and east, rather than, as in the past, in the north and west. This is reinforced by personal preferences for living in the south and the east. The north–south movement is overlaid by preferences for living in peripheral areas of cities, small towns and the countryside leading to migration from the inner cities, in all regions but particularly in the north. This movement leaves substantial areas, particularly in the inner cities but also in some smaller industrial towns and remoter villages, under-used and subject to decline. The pressure of population and activities in areas receiving migration creates demands on the countryside for additional urban development for housing, industry, commerce, roads and other services.

There is no agreement as to whether economic activities wishing to develop or expand in the south and east can and should be persuaded to develop in the north; whether such a policy, if successful, would increase or reduce national output and employment; and whether such a policy is practical. In the past, regional strategies aimed at this end have not been notably effective and have now to a large extent been abandoned. The regional policies were aimed both at limiting opportunities for development in the south and east, and at encouraging it elsewhere. Some development policies, however, such as those for London Airports and the Channel Tunnel, are likely to increase the market pull of the south and east.

Many industrial and service enterprises would appear to be able to operate in a range of locations but most appear to prefer to remain and expand in their area of origin, with firms in the same trade, where subcontractors, ancillary services, skilled labour and management have developed. Firms look for areas with sympathetic local authorities, low rates, good communications, and an industrious and adaptable labour force, while their managements and senior

staff prefer locations with attractive environments and good social, educational, leisure and other services. Generally these conditions are more likely
to be found in the south and east and outside rather than inside cities and
conurbations. Subsidizing the development of firms has often resulted in the
creation of capital rather than labour intensive firms. Often the firms obtaining subsidies are ones which would have developed in those areas in any case.
Many of the plans which have been subsidized have lacked long-term viability. An alternative strategy, now being given more weight, is to attempt to
create market demand in areas needing economic revival by such policies as
environmental improvement, shifting government activities and market
demands to them and trying to stimulate additional enterprise, particularly
local enterprise, by creating appropriate local business services, providing
training in management and skills, assisting in start-up operations and so on.
The driving force for such policies has come from both central and local
government, and private initiatives. For reasons indicated above, success is
generally more difficult to achieve in run-down inner city areas than elsewhere.

Reviving the economies and restoring the services and environments of
cities and conurbations, and even towns and villages which have lost their
economic purpose, is difficult and costly. The alternative of continued decline
and eventual closure creates considerable economic, social and political
difficulties. If the former option is chosen there is a choice between concentration on one or two areas at a time, giving priority to areas likely to respond
rapidly and start a chain reaction, or to areas most in need, and operating
through development corporations rather than local authorities.

Many of the problems of town development stem from the continuing
growth of road traffic, both passenger and goods, and in particular the
considerable convenience most people find in the use of the private car.
Policies for road traffic have been conflicting. Outside the built-up areas road
space is gradually being increased and its layout improved to meet the
increasing flow of traffic, but provision in towns (both for traffic movement
and parking) lags far behind demand, resulting in declining traffic speeds,
parking difficulties and increased costs. At the same time potential traffic in
towns is rising not only because of rising car ownership and transfer of goods
transport to roads but also because potential traffic terminals are increasing.
Redevelopment generally creates more floor space and workers, while the
decline in retail deliveries increases the convenience of shopping by car.
Traffic congestion and lack of parking reduces the attraction of towns for
retailing, other commerce and industry, and encourages development on
out-of-town sites. This reduces the advantages of living in towns and increases
the demand for out-of-town housing. The two forces interact to increase the
rate of decline of the town's economy, revenues, services and environment,
and to increase pressure on the countryside for urban development.

The protection of the countryside from further development has rested on the twin claims of agriculture and the environment. With surplus agricultural output the need to safeguard the countryside for farming has disappeared. The environmental strategy aims at preventing ribbon development, the infinite extension of cities and conurbations and their coalescence, random development, preserving undeveloped space around towns and between arms of development, and preserving unspoilt countryside, particularly in areas of special scenic merit and scientific and historical interest. While many areas have been officially designated as protected areas, the protection does not appear to prevent public development for such purposes as airfields, defence, water provision and power generation. Planning control of agricultural land is far less than for urban land. In its absence agriculture has transformed the rural environment in its development of high input–high output farming and destroyed the rural scene many valued along with much of the natural flora and fauna, and increased chemical pollution. Unless the growing agricultural surplus is accepted, or low input–low output husbandry is quickly adapted, increasing amounts of farmland are likely to be taken out of production. Unless alternative uses can be found, such land is likely to revert to untidy scrub and will be a temptation to developers, especially around settlements and in areas of urban pressure.

Development depends in the first place on demand and the availability of funds for investment in it. It needs the support of appropriate monetary and fiscal policy. If development resources are to be used efficiently and effectively, development needs to proceed within the context of a well thought-out long-term development plan, within the context of which planning consent is handled flexibly to ensure an adequate balance between the interests of developers and the community. Options between central and local decision-taking depend on judgements of the balance between the wider national and regional views of development needs and the more detailed local knowledge, and the importance of national consistency and objectivity. Further options for the development of planning policy include more or less dependency on planning machinery, and other central and local government initiatives, and more or less response to and analysis of local opinion.

A substantial part of the built infrastructure is developed and maintained by the public sector but there is considerable doubt as to how efficiently and effectively this is provided and managed. Options arise for the priorities to be accorded to the scale, quality and direction of public development, for the forms of organization best suited to handle public investment and maintenance of development and for techniques of management.

Index